Advanced Reactive Programming
Integrating RxJava with Spring Boot Applications

Contents

1   Introduction to Reactive Programming   11

   1.1   Understanding the Paradigm: Imperative vs. Reactive . 11

   1.2   Core Concepts of Reactive Programming 13

   1.3   The Advantages of Reactive Programming 15

   1.4   Reactive Programming Use Cases 17

   1.5   Key Components in Reactive Systems 19

   1.6   The Reactive Manifesto Explained 20

   1.7   Introduction to Reactive Streams 24

   1.8   Understanding Observables and Subscribers 26

   1.9   The Role of Non-Blocking I/O 27

  1.10   Challenges and Solutions in Reactive Programming . . . 29

  1.11   An Overview of Reactive Programming Libraries 31

  1.12   Preparing for a Shift to Reactive Programming 33

2   Reactive Programming with RxJava   37

   2.1   Getting Started with RxJava 37

   2.2   Key Concepts and Components of RxJava 39

   2.3   Creating Observables from Scratch 41

   2.4   Transforming Items in a Stream 43

   2.5   Filtering Observables in RxJava 44

   2.6   Combining Multiple Data Streams 47

2.7   Error Handling in RxJava   49

2.8   Working with Schedulers and Concurrency   51

2.9   Backpressure in RxJava   52

2.10   Hot vs. Cold Observables   54

2.11   Advanced RxJava Operators   56

2.12   Best Practices for Using RxJava   58

3   Spring Boot Essentials for Reactive Applications   61

3.1   Introduction to Spring Boot for Reactive Applications   . .   61

3.2   Configuring a Reactive Spring Boot Application   63

3.3   Understanding the Spring WebFlux Framework   65

3.4   Developing Reactive RESTful APIs   68

3.5   Reactive Database Access with Spring Data   70

3.6   Integrating Reactive Streams with Spring Boot   72

3.7   Securing Reactive Applications with Spring Security   . . .   74

3.8   Event-Driven Microservices with Spring Boot   77

3.9   Testing Reactive Applications with Spring Boot   79

3.10   Monitoring and Managing Reactive Spring Boot Applications   81

3.11   Optimizing Spring Boot Application Performance   83

3.12   Deploying Reactive Spring Boot Applications   85

4   Combining RxJava and Spring Boot   89

4.1   Setting Up the Development Environment   89

4.2   Creating a Reactive Spring Boot Application with RxJava   91

4.3   Integrating RxJava with Spring WebFlux   94

4.4   Implementing Reactive Data Access with RxJava and Spring Data   96

4.5   Building a Reactive RESTful API with RxJava and Spring Boot   98

4.6   Reactive Error Handling in Spring Boot and RxJava   . . . 101

4.7 Achieving Concurrency and Parallelism 103

4.8 Implementing Backpressure with RxJava in Spring Boot Applications 105

4.9 Reactive Caching Strategies 107

4.10 Securing your Reactive Application 109

4.11 Monitoring and Metrics for RxJava and Spring Boot Applications 111

4.12 Best Practices for Combining RxJava and Spring Boot . . 113

5 Data Streams and Back-Pressure   117

5.1 Understanding Data Streams in Reactive Programming . 117

5.2 The Concept of Back-Pressure Explained 119

5.3 Creating Responsive Data Streams 121

5.4 Flow Control Strategies in Reactive Programming 123

5.5 Implementing Back-Pressure with Reactive Streams . . . 125

5.6 Back-Pressure in RxJava Explained 127

5.7 Dealing with Back-Pressure in Project Reactor 129

5.8 Strategies for Handling Overflow in Reactive Systems . . 131

5.9 Implementing Custom Back-Pressure Mechanisms 133

5.10 Testing and Debugging Back-Pressure Issues 135

5.11 Back-Pressure and Resilience Patterns 137

5.12 Real-World Examples of Back-Pressure Management . . 140

6 Reacting to Data with RxJava Operators   143

6.1 Operators Overview: The Building Blocks of RxJava . . . 143

6.2 Creating Observables with Creation Operators 145

6.3 Transforming Data with Transformation Operators 147

6.4 Filtering Data Stream with Filtering Operators 150

6.5 Combining Observables with Combination Operators . . 152

6.6 Managing Time with Time-Based Operators 154

6.7 Error Handling Operators 156

6.8   Controlling Back-Pressure with Reactive Operators . . . 158

6.9   Conditional and Boolean Operators 159

6.10 Mathematical and Aggregate Operators 161

6.11 Converting Observables with Conversion Operators . . . 163

6.12 Utility Operators to Debug and Test 165

7   **Handling Errors in Reactive Streams**   **167**

7.1   Understanding Error Handling in Reactive Streams . . . 167

7.2   Error Propagation in Reactive Systems 169

7.3   Catching and Handling Errors with RxJava 171

7.4   Using onErrorReturn, onErrorResume, and retry Opera-
      tors 173

7.5   Error Handling Best Practices in Reactive Programming . 175

7.6   Implementing Custom Error Handling Strategies 177

7.7   Dealing with Timeout Errors 179

7.8   Handling Errors in Project Reactor 181

7.9   Fallback Strategies for Resilient Systems 183

7.10 Integrating Error Handling with Spring WebFlux 185

7.11 Testing Error Handling in Reactive Applications 187

7.12 Real-World Scenarios and Solutions for Error Handling . 189

8   **Building Reactive APIs with Spring WebFlux**   **193**

8.1   Introduction to Spring WebFlux 193

8.2   Setting Up a Spring WebFlux Project 195

8.3   Creating Reactive Endpoints with Spring WebFlux . . . 197

8.4   Handling Requests with Server-Side Events (SSE) 199

8.5   Implementing Reactive CRUD Operations 201

8.6   Error Handling in Spring WebFlux Applications 203

8.7   Functional Endpoint Routing in WebFlux 205

8.8   Securing Spring WebFlux APIs 207

8.9   Integrating Reactive Client with WebFlux 209

8.10 WebFlux and Database Reactive Transactions 211

8.11 Building Real-time WebSocket APIs with WebFlux 213

8.12 Performance Monitoring and Optimization for WebFlux
APIs 215

9   Reactive Database Access with R2DBC   **219**

9.1 Introduction to R2DBC 219

9.2 Setting up R2DBC with Spring Boot 222

9.3 Configuring Database Connections 223

9.4 Implementing CRUD Operations with R2DBC 226

9.5 Advanced Query Techniques 227

9.6 Transaction Management in R2DBC 230

9.7 R2DBC with Spring Data 232

9.8 Error Handling and Exception Translation 234

9.9 Performance Considerations for Reactive Database Access 236

9.10 Migrating from JDBC to R2DBC 238

9.11 Testing R2DBC Applications 240

9.12 Real-World Use Cases and Patterns 243

10 Testing and Debugging Reactive Applications   **247**

10.1 Overview of Testing Reactive Applications 247

10.2 Unit Testing Reactive Flows with JUnit 250

10.3 Integration Testing Strategies 251

10.4 Testing with Testcontainers for Reactive Services 255

10.5 Debugging Techniques for Reactive Streams 257

10.6 Using Spring Boot Actuator for Monitoring 259

10.7 Performance Testing Reactive Applications 262

10.8 Error Handling and Exception Testing 264

10.9 Mocking and Stubbing Reactive Components 266

10.10 End-to-End Testing of Reactive Applications 268

10.11 Automating Reactive Testing with CI/CD 271

10.12Common Pitfalls and How to Avoid Them 273

Introduction

As the landscape of software development continues to evolve, the demand for highly responsive, resilient, and scalable applications has grown exponentially. With "Advanced Reactive Programming: Integrating RxJava with Spring Boot Applications," this book aims to serve as a comprehensive guide for developers seeking to master the art and science of reactive programming. This volume offers an in-depth exploration into utilizing the potent combination of RxJava and Spring Boot, empowering you to construct applications that meet the rigorous demands of modern software environments.

Reactive programming represents a shift from traditional imperative programming paradigms, focusing on asynchronous data streams and the propagation of change. This approach promises enhanced performance, better resource utilization, and improved system resilience by naturally handling errors and gracefully managing back-pressure scenarios. In this book, we delve into these foundational principles to provide you with a robust understanding of why and when to adopt a reactive programming approach in building Java applications.

The integration of RxJava with Spring Boot exemplifies the synergy between a powerful reactive library and a versatile microservices framework, allowing developers to leverage the full capabilities of functional reactive programming. This integration allows for seamless reactive data processing, enables the management of asynchronous event-driven systems, and enhances the ability to handle extensive I/O-bound workloads efficiently. Our guide caters to developers and architects aiming to design reactive systems that are not only functionally robust but also maintainable and efficient.

The book is structured to take you through a logical and practical journey, beginning with the essentials of setting up your reactive development environment. It then delves into more sophisticated topics such as advanced stream processing with RxJava, handling concurrency, integrating with Spring WebFlux for reactive API development, and interacting with databases using R2DBC. Throughout, emphasis is placed on real-world applications, showcasing how to implement patterns that mitigate common challenges and pitfalls associated with reactive system development.

Each chapter is laden with practical examples and hands-on exercises that transition from foundational topics to advanced reactive scenarios. This methodical progression ensures that, whether you are a Java developer keen to expand your skillset or a seasoned software architect, you will gain actionable insights that enhance your reactive programming proficiency with RxJava and Spring Boot.

The book also addresses strategies for effectively troubleshooting reactive applications, optimizing performance, and ensuring that your applications remain resilient under stress. By integrating RxJava with Spring Boot, developers can achieve a cohesive technology stack that enables the construction of lightweight, flexible, and highly responsive microservices.

In conclusion, "Advanced Reactive Programming: Integrating RxJava with Spring Boot Applications" serves as a vital resource for anyone intent on mastering the reactive paradigm. By merging theoretical foundations with practical applications, this book prepares you to tackle the next generation of software development challenges—equipping you with the knowledge and tools to architect high-performing, scalable, and robust reactive applications.

Chapter 1

Introduction to Reactive Programming

Reactive programming represents a paradigm shift in the way developers conceptualize and build software applications, centering around data streams and the propagation of change. This approach allows for more flexible, scalable, and responsive applications by embracing asynchronous data flow and non-blocking operations. It addresses the challenges presented by modern computing environments that demand efficient handling of real-time data and complex data pipelines. Understanding the fundamentals of reactive programming is essential for developers looking to adopt this model in their application architecture to improve performance and user experience.

1.1 Understanding the Paradigm: Imperative vs. Reactive

In the sphere of software development, a paradigm provides a fundamental approach to solving problems. Over the years, several paradigms have emerged, but this section will focus on contrasting imperative programming with reactive programming. Understanding the distinction between these two paradigms is instrumental in comprehending the transformative potential of reactive programming.

Imperative programming, one of the oldest paradigms, centers on describing how a program operates through statements that change its state. It follows a sequential execution model, where commands are executed one after the other, leading to a predictable state change. This paradigm is subdivided into procedural programming, which relies on procedure calls, and object-oriented programming, which encapsulates state changes within objects.

To illustrate, consider a simple example of reading and processing a file in an imperative style:

```
1  File file = new File("data.txt");
2  Scanner scanner = new Scanner(file);
3  while(scanner.hasNext()){
4      String line = scanner.nextLine();
5      // Process the line
6  }
7  scanner.close();
```

In this example, the code explicitly describes the steps to read from a file and process its contents line by line. Each step is executed in the sequence it is written, and the state of the program changes as it moves through the lines of the file.

In contrast, reactive programming is a declarative paradigm that focuses on the flow of data and the propagation of changes. Instead of explicitly stating the steps to achieve a goal, a reactive program will define the relationships between data sources and the operations to be performed when new data is available. This paradigm leverages asynchronous data streams and non-blocking operations, enabling systems to be more responsive, scalable, and resilient.

A reactive approach to the previous file reading example might involve creating a data stream from the file and applying a function to process each line as soon as it's available:

```
1   Flux<String> lines = Flux.using(
2       () -> Files.lines(Paths.get("data.txt")),
3       Flux::fromStream,
4       BaseStream::close
5   );
6
7   lines.subscribe(
8       line -> {
9           // Process the line
10      }
11  );
```

Here, Flux is a type from Project Reactor, a reactive library for the Java Virtual Machine, which represents an asynchronous sequence of data.

12

Instead of controlling the reading and processing sequence explicitly, this code declares a source of data (`Flux`) and an operation to be performed on each piece of data (`subscribe` method). The underlying library handles the data flow, including opening and closing the file, reading lines, and invoking the subscriber's callback method for each line asynchronously. This means the program can process other tasks while waiting for new lines to be read.

The transition from imperative to reactive programming entails a shift from a command-oriented perspective, where every operation's execution path is clearly defined, to a reactive stance, focusing on data relations and transformations. Imperative programming tends to be straightforward but can lead to complex and inefficient code in scenarios involving asynchronous operations or real-time data. Reactive programming, with its emphasis on data streams and propagation of changes, provides a more natural and scalable approach to handling such scenarios, although it requires a rethinking of how to architect applications.

Imperative and reactive paradigms offer different tools and abstractions to solve software development problems. While imperative programming gives developers fine-grained control over program flow and state management, reactive programming excels in scenarios where data is asynchronous, concurrent, or real-time by abstracting away explicit control flow in favor of expressing data dependencies and transformations. As modern applications increasingly rely on these characteristics, understanding and effectively leveraging the reactive programming paradigm can significantly enhance application performance and user experience.

1.2 Core Concepts of Reactive Programming

Reactive programming is a programming paradigm focused on data streams and the propagation of change. This model encourages developers to think in terms of asynchronous data flows that enable applications to react to changes in their environment in real-time. Central to understanding reactive programming are several key concepts: Observables, Observers, Operators, and Schedulers. These concepts work together to create a cohesive ecosystem for developing highly responsive and scalable applications.

The first foundational concept of reactive programming is the Observable. An Observable represents a data stream that emits items over time. These items can be any type of data, from simple scalar values to complex data structures. An Observable is essentially a producer of data items.

```
1  Observable<String> dataStream = Observable.create(subscriber -> {
2      subscriber.onNext("Hello");
3      subscriber.onNext("Reactive");
4      subscriber.onNext("Programming");
5      subscriber.onComplete();
6  });
```

In this example, an Observable named dataStream is created, emitting three strings before signaling completion. This demonstrates how an Observable can asynchronously push data to its consumers.

Next is the Observer, which is the consumer of the data items emitted by an Observable. An Observer subscribes to an Observable to receive its data items. It defines methods to handle received items, errors, and completion notifications.

```
1   Observer<String> observer = new Observer<String>() {
2       @Override
3       public void onNext(String value) {
4           System.out.println(value);
5       }
6
7       @Override
8       public void onError(Throwable e) {
9           e.printStackTrace();
10      }
11
12      @Override
13      public void onComplete() {
14          System.out.println("Completed");
15      }
16  };
```

Upon subscribing the observer to the dataStream Observable, the observer receives the emitted items, prints them, and upon completion, prints a completed message.

Operators are powerful tools within reactive programming, enabling complex processing and transformation of data streams. Operators allow for operations such as filtering, transformation, combination, and error handling on streams.

```
1  dataStream
2      .filter(value -> value.length() > 5)
3      .map(String::toUpperCase)
4      .subscribe(System.out::println);
```

This chain of operators filters strings longer than five characters, converts them to uppercase, and then subscribes to print each transformed item. It exemplifies how operators can be used to modify data streams.

Schedulers manage concurrency in reactive programming. They control the threads on which Observables emit items and on which Observers receive those items. By default, Observables operate on the same thread as their subscribers. However, Schedulers can modify this behavior, allowing developers to easily implement concurrent and parallel data flows.

```
dataStream
    .subscribeOn(Schedulers.io())
    .observeOn(Schedulers.newThread())
    .subscribe(observer);
```

In this code snippet, the Observable's emissions and the observer's receptions are scheduled to run on different threads, showcasing the flexible concurrency model provided by Schedulers.

Reactive programming, by leveraging the described core concepts, facilitates building applications that can efficiently process data streams. This empowerment allows handling complex asynchronous and event-driven scenarios, enhancing scalability and responsiveness. Understanding Observables, Observers, Operators, and Schedulers is fundamental for effectively applying the reactive programming paradigm in modern software development.

1.3   The Advantages of Reactive Programming

Reactive programming offers several distinct advantages over more traditional programming paradigms, particularly when dealing with asynchronous data flows and systems that require high levels of responsiveness and resilience. This section will discuss the key benefits of adopting reactive programming, including improved scalability, enhanced performance, increased responsiveness, and better resource utilization.

Improved Scalability: One of the foremost benefits of reactive programming is its ability to significantly enhance the scalability of applications. By adopting a non-blocking and asynchronous approach, reactive applications can handle a large number of concurrent users and data streams without compromising on performance. This is particularly beneficial for applications that must scale dynamically in response to fluctuating load demands. Reactive programming achieves this by minimizing the dependency on thread-based concurrency, which is often a limiting factor in the scalability of traditional applications.

Enhanced Performance: Reactive programming contributes to improved performance through efficient utilization of system resources. Since it operates on an event-driven and non-blocking model, it avoids the overhead associated with thread context switches and blocking I/O operations. This results in lower latency and higher throughput for applications, making them capable of processing real-time data streams more effectively. Moreover, the reactive model facilitates better error handling and backpressure mechanisms, which further contribute to the overall performance by preventing system overloads and ensuring smooth data flow.

Increased Responsiveness: Responsiveness is a critical attribute of modern applications, especially those providing interactive user experiences or handling real-time data. Reactive programming directly targets this requirement by ensuring that applications remain responsive under various conditions, including high load, network latency, and partial failures. The paradigm's emphasis on non-blocking operations and asynchronous data processing means that applications can remain responsive to user interactions and incoming data, even while executing long-running operations or waiting on external resources.

Better Resource Utilization: Traditional synchronous programming models often result in inefficient resource utilization, particularly in scenarios requiring I/O operations or external service calls. Threads may be left idle waiting for resources or data, leading to underutilization of computational resources. Reactive programming addresses this inefficiency through its non-blocking nature, allowing applications to make optimal use of available CPU cycles and memory. By decoupling the application logic from I/O operations, it enables more tasks to be processed concurrently without additional resource consumption, leading to more efficient and cost-effective applications.

Facilitation of Complex Data Flows: The handling of complex, asynchronous data streams is another area where reactive programming excels. Its foundational concepts, such as observables and streams, provide a robust framework for composing and managing data flows that are inherently asynchronous. This makes it particularly suited for applications that require real-time data processing, event handling, and complex transformation and aggregation of data streams. Reactive programming simplifies the development of these complex data pipelines, offering developers powerful tools to express data dependencies and flow control in a declarative manner.

The adoption of reactive programming offers a multitude of advantages for developing modern applications. Its emphasis on non-blocking, asynchronous processing aligns well with the requirements of today's computing environments, characterized by the need for real-time data processing, high scalability, and responsive user interfaces. By leveraging the benefits outlined above, developers can build more efficient, scalable, and user-friendly applications, ready to meet the challenges of current and future digital landscapes.

1.4 Reactive Programming Use Cases

Reactive Programming has found a niche in various application domains where data's asynchronous nature and the requirement for non-blocking operations are predominant. This section elaborates on specific scenarios where the reactive programming model significantly enhances performance, scalability, and overall system responsiveness.

- **Real-Time Data Processing:** Applications that require the continual processing of live data streams, such as financial tickers, IoT sensor data, or social media feeds, benefit immensely from reactive programming. The ability to operate on a stream of data asynchronously allows these applications to provide instant insights and reactions to incoming data.

- **User Interface Development:** Modern UI development frameworks and libraries have started to employ reactive programming principles to manage state changes dynamically. This reactive approach facilitates a more intuitive and responsive user experience by efficiently handling user interactions, routing, and view updates without blocking the main thread.

- **Microservices Architecture:** In a microservices architecture, services often communicate through asynchronous messaging. Reactive programming enables these services to handle requests non-blockingly and maintain backpressure, which is critical for preventing system overloads and ensuring resilience and elasticity.

- **Networking Applications:** Application protocols that operate over networks, such as HTTP/2 and WebSockets, inherently support asynchronous operations and streams. Reactive programming models align well with these protocols by enabling efficient, non-blocking I/O operations, which is crucial for high-performance web servers and clients.

- **Complex Event Processing (CEP):** In scenarios where applications must react to a series of events in real-time, such as fraud detection, algorithmic trading, or monitoring systems, reactive programming provides the tools to filter, aggregate, and analyze streams of events efficiently.

The practical implementation of reactive programming in these use cases typically involves the composition of data streams and the definition of how data flows through operators, ultimately reaching subscribers who take action based on the data. An example of creating a simple data stream with a reactive library (RxJava) might look like the following:

```
1  Flowable.just("Reactive", "Programming", "Use", "Cases")
2      .subscribe(System.out::println);
```

The above example demonstrates the creation of a `Flowable` object that emits a stream of strings. Each string is then passed to `System.out :println`, which acts as a subscriber and prints each string to the console. This simplistic example illustrates the foundation of reactive programming, where data streams are first-class citizens, and the focus is on the data flow and the operations performed on the data.

As reactive programming continues to gain popularity, its application has spread across various domains, proving its usefulness in dealing with asynchronous data streams and systems requiring high levels of interactivity and scalability. The integration of reactive programming models into development practices requires a shift in mindset from traditional imperative programming, but the benefits in terms of application performance, responsiveness, and scalability are substantial.

1.5 Key Components in Reactive Systems

Reactive systems are characterized by their responsiveness, resilience, elasticity, and message-driven architecture. These characteristics are

18

not emergent properties but are the result of specific architectural decisions. This section will discuss the foundational components that are integral to the functioning of reactive systems, including the data stream, the publisher-subscriber pattern, backpressure, and event loops.

First and foremost, at the heart of reactive systems lies the concept of a data stream. A data stream is a sequence of asynchronous data items that can be processed in a non-blocking manner. In the reactive paradigm, almost everything can be modeled as a stream—user interactions, messages from a queue, and even variable changes. The data stream is the conduit through which data flows from its source to potential consumers.

The publisher-subscriber pattern is fundamental to the operation of reactive systems. This pattern allows components to emit data (publishers) without knowing who will consume them (subscribers). This decoupling of data production from consumption enhances modularity and scalability. The reactive streams specification, a foundational standard in reactive programming, formalizes this interaction through the Publisher and Subscriber interfaces. A simple example in code might look like the following:

```
1  Publisher<Integer> publisher = Flux.just(1, 2, 3, 4);
2  Subscriber<Integer> subscriber = new BaseSubscriber<>() {
3      @Override
4      protected void hookOnNext(Integer value) {
5          System.out.println("Received: " + value);
6      }
7  };
8  publisher.subscribe(subscriber);
```

Here, Flux is a reactive type that represents a data stream which can emit 0 to N elements. In this example, the publisher is emitting a sequence of integers, while the subscriber processes each item as it arrives.

Backpressure is a critical mechanism within reactive systems for managing data flow. It allows subscribers to signal to publishers how much data they are ready to process, preventing them from being overwhelmed. This feedback loop ensures that subscribers can process data at their own pace, leading to more stable and resilient systems. Without backpressure, fast producers could easily overwhelm slow consumers, leading to out-of-memory errors and other issues.

Event loops are another key component, especially in the implementation of non-blocking I/O operations. An event loop runs a loop that waits for and dispatches events or messages in a program. It works hand-in-hand with non-blocking I/O operations, allowing a single thread to manage multiple concurrent operations. The event loop ensures that I/O operations do not block the execution thread, enhancing the system's scalability and responsiveness.

```
Received: 1
Received: 2
Received: 3
Received: 4
```

The output above demonstrates how the subscriber processes each element emitted by the publisher.

In addition to these components, reactive systems often leverage additional patterns and utilities, such as Futures, Promises, and Callbacks, to facilitate asynchronous programming. These tools work together to enable developers to write code that is more responsive and efficient.

In summary, the transition to building reactive systems requires a fundamental shift in mindset from traditional synchronous and blocking interaction models. By understanding and correctly implementing key components like data streams, the publisher-subscriber pattern, backpressure, and event loops, developers can construct systems that are significantly more resilient, responsive, and scalable. This underlying architecture not only supports the volume and velocity of data in modern applications but also provides a more efficient way to manage resources, thus fulfilling the reactive manifesto's goals.

1.6 The Reactive Manifesto Explained

The Reactive Manifesto, formalized in 2013, is a pivotal document that lays the foundation for understanding and implementing reactive programming in software development. It articulates the guiding principles that reactive systems must adhere to, aiming to furnish a more coherent, resilient, and interactive application architecture. The Manifesto delineates four cardinal attributes that are quintessential for reactive systems: responsiveness, resilience, elasticity, and message-driven architecture. In this section, we will discuss each of these attributes in detail, elucidating their significance and implications for software development practices.

Firstly, responsiveness is the cornerstone of the Reactive Manifesto. A responsive system is prompt in handling requests, ensuring timely outcomes that contribute to a satisfactory user experience. Responsiveness is crucial not only in the face of user interactions but also under variable load conditions. The necessity for responsiveness stipulates that systems must be designed to return feedback within a predictable time frame, thus maintaining a reliable service quality.

To illustrate responsiveness, consider the following 1stlisting example of a non-blocking REST endpoint using Spring WebFlux, a reactive web framework:

```
1  @GetMapping("/events")
2  public Flux<Event> getEvents() {
3      return eventService.findAll(); // Non-blocking I/O operation
4  }
```

In this example, the use of Flux<Event> as the return type showcases the non-blocking nature of the operation, allowing for a responsive system that can serve numerous concurrent requests efficiently.

Secondly, resilience refers to the system's capacity to remain responsive even in the event of failure. Resilience in reactive systems is achieved through replication, containment, isolation, and delegation. Failures are contained within each component, ensuring that a single component's failure doesn't cascade through the system. Delegation is used to recover from failures where appropriate, with recovery measures treated as a first-class concern.

One effective strategy for implementing resilience is the Circuit Breaker pattern, which prevents a failure in one service from cascading to other services. The following pseudocode illustrates the Circuit Breaker's conceptual operation:

21

Algorithm 1: Pseudocode for a Circuit Breaker pattern

Data: request to a microservice

Result: response from the microservice or a fallback
mechanism

1 circuitBreaker ← getCircuitBreakerForService()
2 **if** *circuitBreaker.isClosed()* **then**
3 | response ← forwardRequestToService()
4 | **if** *response.isSuccessful()* **then**
5 | | return response
6 | **else**
7 | | circuitBreaker.recordFailure()
8 | | return fallbackResponse
9 **else**
10 | return fallbackResponse

Thirdly, elasticity pertains to the system's ability to adapt to changing loads by allocating and de-allocating resources in an efficient manner. Unlike scalability, which is merely the capability to handle growth, elasticity implies the system's prowess in both scaling up and down as necessary. Elastic systems can thus optimize resource utilization dynamically, aligning closely with the pay-per-use models used in cloud environments.

For a visualization of elasticity, consider a hypothetical scenario where system load is plotted against time:

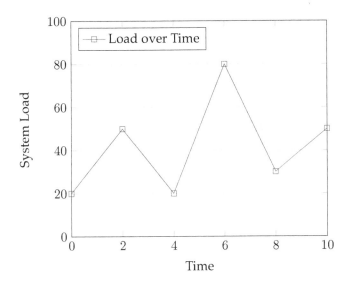

This plot demonstrates how an elastic system's consumption of resources fluctuates in tandem with the load, ensuring optimal performance and cost efficiency.

Lastly, being message-driven is integral to reactive systems, facilitating loose coupling, isolation, and location transparency. Message-driven architectures revolve around the asynchronous exchange of messages, allowing components to communicate reliably and efficiently without necessitating a direct invocation of methods. This promotes a non-blocking behavior, enhancing overall system responsiveness.

In sum, the Reactive Manifesto propounds a paradigm centered on building systems that are more aligned with the contemporary demands of software development. These systems are designed to be responsive, resilient, elastic, and message-driven, each of which contributes significantly to the manifesto's vision of a high-quality interactive user experience. Through adherence to these principles, developers can craft systems that are better equipped to deal with modern computing challenges, including real-time data processing and high concurrency demands.

1.7   Introduction to Reactive Streams

Reactive Streams is an initiative to provide a standard for asynchronous stream processing with non-blocking back pressure. This concept plays a crucial role in the reactive programming paradigm, especially when dealing with streams of data that need to be handled in a performant and resource-efficient manner. The key motivation behind Reactive Streams is to create a protocol that facilitates the exchange of data across asynchronous boundaries without overwhelming any participant in the communication chain.

In essence, Reactive Streams specify four main interfaces: `Publisher`, `Subscriber`, `Subscription`, and `Processor`. Let's break down each component and its responsibilities in the data flow.

- `Publisher`: This interface represents a data source that can emit items to one or more `Subscribers`. It is responsible for publishing data when requested by its subscribers.

- `Subscriber`: Subscribers consume data items emitted by a `Publisher`. They need to handle received data and manage the data flow through back pressure. This mechanism allows subscribers to signal the publisher how much data they are ready to process, preventing potential overflow or resource exhaustion.

- `Subscription`: A `Subscription` represents a one-to-one lifecycle handling contract between a `Publisher` and a `Subscriber`. It provides mechanisms for requesting items from the publisher and for canceling the subscription, offering subscribers control over the data flow.

- `Processor`: This interface acts as both a `Subscriber` and a `Publisher`, essentially bridging a data processing component that can both consume and produce data. It allows for the creation of transformation pipelines that can process data as it passes from one `Publisher` to the next `Subscriber`.

The concept of back pressure is central to understanding Reactive Streams. It is a strategy that ensures consumers of data don't get overwhelmed by too much data being pushed to them faster than they can handle. Through the `Subscription` mechanism, a `Subscriber` can request a specific amount of data items from the `Publisher`, ensuring that the subscriber dictates the pace of the data flow. This interaction pattern allows reactive systems to operate efficiently, even in resource-constrained environments or under heavy load, by preventing unbounded resource usage and system crashes.

To illustrate how these components interact within a reactive stream, consider the following example:

```
1   Publisher<String> publisher = ...; // A source of strings
2   Subscriber<String> subscriber = new Subscriber<>() {
3       @Override
4       public void onSubscribe(Subscription s) {
5           s.request(Long.MAX_VALUE); // Request all data
6       }
7
8       @Override
9       public void onNext(String s) {
10          // Process each string as it is received
11      }
12
13      @Override
14      public void onError(Throwable t) {
15          // Handle any errors that occur during processing
16      }
17
18      @Override
19      public void onComplete() {
20          // Perform cleanup or final actions after all data is processed
21      }
22  };
23
24  publisher.subscribe(subscriber);
```

In this code snippet, a `Subscriber` subscribes to a `Publisher`, indicating readiness to receive and process data. By calling `s.request(Long.MAX_VALUE)`, the subscriber effectively requests an unbounded amount of data. However, in a real-world scenario, the subscriber would typically request a more manageable chunk of data, processing that set of items before requesting more, thereby implementing back pressure.

Reactive Streams offer a firm foundation for building responsive and resilient applications that can handle asynchronous data flows and dynamic data volumes gracefully. By adhering to this standard, developers can architect systems that are both scalable and reactive, effectively addressing modern software application challenges.

1.8 Understanding Observables and Subscribers

Let's start with the concept of Observables in the context of Reactive Programming. An Observable is an object that emits a stream of data or events over time. This could be anything from a simple sequence of integer values, a stream of mouse events in a graphical user interface, or more complex data streams like financial tickers. The fundamental idea behind an Observable is that it represents a collection of future events or asynchronous data that a Subscriber can listen to.

To illustrate how Observables work, consider the following example using pseudocode:

```
1  Observable<int> observable = new Observable();
2  observable.subscribe(data -> print(data));
3  observable.emit(1);
4  observable.emit(2);
5  observable.emit(3);
```

In this example, an `Observable` object is created that will emit integer values. A Subscriber expresses interest in those values by subscribing to the Observable and providing a lambda function that prints the data. When the Observable emits values using `.emit()`, the Subscriber's function is invoked with the emitted data.

Subscribers are essentially observers that react to the data or events emitted by an Observable. For each piece of emitted data, a Subscriber will perform a predefined action, which can be anything from a side-effect like logging to more complex transformations and processing. It is important to note that a Subscriber only receives data after it subscribes to an Observable; data emitted before a subscription are not received by the Subscriber.

The relationship between Observables and Subscribers is fundamentally asynchronous. This means that in a Reactive system, the code does not block or wait for all the data to be generated before moving on to another task. Instead, data is consumed and reacted to as it becomes available, which is a key aspect of non-blocking I/O operations and contributes significantly to the efficiency and scalability of Reactive systems.

Moreover, Observables support various operations that can transform, filter, combine, or otherwise manipulate the streams of data before they reach the Subscriber. These operations can be chained together to construct complex data processing pipelines in a declarative manner. For instance:

```
1  observable
2    .filter(data -> data % 2 == 0)
3    .map(data -> data * 2)
4    .subscribe(data -> print(data));
```

This code snippet modifies the original data stream by first filtering out odd integers and then doubling the remaining even integers before they are printed by the Subscriber.

Understanding Observables and Subscribers involves grasping the push-based nature of data flows in Reactive Programming. Unlike traditional pull-based models where the consumer requests data when ready, in Reactive Programming, the Observable pushes data to Subscribers as it becomes available, inversely controlling the flow of data.

Error handling is an integral aspect of working with Observables and Subscribers. Observables can emit errors alongside regular data events, which Subscribers can handle gracefully, often without terminating the data stream. This approach to error handling emphasizes resilience and supports the development of robust, fault-tolerant systems.

In summary, Observables and Subscribers form the backbone of Reactive Programming, enabling efficient, asynchronous data streams that underpin Reactive systems. Through their interactions, complex data flows can be easily composed, managed, and reacted to, fostering the development of responsive, scalable, and performant applications.

1.9 The Role of Non-Blocking I/O

Non-Blocking I/O, or Non-Blocking Input/Output, plays a critical role in the reactive programming paradigm. It is a technique that allows a system to perform other tasks while waiting for I/O operations to complete, essentially not blocking the thread on which the I/O operation is being performed. This is in stark contrast to traditional blocking I/O, where the application thread is halted, waiting for the operation to finish, thus potentially leading to inefficient use of resources and poor application performance, especially in high-load scenarios.

In the context of reactive programming, Non-Blocking I/O is fundamental as it complements the asynchronous data flow and contributes significantly to the system's scalability and responsiveness. When an application leverages Non-Blocking I/O, it can manage numerous connections and requests concurrently without requiring a proportional increase in the number of threads or the amount of hardware resources. This is achieved by utilizing mechanisms such as callbacks, futures, promises, and reactive streams, which allow the application to react to I/O events rather than waiting for them.

An example to illustrate the use of Non-Blocking I/O in a simple HTTP request scenario is as follows:

```
1  WebClient.create("http://example.com")
2    .get()
3    .retrieve()
4    .bodyToMono(String.class)
5    .subscribe(content -> System.out.println(content));
```

In the above example, `WebClient` from the Spring WebFlux framework is used to perform a non-blocking HTTP GET request. The `subscribe()` method is non-blocking. It registers a callback that prints the HTTP response content once it's available, without blocking the thread in the meantime.

Key benefits of adopting Non-Blocking I/O include:

- **Improved Resource Utilization:** As threads are not blocked waiting for I/O operations to complete, they can be used to handle other tasks. This leads to more efficient use of system resources.

- **Higher Scalability:** The ability to handle more concurrent requests with fewer resources greatly improves the application's scalability.

- **Better Performance:** Applications can serve more users and handle more data with lower latency, leading to an improved overall performance.

- **Enhanced User Experience:** Users benefit from faster responses and a smoother interaction with the application, given the reduced latency in processing their requests.

However, implementing Non-Blocking I/O is not without challenges. It introduces complexity in error handling, flow control, backpressure management, and the understanding of the underlying asynchronous programming models. Developers must embrace these complexities and be proficient in the patterns and best practices of asynchronous and event-driven programming to build efficient, robust, and scalable reactive systems.

Furthermore, the choice of frameworks and libraries that support Non-Blocking I/O is critical. In the Java ecosystem, for example, libraries such as Reactor (used by Spring WebFlux) and RxJava provide comprehensive support for building non-blocking applications. They offer abstractions like Flux and Mono in Reactor, or Observable and Single in RxJava, that conform to the Reactive Streams specification, ensuring seamless flow control and backpressure management.

Non-Blocking I/O is indispensable in the world of reactive programming. It is a cornerstone that enables applications to achieve high levels of performance, scalability, and responsiveness. By carefully adopting and correctly implementing Non-Blocking I/O patterns, along with choosing the appropriate libraries and frameworks, developers can significantly improve the efficiency and quality of their applications in a reactive programming model.

1.10 Challenges and Solutions in Reactive Programming

Reactive programming, despite its numerous advantages for building responsive, scalable applications, presents several challenges to developers, particularly those accustomed to the imperative programming paradigm. This section discusses these challenges and explores potential strategies and solutions to overcome them, ensuring a smooth transition and effective implementation of reactive programming principles in software development projects.

Backpressure: One of the fundamental challenges in reactive programming is managing backpressure. Backpressure occurs when data producers generate data at a faster rate than consumers can process, leading to potential system overloads and performance degradation.

```
Example of a potential backpressure scenario:
- A sensor network producing data readings every millisecond
- A processing unit capable of handling data readings every second
```

To address this issue, reactive streams specification includes a backpressure mechanism that allows consumers to signal producers about how much data they are ready to process, effectively controlling the flow of data. Implementations such as Project Reactor and RxJava

29

provide built-in support for backpressure, ensuring that applications can manage data flow efficiently.

Complex Error Handling: Compared to imperative programming, error handling in reactive programming can become more complex due to the asynchronous and non-blocking nature of data streams. Errors can occur at any point in the data pipeline and need to be propagated through the stream to be handled appropriately.

To facilitate effective error handling, reactive programming libraries offer operators that allow developers to intercept and manage errors. The onErrorReturn, onErrorResumeNext, and retry operators, for example, enable developers to specify fallback mechanisms, alternate data streams, or retry logic in case of errors, thus ensuring that applications can recover gracefully from failures.

```
1  Example of using onErrorReturn in RxJava:
2  Observable<String> observable = Observable
3     .fromCallable(() -> { throw new RuntimeException("Error!"); })
4     .onErrorReturn(error -> "Fallback Value");
5
6  observable.subscribe(
7     item -> System.out.println(item),
8     error -> error.printStackTrace()
9  );
```

- Performance Concerns: Reactively architecting systems introduces the challenge of ensuring performance does not suffer due to overhead associated with managing asynchronous data streams and backpressure. Strategies for addressing performance concerns include optimizing data flow paths, leveraging parallel processing where applicable, and using profiling tools to identify and eliminate bottlenecks.

- Steep Learning Curve: Developers accustomed to synchronous and blocking operations often find the reactive programming model challenging to grasp. Concepts such as observables, subscribers, backpressure, and non-blocking I/O represent a significant paradigm shift.

To mitigate the learning curve, it is recommended to start with foundational concepts, progressively building towards more complex structures and operations. Additionally, practical, hands-on exercises and examples play a crucial role in solidifying understanding.

Debugging Asynchronous Streams: Debugging applications that use reactive programming can be more challenging than traditional imperative counterparts due to the asynchronous nature of data flows. Challenges include tracking data across thread boundaries, understanding the state of the application at any given moment, and identifying the source of errors that may not manifest immediately.

Solutions for easing the debugging process include using advanced debugging tools and features provided by reactive programming libraries, such as detailed logging mechanisms and the ability to introspect data streams. For instance, Project Reactor offers the `log` operator to provide insight into the events passing through the stream, helping developers trace and diagnose issues more effectively.

```
1   Example of using the log operator in Project Reactor:
2   Flux<String> flux = Flux.just("A", "B", "C")
3       .map(String::toLowerCase)
4       .log();
5
6   flux.subscribe(System.out::println);
```

While reactive programming introduces new challenges, understanding and employing the right strategies and tools can significantly mitigate these issues. Emphasizing backpressure management, effective error handling, proactive performance optimization, gradual learning, and efficient debugging practices ensures developers can harness the full potential of reactive programming to build responsive, resilient, and scalable applications.

1.11 An Overview of Reactive Programming Libraries

Reactive programming has gained substantial prominence in the software development community, particularly with the rise in demand for non-blocking, event-driven applications that can elegantly handle real-time data streams. A variety of libraries have emerged to facilitate the adoption of reactive programming paradigms across different programming languages. This section will discuss several pivotal libraries that have significantly contributed to the reactive programming ecosystem, namely RxJava, Project Reactor, and Akka Streams, along with a brief mention of others that play a crucial role in specific contexts.

RxJava is a Java VM library that implements the Reactive Extensions (Rx) API. It offers a comprehensive collection of operators that allow developers to compose asynchronous and event-based programs in a declarative manner. Its core abstraction is the `Observable` class, which represents data sources that push items to the subscriber. The code snippet below illustrates a simple RxJava example:

```
1  Observable<String> observable = Observable.just("Hello", "Reactive", "World");
2  observable.subscribe(System.out::println);
```

The snippet demonstrates creating an `Observable` that emits strings and subscribing to it to print each emitted item. This simplicity masks the library's profound capability to handle complex asynchronous data flows.

Project Reactor is another influential library in the Java ecosystem, specifically designed to work with the Spring Framework. It implements the Reactive Streams specification and offers two main reactive types: `Flux`, which represents a reactive sequence of 0 to N items, and `Mono`, representing a single or empty value. Project Reactor is tightly integrated with Spring WebFlux, enabling developers to build reactive applications seamlessly within the Spring ecosystem. An example of creating a `Flux` is as follows:

```
1  Flux<String> flux = Flux.just("Reactor", "is", "powerful");
2  flux.subscribe(System.out::println);
```

This code snippet generates a `Flux` that emits three strings sequentially and subscribes to it to print each string to the console.

Akka Streams is part of the Akka toolkit and offers an actor-based approach to reactive streams. It is designed for building scalable, resilient, and responsive applications and excels in back-pressure management across asynchronous boundaries. Akka Streams facilitate the design of complex data transformation pipelines with ease.

In addition to these libraries, there are others worth mentioning that cater to different programming languages and use cases:

- **RxJS**: A reactive programming library for JavaScript, which plays a crucial role in handling asynchronous data streams in web applications.

- **RSocket**: A binary protocol for use on byte stream transports such as TCP, WebSocket, and Aeron. It supports Reactive

Streams backpressure and is designed for high-performance and resilience in distributed systems.

- **ReactiveX**: An API for asynchronous programming with observable streams, which has implementations in multiple programming languages.

The proliferation of reactive programming libraries across various ecosystems underscores the paradigm's relevance in modern software architecture. Each library has been fine-tuned for specific runtime environments, frameworks, and programming models, yet they all share the fundamental principles of reactive programming—facilitating an event-driven, non-blocking, and composable approach to software development.

It is essential for developers to understand the capabilities and idiosyncrasies of each library to make informed decisions when architecting reactive systems. While the adoption of reactive programming introduces a steep learning curve, the payoff in application performance, scalability, and responsiveness is substantial, making it a worthwhile investment for the evolving demands of contemporary computing environments.

1.12 Preparing for a Shift to Reactive Programming

Preparing for a shift to reactive programming involves a series of strategic steps and considerations, given its fundamentally different approach from traditional programming models. This transition requires not only a change in the tools and libraries used but also a significant shift in mindset regarding how data flows and is processed within applications. This section will discuss the key aspects of gearing up for adopting reactive programming in software development projects, focusing on understanding the necessary conceptual shift, selecting appropriate tools and libraries, integrating with existing codebases, and evolving the development mindset.

Let's start with the essential conceptual shift. At the heart of reactive programming is the principle of non-blocking, asynchronous data streams. This requires developers to think in terms of events rather than the sequential execution of code. Data in reactive programming is seen as a sequence of events that can be observed and manipulated using a variety of operators. This represents a paradigmatic change from imperative programming models that require a mental model adjustment for developers. One way to facilitate this shift is through hands-on experience, engaging with small, reactive projects to internalize the asynchronous, event-driven nature of reactive programming.

Selecting the appropriate tools and libraries is pivotal in moving to reactive programming. For Java developers, Reactor and RxJava are two prominent libraries that provide extensive functionality for creating reactive applications. Additionally, when working with Spring Boot, the Spring WebFlux module offers powerful support for building reactive APIs and services. It is crucial to evaluate these libraries in the context of the specific requirements of your project, considering factors such as learning curve, community support, and compatibility with existing tools and frameworks.

Integrating reactive programming concepts into existing codebases presents another layer of complexity. Transitioning an existing application to a reactive model often involves identifying components that can benefit most from reactive features, such as those handling I/O operations or requiring high scalability and responsiveness. This phased integration approach can mitigate the risk of disrupting the current functionality, allowing teams to gain familiarity with reactive principles and identify potential challenges in a controlled manner.

```
1  // Example of integrating a simple reactive component in a Spring Boot application
2  Flux<String> dataStream = Flux.just("Alpha", "Beta", "Gamma");
3  dataStream.subscribe(System.out::println);
```

```
Alpha
Beta
Gamma
```

Evolving the development mindset is perhaps the most crucial aspect of preparing for a shift to reactive programming. This involves embracing the principles of the Reactive Manifesto, focusing on building systems that are Responsive, Resilient, Elastic, and Message Driven. Developers need to prioritize non-blocking operations, leverage asynchronous processing, and design systems capable of back-pressure management. Cultivating this mindset requires ongoing learning and experimentation, often benefiting from community engagement through forums, conferences, and online resources.

34

- Understand and internalize the asynchronous, non-blocking nature of reactive programming.

- Select and experiment with reactive programming libraries that align with project needs.

- Adopt a phased approach to integrating reactive programming principles into existing projects.

- Embrace the reactive development mindset, focusing on building responsive, resilient, and elastic systems.

Preparing for a shift to reactive programming demands a comprehensive approach that encompasses a conceptual shift, tool selection, integration strategies, and mindset evolution. The asynchronous, non-blocking nature of reactive programming offers significant advantages in handling real-time data and complex data pipelines, catering to modern application demands. By carefully navigating these preparatory steps, developers can effectively harness the power of reactive programming to build more scalable, responsive, and efficient applications.

Chapter 2

Reactive Programming with RxJava

RxJava, a prominent library for composing asynchronous and event-based programs using observable sequences, stands at the forefront of implementing reactive programming in Java applications. By providing a rich toolkit for dealing with asynchronous data streams, RxJava enables developers to write highly concurrent, scalable, and resilient applications. This chapter delves into the core concepts, components, and practical applications of RxJava, equipping developers with the knowledge to effectively employ reactive programming patterns in their projects for improved data handling and application responsiveness.

2.1 Getting Started with RxJava

Let's start with the initial steps required to integrate RxJava into a Java project. RxJava can be added to your project using build automation tools like Gradle or Maven. For Gradle, add the dependency to the `build.gradle` file:

```
1  dependencies {
2      implementation 'io.reactivex.rxjava3:rxjava:3.x.y'
3  }
```

For Maven, include it in your `pom.xml`:

```
1  <dependency>
2    <groupId>io.reactivex.rxjava3</groupId>
3    <artifactId>rxjava</artifactId>
4    <version>3.x.y</version>
5  </dependency>
```

Replace "3.x.y" with the latest version of RxJava. After integrating RxJava into your project, the fundamental concept to grasp is the Observable. An Observable is an entity that emits a stream of data or events. Subscribers observe these emissions and react accordingly. To illustrate, consider creating a simple Observable that emits a sequence of integers:

```
1  Observable<Integer> observable = Observable.just(1, 2, 3, 4, 5);
```

Subscribing to the Observable and printing each emitted item can be done as follows:

```
1  observable.subscribe(item -> System.out.println(item),
2                  error -> error.printStackTrace(),
3                  () -> System.out.println("Completed"));
```

This code subscribes to the `Observable` and defines three handlers: one for handling emitted items, one for handling errors, and one that executes upon completion of the emission sequence. The output of subscribing to this Observable is:

```
1
2
3
4
5
Completed
```

Creating Observables from scratch provides insight into how emission patterns work. For more dynamic examples, RxJava provides several methods to create Observables. The `fromIterable` method, for example, converts an `Iterable` (such as a list) into an Observable:

```
1  List<Integer> list = Arrays.asList(1, 2, 3, 4, 5);
2  Observable<Integer> observableFromList = Observable.fromIterable(list);
```

Another vital component in RxJava is the `Observer`, which subscribes to an `Observable`. An Observer must implement three methods: onNext, onError, and onComplete. The onNext method is called for each item emitted by the Observable, onError is called if an error occurs, and onComplete is called once the Observable has finished emitting items.

38

```
1   Observer<Integer> observer = new Observer<Integer>() {
2       @Override
3       public void onNext(Integer item) {
4           System.out.println(item);
5       }
6
7       @Override
8       public void onError(Throwable e) {
9           e.printStackTrace();
10      }
11
12      @Override
13      public void onComplete() {
14          System.out.println("Completed");
15      }
16  };
```

Subscribing the Observer to the Observable is straightforward:

```
1   observable.subscribe(observer);
```

Understanding Observables and Observers is crucial, as they form the cornerstone of RxJava's data flow paradigm. They enable RxJava to handle streams of data efficiently, particularly in applications where data changes frequently or operations need to be performed asynchronously. Reactive programming with RxJava, therefore, allows developers to manage data streams and propagation of changes in a scalable manner, ensuring applications remain responsive and performant.

In the next sections, we will discuss more advanced topics and scenarios, further exploring the capabilities and versatility of RxJava in building reactive applications.

2.2 Key Concepts and Components of RxJava

In this section, we will discuss the foundational ideas and structural elements that underpin RxJava, a library designed to handle asynchronous and event-driven programming paradigms. RxJava, grounded in the Observer pattern, extends its capabilities to offer a comprehensive toolkit for working with and manipulating streams of data asynchronously. The core concepts include Observables, Observers, Subscriptions, and Operators. Understanding these components is essential for harnessing the power of RxJava to create efficient, responsive, and robust applications.

Observables: At the heart of RxJava are Observables. They form the primary source of data and events in a reactive program. Observables emit items or sequences of items over time, which are then consumed by Observers. Code block below demonstrates the creation of a simple Observable emitting a sequence of integers.

```
1   Observable<Integer> simpleObservable = Observable.just(1, 2, 3, 4, 5);
```

Observables can be cold or hot, determining the behavior of data emission with respect to multiple subscribers. Cold Observables start emitting data from the beginning for each new subscriber, whereas Hot Observables emit data in real-time regardless of when a subscriber starts listening.

Observers: Observers, or subscribers, are entities that consume the data or events emitted by Observables. They define how to handle the received items, dealing with the completion of the sequence, or managing errors that may arise during the data stream processing. The example below illustrates an Observer subscribing to the simpleObservable defined earlier.

```
1   simpleObservable.subscribe(
2       item -> System.out.println(item), // OnNext
3       error -> error.printStackTrace(), // OnError
4       () -> System.out.println("Completed") // OnCompleted
5   );
```

Subscriptions: When an Observer subscribes to an Observable, a Subscription is created. This Subscription represents the connection between the Observable and the Observer, providing a way to unsubscribe and terminate the data stream before it completes, freeing up resources and preventing potential memory leaks.

Operators: RxJava introduces the concept of Operators, which allow for the transformation, filtration, combination, and manipulation of data streams emitted by Observables. Operators are what make RxJava exceptionally powerful, enabling complex asynchronous operations to be performed with minimal and straightforward code. An example of an Operator is map, which applies a function to each item emitted by an Observable, effectively transforming the items according to the provided function. The following code applies a simple transformation to each item emitted.

```
1   Observable<Integer> transformedObservable = simpleObservable.map(item -> item * 2);
```

This section also outlines other vital components and concepts of Rx-Java, such as:

- **Schedulers**: RxJava's concurrency model, which allows specifying the thread or thread pool on which an Observable operates and the Observer receives notifications. This enables fine-grained control over the execution context of asynchronous operations, improving application performance and responsiveness.

- **Backpressure**: A strategy for dealing with scenarios where data is being emitted by an Observable faster than it can be consumed by an Observer. RxJava provides mechanisms to handle backpressure, ensuring that applications remain stable and responsive under heavy data loads.

- **Disposable**: A representation of a resource or a task that can be disposed of. In the context of RxJava, Disposables help manage the lifecycle of a Subscription, allowing for precise control over memory and resource management.

By mastering Observables, Observers, Subscriptions, and Operators, along with understanding Schedulers, Backpressure, and Disposables, developers can leverage the full capability of RxJava in creating sophisticated, asynchronous, and event-driven applications. The subsequent sections will delve deeper into these components, demonstrating their practical applications and providing insights into effective RxJava programming practices.

2.3 Creating Observables from Scratch

Creating observables from scratch is a fundamental skill in RxJava, enabling developers to encapsulate asynchronous data streams that can emit zero or more items, complete normally, or terminate with an error. This section will discuss the creation of observables using RxJava's factory methods: `create`, `just`, `fromIterable`, and `range`.

`create` is the most versatile factory method in RxJava, allowing for manual control over the emission of items, completion signals, and error notifications. The `create` method requires an `ObservableOnSubscribe` implementation, within which developers can call the `onNext`, `onComplete`, and `onError` methods to control the observable's behavior.

41

A simple usage of `create` method to emit three integer values could be as follows:

```
Observable<Integer> observable = Observable.create(emitter -> {
    emitter.onNext(1);
    emitter.onNext(2);
    emitter.onNext(3);
    emitter.onComplete();
});
```

This observable, when subscribed to, will emit the numbers 1, 2, and 3 sequentially before indicating completion.

The `just` method simplifies the creation of observables that emit a known set of items and then complete. `just` can take from one to ten arguments, which will be emitted in the sequence they're provided. An example usage of `just` to emit a string series is shown below:

```
Observable<String> observable = Observable.just("RxJava", "Reactive Programming", "
    Spring Boot");
```

`fromIterable` method converts an existing iterable, such as a list or a set, into an observable that emits each item contained within the iterable. It is particularly useful when working with collections of data:

```
List<String> list = Arrays.asList("Alpha", "Beta", "Gamma");
Observable<String> observable = Observable.fromIterable(list);
```

`range` method creates an observable that emits a sequence of integers in range, starting from a specified value and containing a specific count of sequential numbers:

```
Observable<Integer> observable = Observable.range(1, 5);
```

This will produce an observable emitting integers from 1 through 5.

Each of these factories offers flexibility in how observables are created and what they emit, forming the bedrock for building complex data streams in RxJava applications. It is important to select the most appropriate factory method based on the characteristics of the data source and the desired behavior of the observable sequence.

In terms of best practices, prefer `fromIterable` over `create` when dealing with collections to avoid manual iteration and potential errors. Moreover, `just` and `range` are more suitable for emitting a fixed series of known items or ranges, ensuring clear and concise code.

To encapsulate, understanding and employing these factory methods judiciously allows for the efficient creation of observables, facilitating

42

the powerful reactive programming model RxJava offers for handling asynchronous data streams in a consistent and resilient manner.

2.4   Transforming Items in a Stream

Transforming items in a stream is a cornerstone operation in reactive programming, particularly when using RxJava. This process involves taking each item emitted by an Observable and applying a function to each item to produce a new item. The transformation operators provided by RxJava are versatile, allowing for the modification, combination, and generally, the manipulation of data streams to suit specific application needs.

One of the primary operators for transformation in RxJava is the map operator. The map operator takes each item emitted by an Observable, applies a function to it, and then emits the resulting item. This operator is particularly useful for converting the items of a stream from one type to another or for applying any function to modify the items.

```
1  Observable<Integer> observable = Observable.just(1, 2, 3, 4, 5);
2  Observable<Integer> squaredNumbers = observable.map(x -> x * x);
3  squaredNumbers.subscribe(System.out::println);
```

```
1
4
9
16
25
```

The above code snippet demonstrates the use of the map operator to square each number in a stream of integers. The subscribe method is then used to print each squared number.

Another essential transformation operator is the flatMap operator. Unlike the map operator, which applies a function to each item and emits one item at a time, the flatMap operator is used when each item in the stream is transformed into an Observable, and the outputs of these Observables are then flattened into a single Observable.

```
1  Observable<String> names = Observable.just("John", "Doe", "Jane", "Doe");
2  Observable<String> initials = names.flatMap(name -> Observable.just(name.charAt(0)
       + "."));
3  initials.subscribe(System.out::println);
```

J.

```
D.
J.
D.
```

This example demonstrates converting a stream of names into a stream of initials using the `flatMap` operator. Each name is transformed into an Observable emitting the initial, and then `flatMap` merges these Observables into one stream.

The `buffer` operator is another transformative tool that gathers items emitted by an Observable into batches and emits each batch instead of emitting one item at a time. This operator is particularly useful in scenarios where processing or handling a batch of items at once is more efficient than processing each item individually.

```
1  Observable<Integer> numbers = Observable.range(1, 10);
2  Observable<List<Integer>> buffered = numbers.buffer(3);
3  buffered.subscribe(System.out::println);
```

```
[1, 2, 3]
[4, 5, 6]
[7, 8, 9]
[10]
```

In the provided code, the `buffer` operator collects items emitted by an Observable into lists of three items. The last buffer contains the remainder, which in this case, is only one item.

RxJava provides a rich set of operators for transforming data streams, enabling developers to solve complex data processing problems efficiently. The `map`, `flatMap`, and `buffer` operators are fundamental tools in the repertoire of an RxJava developer, offering straightforward solutions for data transformation. By applying these operators, developers can significantly enhance the flexibility and capability of their reactive programming solutions, making the handling of asynchronous data streams both effective and manageable.

2.5   Filtering Observables in RxJava

Filtering is a pivotal operation in dealing with observables in RxJava, particularly when it comes to processing substantial data streams. This operation allows developers to sift through a stream of items emitted by an Observable, selecting those that meet specific criteria. Filtering operations can significantly improve the efficiency and responsiveness of applications by narrowing down the data set to work with, thereby facilitating more targeted operations on these data streams.

RxJava provides several operators for filtering observables, each tailored to different scenarios and types of criteria. In this section, we will discuss some of the most commonly used filtering operators, such as filter, take, takeWhile, skip, and distinct. Additionally, practical examples will elucidate how these operators can be applied in real-world applications.

```
1  Observable<Integer> observable = Observable.range(1, 10);
```

One of the most straightforward filtering operators is filter. This operator applies a predicate to each item emitted by an Observable and only emits those items that satisfy the predicate.

```
1  observable.filter(item -> item % 2 == 0)
2          .subscribe(System.out::println);
```

Consider the above code snippet where the filter operator is applied to an Observable that emits integers from 1 to 10. The predicate in this instance checks for even numbers. Consequently, the output is:

```
2
4
6
8
10
```

The take operator is another useful operator that allows taking a specific number of items from the beginning of a stream.

```
1  observable.take(4)
2          .subscribe(System.out::println);
```

The code above will result in the first four integers being emitted:

```
1
2
3
4
```

Contrastingly, the takeWhile operator emits items as long as a specified condition remains true. Once the condition evaluates to false, it stops emitting items.

```
1  observable.takeWhile(item -> item < 5)
2          .subscribe(System.out::println);
```

This code snippet emits integers until it encounters a number that is not less than 5:

```
1
2
3
4
```

In scenarios where it is desirable to skip a certain number of items before beginning to emit, the skip operator proves to be useful.

```
1  observable.skip(3)
2        .subscribe(System.out::println);
```

In this example, the first three items are skipped:

```
4
5
6
7
8
9
10
```

Additionally, when dealing with streams that may contain duplicate items, the distinct operator provides a means to ensure that only unique items are emitted.

```
1  Observable.just(1, 2, 2, 3, 4, 4, 5)
2        .distinct()
3        .subscribe(System.out::println);
```

The output from the above snippet ensures that all the numbers emitted are distinct:

```
1
2
3
4
5
```

In summary, the ability to filter observables in RxJava is an essential aspect of writing efficient and effective reactive applications. Through the use of various filtering operators such as filter, take, takeWhile, skip, and distinct, developers can precisely control the data that flows through their application's reactive pipelines. These operators, when used correctly, enable the handling of complex data streams with greater agility and specificity, ultimately leading to more responsive and performant applications.

2.6   Combining Multiple Data Streams

Combining multiple data streams in RxJava is a fundamental aspect of building reactive applications that require data from various sources to be merged, concatenated, or otherwise combined into a single stream for further processing. RxJava provides several operators to accomplish these tasks, each tailored for specific use cases. This section will discuss the `merge`, `concat`, `zip`, and `combineLatest` operators, offering insight into their unique characteristics and practical applications.

`merge` operator is used when it is necessary to combine multiple Observables into one, without waiting for any of them to complete before starting to emit items from the next observable. This is particularly useful in scenarios where the order of items is not critical, and you want to process items as soon as they are emitted by any of the source Observables. Here is an example of how the `merge` operator can be utilized:

```
1  Observable<String> stream1 = Observable.just("A", "B");
2  Observable<String> stream2 = Observable.just("C", "D");
3
4  Observable<String> mergedStream = Observable.merge(stream1, stream2);
5
6  mergedStream.subscribe(System.out::println);
```

```
A
B
C
D
```

`concat` operator, in contrast to `merge`, combines multiple Observables by waiting for each one to complete before starting to emit items from the next observable. This operator is suitable for situations where the order of items is important. The following code snippet demonstrates how to use the `concat` operator:

```
1  Observable<String> stream1 = Observable.just("A", "B").delay(1, TimeUnit.SECONDS);
2  Observable<String> stream2 = Observable.just("C", "D");
3
4  Observable<String> concatenatedStream = Observable.concat(stream1, stream2);
5
6  concatenatedStream.subscribe(System.out::println);
```

```
A
B
C
D
```

The `zip` operator combines the emissions of multiple Observables together via a specified function and emits single items for each combination based on the results of this function. It is typically used when there is a need to combine items from different streams based on their relative positions. The `zip` operator can be illustrated with the following example:

```
1  Observable<String> titles = Observable.just("Mr.", "Mrs.");
2  Observable<String> names = Observable.just("John", "Jane");
3
4  Observable<String> zippedStream = Observable.zip(titles, names,
5      (title, name) -> title + " " + name);
6
7  zippedStream.subscribe(System.out::println);
```

```
Mr. John
Mrs. Jane
```

Finally, the `combineLatest` operator is used to combine the latest items emitted by multiple Observables. Whenever any of the source Observables emits an item, `combineLatest` combines the latest item emitted by each of the other observables and applies a function to the combination, emitting the result. This operator is particularly useful for cases where you want to perform operations on the latest data from each of multiple sources. Here is how the `combineLatest` operator works:

```
1  Observable<Long> interval1 = Observable.interval(1, TimeUnit.SECONDS);
2  Observable<Long> interval2 = Observable.interval(2, TimeUnit.SECONDS);
3
4  Observable<String> combinedStream = Observable.combineLatest(
5      interval1,
6      interval2,
7      (i1, i2) -> "interval1: " + i1 + ", interval2: " + i2);
8
9  combinedStream.subscribe(System.out::println);
```

RxJava provides a powerful set of operators to combine multiple data streams, allowing developers to elegantly handle complex data-driven scenarios in their reactive applications. By selecting the appropriate combining operator based on the specific requirements of the application - whether it's the order of emissions, combining based on relative positions, or handling the latest data from each source - developers can enhance the functionality and responsiveness of their reactive applications.

2.7 Error Handling in RxJava

Error handling in RxJava is a critical aspect of developing resilient reactive applications. RxJava provides a comprehensive set of operators for handling errors that allow developers to manage exceptions in a declarative and flexible manner. This section discusses the strategies for handling errors in observables, including the use of the onErrorReturn, onErrorResumeNext, onExceptionResumeNext, and retry operators. Additionally, the importance of understanding the difference between checked and unchecked exceptions in the context of RxJava error handling is emphasized.

One of the fundamental operators for dealing with errors in RxJava is the onErrorReturn operator. This operator allows the creation of a fallback mechanism in case of an error. When an error occurs, onErrorReturn provides an alternative value to the observer, effectively allowing the sequence to terminate gracefully. The usage of onErrorReturn can be illustrated in the following example:

```
1  Observable<String> source = Observable.just("1", "2", "a", "3", "4")
2      .map(v -> Integer.parseInt(v))
3      .onErrorReturn(e -> -1); // Fallback value
4
5  source.subscribe(System.out::println,
6    Throwable::printStackTrace,
7    () -> System.out.println("Completed"));
```

In the case where parsing "a" fails, onErrorReturn catches the exception and emits -1 as a fallback, allowing the observable to complete.

Another operator, onErrorResumeNext, provides even greater flexibility by allowing an alternate Observable to be subscribed to in case of an error. This is particularly useful when the recovery strategy involves more complex sequences than simply emitting a single fallback value. Below is an example demonstrating onErrorResumeNext:

```
1  Observable<String> source = Observable.just("1", "2", "a", "3", "4")
2      .map(v -> Integer.parseInt(v))
3      .onErrorResumeNext(Observable.just(-1, -2, -3)); // Fallback sequence
4
5  source.subscribe(System.out::println,
6    Throwable::printStackTrace,
7    () -> System.out.println("Completed"));
```

Here, instead of emitting a single value, a new observable with a sequence of fallback values -1, -2, -3 is subscribed to upon encountering an error.

49

The onExceptionResumeNext operator behaves similarly to onErrorResumeNext, with the distinction that it only catches exceptions but not other types of errors such as Throwable. Its usage is identical to onErrorResumeNext, but it is designed for scenarios where only exceptions need to be handled, leaving more serious errors to propagate.

For cases where retrying an operation is desirable, the retry operator becomes invaluable. retry resubscribes to the source observable upon an error, attempting to create a new sequence. This can be particularly useful for transient errors or unstable network connections. An example of using retry is shown below:

```
Observable<String> source = Observable.just("remoteServiceCall")
    .map(this::someUnreliableFunction)
    .retry(2); // Retry max 2 times

source.subscribe(System.out::println,
  Throwable::printStackTrace,
  () -> System.out.println("Completed"));
```

Here, retry(2) specifies that the subscription should be attempted up to two more times upon encountering an error before ultimately failing.

It is important to note the distinction between checked and unchecked exceptions in Java when dealing with RxJava error handling. Unchecked exceptions, deriving from RuntimeException, are the primary exception type expected by RxJava's error handling operators. Checked exceptions, although can be managed, typically require additional boilerplate code to wrap them into unchecked exceptions or Throwable objects. Understanding this distinction is crucial for implementing effective error handling strategies in reactive programming with RxJava.

In summary, RxJava offers a sophisticated toolkit for managing errors in reactive sequences. By leveraging operators such as onErrorReturn, onErrorResumeNext, onExceptionResumeNext, and retry, developers can create resilient and fault-tolerant applications. Mastery of these error handling mechanisms is essential for effectively managing the asynchronous and event-driven nature of reactive programming.

2.8 Working with Schedulers and Concurrency

In this section we will discuss how RxJava facilitates the execution of code on different threads using Schedulers, which are a fundamental part of achieving concurrency in reactive applications. Concurrency allows for better resource utilization and improved application responsiveness. Understanding how to work with Schedulers and concurrency is crucial for developers aiming to build scalable and efficient reactive systems with RxJava.

Schedulers in RxJava essentially dictate the thread on which an operation (emission, transformation, consumption) is executed. RxJava provides several default Schedulers designed for various use cases, each optimizing different aspects of threading behavior.

- `Schedulers.io()` - optimized for I/O-bound work such as reading and writing to files, database operations, and network calls. It maintains a pool of threads that grows as needed.

- `Schedulers.computation()` - optimized for CPU-bound work that requires computational power. The number of threads is limited to the number of available processors.

- `Schedulers.newThread()` - creates a new thread for each unit of work.

- `Schedulers.single()` - provides a single thread for all tasks to ensure sequential execution, useful for tasks that must not be executed concurrently.

- `Schedulers.trampoline()` - queues work on the current thread to be executed after the current task completes, useful for recursive calls.

To apply a Scheduler in RxJava, the subscribeOn and observeOn operators are used. The subscribeOn operator specifies the Scheduler on which an Observable will operate. Conversely, observeOn changes the Scheduler partway down the chain of operators, affecting downstream operators. It is important to note that while subscribeOn can affect where the source Observable operates, observeOn can be used multiple times to switch execution contexts as needed.

```
1  Observable<String> observable = Observable.just("A", "B", "C")
2      .subscribeOn(Schedulers.io())
3      .map(s -> s.toLowerCase()) // Executed on the I/O Scheduler
4      .observeOn(Schedulers.computation())
5      .map(s -> complexComputation(s)); // Executed on the Computation Scheduler
```

In the example above, the `map` operation following `subscribeOn` operates on the I/O Scheduler, suitable for I/O-bound operations, whereas the `map` operation after `observeOn` switches to the Computation Scheduler, ideal for CPU-intensive work.

One critical aspect of working with concurrency is handling errors that might occur on different threads. RxJava provides mechanisms to deal with exceptions in a thread-safe manner across schedulers. The `onError` callback in an Observable's `subscribe` method is designed to handle exceptions and can be used to specify error handling behavior.

An understanding of backpressure is also necessary when working with concurrency, especially in cases where Observable sources produce items at a faster rate than consumers can process them. RxJava offers strategies such as `Flowable` and `BackpressureStrategy` to handle backpressure effectively.

In summary, Schedulers and concurrency are integral to leveraging the full capabilities of RxJava, allowing developers to write applications that are responsive, efficient, and scalable. By carefully choosing the appropriate Scheduler for the task at hand and understanding how to apply `subscribeOn` and `observeOn` effectively, developers can harness the power of concurrency in their reactive applications.

2.9   Backpressure in RxJava

In reactive programming, backpressure is a critical concept for managing the flow of data between producers and consumers. Backpressure occurs when the producer of data sends items at a faster pace than the consumer can process them. Without proper backpressure management, this mismatch in processing rates can lead to memory issues, such as buffer overflow, which, in turn, might crash the application. RxJava offers mechanisms to handle backpressure efficiently, ensuring that the system remains robust and responsive under various load conditions.

To understand backpressure in RxJava, it is essential to differentiate between two types of observables: 'Flowable' and 'Observable'. Originally, RxJava did not distinguish between these two; however, with the introduction of RxJava 2, this distinction became a cornerstone in handling backpressure:

- 'Observable' does not support backpressure. It is designed for streams where backpressure is not an issue, such as UI events or finite data sources.

- 'Flowable' is designed with backpressure in mind and should be used for streams that might require backpressure handling, typically those dealing with large amounts of data or infinite streams.

When using 'Flowable', RxJava handles backpressure by implementing a strategy called Reactive Pull. In this model, the consumer requests a specific number of items from the producer rather than processing all items at once. This approach aligns the pace at which items are produced and consumed, thereby managing system resources more efficiently.

Consider an example where a 'Flowable' is created to emit a large set of data:

```
1  Flowable.range(1, 1_000_000)
2      .observeOn(Schedulers.io())
3      .subscribe(
4          item -> {
5              System.out.println("Received: " + item);
6              Thread.sleep(100); // Simulated work
7          }
8      );
```

In the example above, the 'Flowable.range' function generates a large range of integers. The 'observeOn' operator directs the 'Flowable' to operate on the 'io' scheduler, simulating a scenario where processing each item takes significant time ('Thread.sleep(100)'). Without backpressure, this would quickly result in a scenario where the system struggles to manage memory efficiently.

To manage backpressure, RxJava provides several strategies through the 'BackpressureStrategy' enum when creating a 'Flowable'. These strategies include:

- MISSING: No backpressure strategy is implemented. It's up to the developer to manage the flow of data.

- ERROR: Throws a 'MissingBackpressureException' when the downstream cannot keep up with the source.

- BUFFER: Buffers all items from the producer, ensuring no data is lost, at the cost of potentially high memory usage.

- DROP: Drops the most recent item if the downstream cannot keep up.

- LATEST: Keeps only the latest item, overriding older values if the consumer is too slow.

Choosing the right backpressure strategy depends on the specific requirements and behavior of the application. For instance, 'BUFFER' is useful when it is crucial not to lose any data, but developers must be wary of the memory implications. On the other hand, 'DROP' or 'LATEST' can be more appropriate when it is acceptable to lose some data for the sake of maintaining application performance.

In addition to choosing a strategy, developers must also design their applications to be aware of backpressure throughout the data pipeline. This includes applying operators that respect backpressure, such as 'flatMap' with maxConcurrency settings, and using 'onBackpressureBuffer', 'onBackpressureDrop', or 'onBackpressureLatest' operators to explicitly manage backpressure behavior in streams where it might not be automatically handled.

In summary, backpressure is a fundamental aspect of building resilient and responsive applications using RxJava. By understanding the mechanisms RxJava provides for managing data flow, developers can ensure that their applications can handle varying loads gracefully, without sacrificing performance or reliability.

2.10   Hot vs. Cold Observables

Understanding the distinction between hot and cold observables is essential for effectively managing data streams in reactive programming with RxJava. This differentiation plays a critical role in how data is published and consumed by subscribers. In this section, we will discuss the characteristics of both hot and cold observables, their use cases, and how to convert between the two.

Cold observables are lazy and do not start emitting data until a subscriber subscribes to them. Each subscriber to a cold observable is guaranteed to receive the data sequence from the beginning, ensuring that all subscribers get the complete data set regardless of when they subscribe. This behavior is analogous to playing a recorded video, where each viewer starts from the beginning, regardless of when they start watching.

```
1  Observable<Integer> coldObservable = Observable.fromArray(1, 2, 3, 4, 5);
2
3  coldObservable.subscribe(item -> System.out.println("Subscriber 1: " + item));
4  coldObservable.subscribe(item -> System.out.println("Subscriber 2: " + item));
```

The output for each subscriber in the code above will be the complete sequence from 1 to 5, illustrating how cold observables behave.

Hot observables, on the other hand, are active and begin emitting data immediately upon creation, independent of the presence of subscribers. When a subscriber subscribes to a hot observable, it begins to receive emissions from that point forward, possibly missing out on previous emissions. This behavior is similar to watching a live broadcast, where viewers only see the content from the point they started watching and cannot view earlier parts of the broadcast.

```
Subscriber 1: 1
Subscriber 1: 2
Subscriber 1: 3
Subscriber 1: 4
Subscriber 1: 5
Subscriber 2: 1
Subscriber 2: 2
Subscriber 2: 3
Subscriber 2: 4
Subscriber 2: 5
```

To demonstrate the concept of hot observables, consider a scenario where an observable wraps a data stream from a live stock ticker. Each subscriber sees the price changes from the moment of subscription, missing any changes that occurred before.

```
1  ConnectableObservable<Integer> hotObservable =
2      Observable.just(1, 2, 3, 4, 5).publish();
3
4  hotObservable.connect();
5
6  hotObservable.subscribe(item -> System.out.println("Subscriber 1: " + item));
7  Thread.sleep(1000); // Simulates delay in subscription
8  hotObservable.subscribe(item -> System.out.println("Subscriber 2: " + item));
```

In this case, 'Subscriber 2' may miss initial emissions if they occur before the subscription.

Conversion between hot and cold observables is a common operation. To convert a cold observable into a hot one, the 'publish()' method from RxJava can be utilized, followed by calling 'connect()' on the resulting 'ConnectableObservable'. This process starts emission, making the observable hot.

```
1  Observable<Integer> cold = Observable.range(1, 5);
2  ConnectableObservable<Integer> hot = cold.publish();
3  hot.connect(); // Starts emission
```

Conversely, converting a hot observable into a cold one involves using operators that inherently multicast and cache emissions, such as 'replay()' and 'cache()'. These operators allow emissions to be stored and replayed to future subscribers, simulating the behavior of a cold observable.

```
1  ConnectableObservable<Integer> hotObservable =
2      Observable.just(1, 2, 3).publish();
3  hotObservable.connect();
4
5  Observable<Integer> coldFromHot = hotObservable.replay().autoConnect();
```

Choosing between hot and cold observables depends on the specific requirements of the application and how data should be delivered to subscribers. Cold observables are suitable for sequences that are generated per subscriber, ensuring all data is available to each subscriber. Hot observables are well-suited for representing live, real-time data streams where it is acceptable or intended for subscribers to only receive data from their point of subscription onward.

In summary, understanding the distinction between hot and cold observables and how to convert between the two is pivotal for effectively utilizing RxJava in reactive programming, ensuring the correct behavior of data streams according to the application's needs.

2.11   Advanced RxJava Operators

Understanding and effectively utilizing RxJava's advanced operators is crucial for developing sophisticated reactive applications. This section will discuss several advanced operators, including `flatMap`, `concatMap`, `switchMap`, `groupBy`, and `scan`, which allow for complex transformations and efficient data manipulation within RxJava's observable streams.

flatMap operator is vital for dealing with nested observables. It transforms the items emitted by an observable into observables themselves and then flattens these observable emissions into a single observable stream. This is particularly useful when dealing with asynchronous operations that return an observable, allowing for elegant handling of sequences of asynchronous tasks.

```
Observable.just("Hello", "World")
    .flatMap(s -> Observable.fromArray(s.split("")))
    .subscribe(System.out::println);
```

In this example, flatMap splits each string into individual characters and merges them into a single observable stream, resulting in each character being emitted separately.

concatMap is similar to flatMap in its functionality of transforming and flattening observables. However, it ensures that the order of items is maintained according to the sequence they are emitted by the source observable. concatMap is preferred when the order of emissions is crucial.

```
Observable.range(1, 3)
    .concatMap(i -> Observable.range(i * 10, 2))
    .subscribe(System.out::println);
```

This emits items in a strict order, producing an ordered sequence of values starting from 10.

switchMap also transforms items emitted by an observable into observables. It differs in that it only emits items from the most recently transformed observable, disposing of any previous ones. This is particularly useful in scenarios where only the latest response is relevant, such as in search queries where only the latest entered query's result matters.

```
Observable.just("a", "b", "c")
    .switchMap(s -> Observable.just(s + "1"))
    .subscribe(System.out::println);
```

groupBy operator partitions the items emitted by an observable into separate observables that group items into different categories. This is analogous to the 'GROUP BY' operation in SQL and is useful for categorizing items based on some criteria.

```
Observable.just("banana", "apple", "pear", "kiwi")
    .groupBy(fruit -> fruit.charAt(0))
    .subscribe(groupedObservable ->
        groupedObservable.subscribe(
            item -> System.out.println("Key: " + groupedObservable.getKey() + ",
                Item: " + item)));
```

`scan` operator applies a function to the first item emitted by the source observable and then continues to combine the subsequent items cumulatively. This is particularly useful for running totals or iterative calculations.

```
Observable.range(1, 5)
    .scan(0, (acc, v) -> acc + v)
    .subscribe(System.out::println);
```

In this example, `scan` accumulates the sum of the numbers emitted, outputting an incremental total at each step.

```
0
1
3
6
10
15
```

The advanced RxJava operators `flatMap`, `concatMap`, `switchMap`, `groupBy`, and `scan` provide powerful mechanisms for transforming, combining, and managing observable streams in sophisticated and efficient ways. Mastering these operators is essential for leveraging the full potential of RxJava in developing reactive applications.

2.12 Best Practices for Using RxJava

In leveraging RxJava to build reactive applications, adhering to best practices ensures the creation of efficient, readable, and maintainable code. This section will discuss several guidelines imperative for developers utilizing RxJava in their reactive programming endeavors.

First, understanding and judiciously applying the correct operators is fundamental. RxJava offers a plethora of operators for various purposes, including creation, transformation, filtering, and combination of Observables. Developers must familiarize themselves with these operators to select the most appropriate ones for their specific use cases. For instance, using the `flatMap` operator allows for the transformation of items emitted by an Observable into Observables themselves, thus enabling the handling of nested asynchronous operations in a seamless manner.

```
Observable.just("Request1", "Request2", "Request3")
    .flatMap(request -> performAsyncOperation(request))
    .subscribe(result -> System.out.println(result));
```

Second, managing subscription lifecycles is crucial. Memory leaks and unintended behavior often occur due to improperly managed subscriptions. Utilizing the `CompositeDisposable` class to hold and dispose of subscriptions can effectively mitigate such issues. It is essential to clear these disposables, typically in a lifecycle method such as `onDestroy` in Android or a similar teardown method in Java applications.

```
1  CompositeDisposable disposables = new CompositeDisposable();
2
3  disposables.add(
4      observable.subscribe(item -> System.out.println(item))
5  );
6
7  // Later on
8  disposables.dispose();
```

Third, error handling is pivotal for developing resilient applications. RxJava provides mechanisms such as the `onError` event in subscriptions and operators like `onErrorReturn`, `onErrorResumeNext`, and `retry`, which can be used to elegantly handle errors and define fallback strategies.

Incorporating error handling directly into the Observable chain preserves readability and ensures a clear strategy for dealing with exceptions and boundary cases.

```
1  observable
2      .onErrorResumeNext(fallbackObservable)
3      .subscribe(
4          item -> System.out.println(item),
5          throwable -> throwable.printStackTrace()
6      );
```

Fourth, employing schedulers to control the execution context of an Observable sequence is a powerful feature for achieving desired concurrency patterns without burdening the developer with complex thread management. RxJava abstracts away the intricacies of thread handling, allowing developers to specify execution contexts using schedulers like `Schedulers.io()` for I/O-bound work or `Schedulers.computation()` for CPU-intensive tasks.

```
1  Observable.just("Long", "Running", "Operation")
2      .subscribeOn(Schedulers.io())
3      .observeOn(AndroidSchedulers.mainThread())
4      .subscribe(result -> view.setText(result));
```

Fifth, understanding and utilizing backpressure is essential when dealing with a massive number of events that may overwhelm the consumer. Operators such as `buffer`, `window`, and `debounce` can help manage backpressure by limiting the rate at which items are emitted or processed.

Finally, distinguishing between hot and cold Observables is crucial for correct data flow management. Cold Observables start emitting data upon subscription, making them suitable for one-time or delayed data fetching operations. In contrast, hot Observables emit data independently of subscriptions, thus being ideal for representing ongoing or multi-consumer event streams.

```
1   // Example of a cold Observable
2   Observable<String> cold = Observable.create(subscriber -> {
3       subscriber.onNext("Cold");
4       subscriber.onComplete();
5   });
6
7   // Example of a hot Observable
8   ConnectableObservable<Object> hot = Observable.create(subscriber -> {
9       new Thread(() -> {
10          while(true) {
11              subscriber.onNext("Hot");
12          }
13      }).start();
14  }).publish();
15
16  hot.connect();
```

To encapsulate, adhering to these best practices when using RxJava fosters the development of applications that are not only resilient and scalable but also maintainable and elegant. By effectively applying appropriate operators, managing subscription lifecycles, gracefully handling errors, thoughtfully utilizing schedulers for concurrency, adequately managing backpressure, and distinguishing between hot and cold Observables, developers can fully harness the power of reactive programming with RxJava.

Chapter 3

Spring Boot Essentials for Reactive Applications

Spring Boot offers a comprehensive platform for developing Java-based applications, including support for reactive programming paradigms through its integration with Spring WebFlux and other reactive components. It simplifies building and configuring spring applications, providing a suite of tools and defaults that allow developers to focus on application logic rather than boilerplate configuration. This chapter introduces the essential concepts, configurations, and practices for leveraging Spring Boot in creating reactive applications, emphasizing its role in facilitating scalable, efficient, and easy-to-maintain reactive systems.

3.1 Introduction to Spring Boot for Reactive Applications

Spring Boot is a powerful framework designed to simplify the bootstrap and development of new Spring applications. Its auto-configuration feature, along with a wide array of service and property helpers, allows developers to get up and run quickly, focusing on application-specific features rather than the boilerplate code often associated with setup and configuration. In the context of building reactive applications, Spring Boot's role becomes even more pivotal. It provides a seamless integration with Spring WebFlux, a reactive stack web framework designed for building non-blocking and asynchronous applications that are capable of handling a large number of concurrent users or events.

Reactive programming is a paradigm focused on data flow and the propagation of change. It enables developers to build systems that are scalable, resilient, and responsive, excelling in environments where traditional synchronous processing models falter. The integration of reactive programming paradigms into Spring Boot via Spring WebFlux represents a significant step forward in the development of highly concurrent web applications.

Spring WebFlux, integrated into Spring Boot, leverages project Reactor, a reactive library for building non-blocking applications. It supports backpressure—a mechanism that allows consumers to signal the producer how much data they can process—ensuring that resources are utilized efficiently and systems are not overwhelmed.

A hallmark of reactive applications is their asynchronous execution model, where processes are not bound to any specific thread but can be executed on whichever thread is available, enhancing the application's capability to serve more concurrent requests in a scalable fashion. This model is particularly well-suited for microservices architectures, where independent, loosely-coupled services operate concurrently.

Configuring a Spring Boot application to be reactive involves including the `spring-boot-starter-webflux` dependency in the project's build file. This starter package pulls in all required dependencies, facilitating the development of reactive web applications with minimal configuration. Developers can utilize the familiar Spring MVC annotations within their controllers, while behind the scenes, the application handles requests in a completely non-blocking fashion.

```
1  <dependency>
2      <groupId>org.springframework.boot</groupId>
3      <artifactId>spring-boot-starter-webflux</artifactId>
4  </dependency>
```

Once configured, Spring Boot's reactive capabilities can be leveraged to develop RESTful APIs that are inherently non-blocking and support reactive data access patterns. This is especially beneficial when dealing with operations that are I/O bound, e.g., network calls or database transactions, where the traditional synchronous and blocking nature would significantly hamper performance.

Reactive Database Access with Spring Data is another aspect where Spring Boot shines in the context of reactive programming. By using project R2DBC (Reactive Relational Database Connectivity), a reactive API for SQL databases, Spring Boot applications can perform database operations reactively, thus fully embracing the non-blocking model.

```
Flux<Person> findAllPeople() {
    return databaseClient.select()
                        .from("people")
                        .as(Person.class)
                        .fetch()
                        .all();
}
```

Securing reactive applications with Spring Security is streamlined owing to Spring Boot's autoconfiguration capabilities. It efficiently integrates with Spring Security's reactive support, enabling developers to secure endpoints and enforce authentication and authorization constraints reactively.

Spring Boot's support for reactive programming through its integration with Spring WebFlux and other reactive components not only simplifies the development of reactive applications but also ensures that applications are scalable, efficient, and easy to maintain. By abstracting away much of the tedious configuration work and providing a set of out-of-the-box tools and defaults, Spring Boot allows developers to concentrate on business logic and application features, thereby significantly speeding up the development process.

3.2 Configuring a Reactive Spring Boot Application

Configuring a reactive Spring Boot application involves several key aspects that differentiate it from configuring a standard Spring Boot application. These include dependency setup, application properties configuration, defining the data model, and configuring the reactive Web server. Attention to these aspects ensures that the application utilizes non-blocking I/O operations, a cornerstone of reactive programming, for handling concurrent requests efficiently.

Dependency Setup: The foundational step in configuring a reactive Spring Boot application is to include the appropriate dependencies. The Spring Boot Starter WebFlux must be added to the project's build configuration file to enable reactive web support in the application.

```
1  <dependency>
2      <groupId>org.springframework.boot</groupId>
3      <artifactId>spring-boot-starter-webflux</artifactId>
4  </dependency>
```

This dependency provides all necessary libraries for developing reactive web applications, including Spring WebFlux itself and the Reactor project which powers reactive streams within Spring.

Additionally, for reactive data access, dependencies for the reactive versions of Spring Data repositories should be included. For example, for MongoDB, the following dependency is required:

```
1  <dependency>
2      <groupId>org.springframework.boot</groupId>
3      <artifactId>spring-boot-starter-data-mongodb-reactive</artifactId>
4  </dependency>
```

Application Properties Configuration: Properties configuration plays an essential role in customizing behavior of a Spring Boot application. The `application.properties` or `application.yml` file allows developers to configure server, database, logging, and other operational parameters. For a reactive application, it is critical to configure the server to use a non-blocking web runtime. When using Netty, which is the default with Spring WebFlux, no additional server specific configuration is required. However, developers might want to adjust server properties, such as the port number, by specifying:

```
server.port=8080
```

This snippet sets the application to listen on port 8080.

Defining the Data Model: The data model in a reactive application should be defined with asynchronous processing in mind. Entities should be designed to be non-blocking and should integrate seamlessly with reactive repositories. For instance, when using MongoDB, an entity could be defined as:

```
1  @Data
2  @Document
3  public class Product {
4      @Id
5      private String id;
6      private String name;
7      private double price;
8  }
```

This class uses Lombok annotations @Data for getters and setters, and @Document to mark it as a MongoDB document.

Configuring the Reactive Web Server: The choice of the reactive web server is pivotal in defining the reactive nature of the application. Spring WebFlux supports servers like Netty, Undertow, and Servlet 3.1+ containers. Configurations related to the web server, such as the number of threads for handling I/O operations, can drastically affect the application's scalability and performance. While sensible defaults are provided, tuning these configurations based on specific application requirements and deployment environments is advisable. For instance, configuring the Netty server thread count can be achieved through properties in `application.properties`:

```
server.netty.threads.max=200
```

This configuration limits the maximum number of threads Netty uses to 200, tailoring the server to handle a high number of concurrent non-blocking connections efficiently.

Configuring a reactive Spring Boot application involves setting up the right dependencies, appropriately defining application properties, modeling the data for non-blocking operations, and choosing and configuring the reactive web server. These steps form the backbone of a reactive application, setting the stage for building scalable, efficient, and responsive services. Each aspect requires careful consideration to leverage the full benefits of reactive programming within the Spring ecosystem.

3.3   Understanding the Spring WebFlux Framework

The Spring WebFlux framework provides the foundation for building reactive applications within the Spring ecosystem. It is specifically designed to handle asynchronous operations and stream data efficiently, allowing for non-blocking I/O operations. This capability is critical for developing applications that can serve a large number of concurrent users or processes without tying up server resources unnecessarily.

Unlike the traditional Spring MVC framework, which is built on a servlet API and uses a blocking I/O model, Spring WebFlux operates on an entirely different I/O model, which is non-blocking and reactive. It is built on Project Reactor, an implementation of the Reactive Streams specification, which provides a reactive programming model for Java.

This distinction is crucial for understanding how to develop and scale reactive applications effectively.

Core Components of Spring WebFlux

At the heart of Spring WebFlux are several key components that facilitate the creation of reactive web applications. These include:

- Reactive Streams: This API defines the backpressure mechanism, which allows consumers to control the flow of data from publishers to prevent overwhelming the consumer.

- Project Reactor: As the foundational library for reactive programming in the Spring ecosystem, it extends Reactive Streams with additional operators and features for composing asynchronous and event-based programs.

- Spring WebFlux module: This includes the core functionalities for developing reactive web applications, including annotations, functional programming models, and a non-blocking web runtime.

Developing with Spring WebFlux

Developers can choose between two distinct programming models when using Spring WebFlux: annotation-based and functional. The annotation-based model is similar to Spring MVC and allows for the definition of controller classes with mappings that are declarative and concise. For example:

```
@GetMapping("/users/{id}")
Mono<User> getUser(@PathVariable String id) {
    return userRepository.findById(id);
}
```

This snippet demonstrates how to define a RESTful endpoint that retrieves a user by their ID. The return type Mono<User> is a reactive type from Project Reactor that represents a single or empty asynchronous value.

Alternatively, the functional programming model offers more explicit control over routing and handling through a router and handler functions. For instance:

66

```
1   RouterFunction<ServerResponse> route =
2       RouterFunctions.route(
3           RequestPredicates.GET("/users/{id}"),
4           request -> ServerResponse.ok().body(userRepository.findById(request.
                pathVariable("id")), User.class)
5       );
```

This example achieves the same goal as the previous annotation-based example but does so in a more explicit and functional manner.

Non-blocking I/O with Spring WebFlux

In traditional servlet-based applications, each client request is processed in a separate thread, potentially leading to scalability issues when the number of requests increases. Spring WebFlux addresses this challenge by using non-blocking I/O operations. This means that threads are not idle while waiting for I/O operations to complete, allowing them to handle other tasks.

The non-blocking nature of Spring WebFlux is made possible through the use of Reactor's Mono and Flux types for single or multiple data items, respectively. These types are fully reactive and support various operations such as map, flatMap, and filter, which can be used to compose complex data processing pipelines.

Integrating with Databases and Other Services

While the reactive programming model provides significant benefits for handling web requests, it also imposes certain requirements on interactions with databases and external services. Specifically, to maintain the non-blocking behavior, it is necessary to use reactive drivers for data access. Spring Data offers reactive support for several databases, including MongoDB, Cassandra, and Redis, through reactive repositories.

For instance, a reactive repository for MongoDB might be defined as follows:

```
1   public interface UserRepository extends ReactiveCrudRepository<User, String> {
2   }
```

This repository extends ReactiveCrudRepository, providing non-blocking CRUD operations for the User entity.

Spring WebFlux offers a robust framework for developing reactive applications within the Spring ecosystem. Its non-blocking I/O model, integration with Reactive Streams and Project Reactor, and support for both annotation-based and functional programming models make it a powerful tool for building scalable and efficient web applications. By leveraging reactive programming principles and Spring WebFlux, developers can create applications that are more responsive and capable of handling a high volume of concurrent requests, thus meeting the modern demands of software development.

3.4 Developing Reactive RESTful APIs

Developing Reactive RESTful APIs with Spring Boot involves understanding the core principles of reactive programming and how they apply to web service development. This section covers the approach to building RESTful web services that operate on the reactive programming model using Spring Boot and Spring WebFlux.

First, it is essential to understand the reactive stack in Spring Boot provided by Spring WebFlux. Unlike the traditional servlet-based stack, Spring WebFlux is designed to work on non-blocking web servers like Netty, allowing for more scalable and efficient handling of concurrent requests. This makes it an ideal choice for applications that require high throughput and low latency.

To define a reactive RESTful API in Spring Boot, one starts by creating a new Spring Boot project with the 'spring-boot-starter-webflux' dependency. This inclusion ensures that the application is equipped with the necessary libraries for building reactive web applications.

```
1  dependencies {
2      implementation 'org.springframework.boot:spring-boot-starter-webflux'
3  }
```

After setting up the project with the required dependencies, the next step involves defining the data model. In reactive applications, it is common to use reactive data types, such as 'Mono' and 'Flux' from Project Reactor, to represent single or multiple data items, respectively. For example, consider a simple 'Book' class that represents the data model in a book management API.

```
1  public class Book {
2      private String id;
3      private String title;
4      private String author;
```

```
5
6      // Getters and Setters
7  }
```

Following the data model definition, one needs to create a repository interface for data access. Spring Data provides reactive support through the 'ReactiveCrudRepository' interface, which offers standard CRUD operations on a reactive API.

```
1  public interface BookRepository extends ReactiveCrudRepository<Book, String> {
2  }
```

With the repository in place, the focus shifts to the controller where the RESTful endpoints are defined. In a reactive Spring Boot application, controllers use annotations such as '@RestController' and '@RequestMapping' to declare RESTful endpoints. The reactive nature of these endpoints is evident in their return types: 'Mono' for single or optional objects and 'Flux' for multiple objects.

```
1  @RestController
2  @RequestMapping("/books")
3  public class BookController {
4
5      private final BookRepository bookRepository;
6
7      public BookController(BookRepository bookRepository) {
8          this.bookRepository = bookRepository;
9      }
10
11     @GetMapping("/{id}")
12     public Mono<Book> getBookById(@PathVariable String id) {
13         return bookRepository.findById(id);
14     }
15
16     @GetMapping("/")
17     public Flux<Book> getAllBooks() {
18         return bookRepository.findAll();
19     }
20
21     @PostMapping("/")
22     public Mono<Book> createBook(@RequestBody Book book) {
23         return bookRepository.save(book);
24     }
25 }
```

In the above example, the 'BookController' class defines three endpoints: 'getBookById', 'getAllBooks', and 'createBook' which demonstrate how to retrieve a single book by ID, retrieve all books, and create a new book entry, respectively.

For reactive APIs, considerations for error handling and backpressure are vital. Error handling can be managed using operators such as 'onErrorReturn' to provide default values or responses in case of failures.

69

Backpressure, which is the ability to control the flow of data based on consumer capacity, is natively supported by reactive streams and can be managed through various operators provided by Project Reactor.

Testing reactive APIs in Spring Boot is facilitated by the 'WebTestClient' class, which allows for binding to controllers and performing requests against the endpoints in a non-blocking manner.

```
1   @SpringBootTest(webEnvironment = SpringBootTest.WebEnvironment.RANDOM_PORT)
2   public class BookControllerTest {
3
4       @Autowired
5       private WebTestClient webTestClient;
6
7       @Test
8       public void testGetBookById() {
9           webTestClient.get().uri("/books/{id}", "1")
10              .exchange()
11              .expectStatus().isOk()
12              .expectBody(Book.class);
13      }
14  }
```

Developing Reactive RESTful APIs with Spring Boot and Spring WebFlux requires an understanding of reactive programming principles, utilizing reactive types for data handling, and making use of Spring WebFlux's support for non-blocking web servers. By following these practices, developers can create scalable, efficient, and responsive web services capable of handling high volumes of concurrent requests with minimal latency.

3.5 Reactive Database Access with Spring Data

Reactive Database Access with Spring Data is pivotal in designing applications that are resilient, scalable, and non-blocking, especially when handling data streams in real-time. In this context, Spring Data provides an abstraction over data store interactions, facilitating reactive programming patterns to manage data operations asynchronously. This section elucidates the integration patterns, configurations, and usage practices of Spring Data in a reactive paradigm, underscoring its efficiency in database access and manipulation within a Spring Boot Reactive application.

Spring Data encompasses a suite of projects each targeting a specific database or data store technology. For reactive support, Spring Data projects such as Spring Data MongoDB, Spring Data Cassandra, and Spring Data R2DBC stand out as primary choices. These projects provide reactive repository support, allowing for non-blocking database access.

Spring Data R2DBC emerges as a cornerstone in the landscape of relational database access in a reactive manner. R2DBC, which stands for Reactive Relational Database Connectivity, offers a non-blocking API to interact with relational databases. Configuring a connection factory for R2DBC within a Spring Boot application requires specifying the database connection properties in the `application.properties` or `application.yml` file. Here is an exemplar configuration for a PostgreSQL database:

```
spring.r2dbc.url=r2dbc:postgresql://host:port/database
spring.r2dbc.username=username
spring.r2dbc.password=password
```

Upon this configuration, Spring Boot auto-configures a `ConnectionFactory` bean to be used for creating database connections reactively.

Repositories in Spring Data play an essential role in abstracting data access logic. For reactive applications, Spring Data provides the `ReactiveCrudRepository` and `ReactiveSortingRepository` interfaces. These interfaces extend the Publisher interfaces from Project Reactor, allowing for asynchronous and non-blocking data access operations. Here is an illustration of defining a reactive repository:

```
public interface BookRepository extends ReactiveCrudRepository<Book, String> {
}
```

Transactions in a reactive context are managed differently compared to the imperative model. The `TransactionalOperator` class in Spring Data R2DBC is utilized to declare transactional boundaries reactively. Transactions can be declared programmatically or declaratively using the `@Transactional` annotation on service methods, enabling reactive transaction management.

```
@Transactional
public Mono<Void> updateBooks(Flux<Book> books) {
    return bookRepository.saveAll(books).then();
}
```

This snippet demonstrates the declarative transaction management by updating a collection of books reactively.

71

Query Methods in Spring Data repositories can also be defined to operate reactively. Spring Data allows for query derivation from method names, as well as the use of the @Query annotation for custom queries. For reactive execution, these methods return types such as Mono or Flux, adhering to the reactive streams specification.

```
1   Flux<Book> findByAuthor(String author);
```

This method signature indicates a reactive query method for fetching books by an author, returning a Flux of Book objects.

Database Migrations are crucial for managing the schema evolution of applications over time. Tools like Flyway and Liquibase offer support for reactive applications, facilitating database migrations in a non-blocking manner when the application starts up.

Leveraging Spring Data for reactive database access significantly enhances the development of non-blocking, scalable, and responsive Spring Boot applications. Through R2DBC support, reactive repositories, and transaction management, developers are equipped with a powerful toolkit for accessing and manipulating databases reactively. Embracing these practices and configurations elevates the efficiency and performance of reactive Spring Boot applications, catering to the demands of modern software architecture patterns.

3.6 Integrating Reactive Streams with Spring Boot

Integrating reactive streams with Spring Boot involves the use of the Project Reactor library. Project Reactor is a fourth-generation reactive library, based on the Reactive Streams specification, which Spring WebFlux uses to provide non-blocking and backpressure-ready components. This section will discuss the principles of reactive streams integration in Spring Boot applications, how to operate with Flux and Mono types from Project Reactor, and best practices for leveraging these within Spring Boot to build efficient, scalable reactive systems.

Reactive streams provide a standard for asynchronous stream processing with non-blocking back pressure. This feature is essential in reactive applications to manage resources and ensure that systems are resilient and responsive under load. Spring Boot's reactive stack, built around Project Reactor, is designed to support these patterns seamlessly throughout the application, from the web layer down to the data store.

To start integrating reactive streams in Spring Boot, developers should first understand the core types provided by Project Reactor: Mono and Flux. Mono represents a stream of 0 to 1 elements, while Flux represents a stream of 0 to N elements. Both types are reactive streams compliant and are fully integrated with Spring's WebFlux module.

```
1  Flux<String> stringFlux = Flux.just("Spring", "WebFlux", "Reactor");
2  Mono<String> stringMono = Mono.just("Spring Boot");
```

Operations on these types are non-blocking and support back pressure, making them ideal for handling stream data in reactive applications. Data operations can be easily chained and composed, with a rich API for transformation, filtering, and aggregation.

```
1  Flux<Integer> numbers = Flux.range(1, 5)
2      .map(i -> i * i)
3      .filter(i -> i % 2 == 0);
```

This code snippet illustrates the creation of a Flux of squared integers, filtering only even numbers. The operations are declarative and composed together in a fluent API style, characteristic of functional programming.

When integrating reactive streams with Spring Boot, developers must also be mindful of error handling strategies. Project Reactor provides several mechanisms for dealing with errors in a stream, such as retry policies, fallback methods, and custom exception handling. This aspect is crucial for maintaining the resilience and reliability of reactive applications.

```
1  Flux<Integer> resilientFlux = numbers
2      .onErrorResume(e -> Flux.just(-1))
3      .doOnError(e -> log.error("Error encountered", e));
```

The snippet above demonstrates handling errors in a Flux by providing a fallback value and logging the error. This pattern aids in the development of resilient, fault-tolerant systems.

Beyond the essentials of working with Mono and Flux, integrating reactive streams with Spring Boot also involves considerations for data access and networking. Spring Data provides reactive repository support for NoSQL databases like MongoDB, Cassandra, and Redis, allowing for fully reactive data access.

```
1  interface ReactivePersonRepository extends ReactiveCrudRepository<Person, String> {
2  }
```

This code defines a reactive repository for a `Person` entity, extending `ReactiveCrudRepository`. Using such repositories, data access operations are asynchronous and non-blocking, fully embracing the reactive programming model.

When developing reactive applications with Spring Boot, it is also essential to consider how reactive streams integrate with Spring Security, transaction management, and message-driven architectures. Reactive support in Spring Security enables the application of security policies on reactive streams. Similarly, transaction management with reactive types ensures that operations are executed reliably and consistently.

Integrating reactive streams with Spring Boot leverages the full power of reactive programming to build scalable, efficient, and responsive applications. By understanding and utilizing Project Reactor's core types, `Mono` and `Flux`, alongside Spring's comprehensive support for reactive data access, networking, security, and transactions, developers can craft resilient and performant systems. The fluent API and comprehensive error handling strategies of Project Reactor further contribute to the elegance and maintainability of the codebase, making the development of reactive Spring Boot applications a rewarding endeavor.

3.7   Securing Reactive Applications with Spring Security

Spring Security is a powerful and highly customizable authentication and access-control framework. It is the de-facto standard for securing Spring-based applications, including those built on the reactive stack. In this section, we will discuss how to leverage Spring Security to secure reactive applications developed with Spring Boot and WebFlux.

Spring Security supports a wide range of authentication mechanisms such as form-based login, OAuth2, JWT tokens, and Basic Authentication, among others. Moreover, it provides comprehensive support for authorization practices ranging from declarative role-based access control to more advanced method-level security.

Configuring Spring Security for Reactive Applications

To integrate Spring Security into a reactive Spring Boot application, the first step involves adding the `spring-boot-starter-security` dependency to the project's build file. This dependency provides auto-configuration options and sensible defaults for a variety of security aspects.

```
1  <dependency>
2      <groupId>org.springframework.boot</groupId>
3      <artifactId>spring-boot-starter-security</artifactId>
4  </dependency>
```

Upon adding the above dependency, Spring Security will secure all endpoints by default, requiring authentication for access. The next step is to create a configuration class that extends `WebSecurityConfigurerAdapter`, where custom security configurations can be defined.

```
1  import org.springframework.security.config.annotation.web.reactive.
        EnableWebFluxSecurity;
2  import org.springframework.context.annotation.Configuration;
3
4  @Configuration
5  @EnableWebFluxSecurity
6  public class SecurityConfig {
7      // Configuration methods go here
8  }
```

In the `SecurityConfig` class, developers can customize authentication mechanisms, configure security filters, and define access control rules.

Basic Authentication

Basic Authentication is a simple authentication scheme built into the HTTP protocol. The clients send requests with a header field in the form of `Authorization: Basic <credentials>`, where `credentials` is the Base64 encoding of ID and password joined by a single colon (:).

To configure Basic Authentication for a reactive application, the `SecurityConfig` class can be modified as follows:

```
1  import org.springframework.security.config.web.server.ServerHttpSecurity;
2  import org.springframework.security.web.server.SecurityWebFilterChain;
3
4  public class SecurityConfig {
5
6      public SecurityWebFilterChain springSecurityFilterChain(ServerHttpSecurity http
            ) {
7          http
8              .authorizeExchange()
9              .pathMatchers("/public/**").permitAll()
10             .anyExchange().authenticated()
11             .and()
12             .httpBasic();
13         return http.build();
```

```
14        }
15    }
```

This configuration permits unauthenticated access to resources under the /public/ path while requiring authentication for all other endpoints.

JWT Authentication

JSON Web Token (JWT) is a compact, URL-safe means of representing claims to be transferred between two parties. In reactive applications, JWT can be used to secure REST APIs by facilitating stateless authentication.

To implement JWT-based authentication, additional dependencies are required. The spring-security-oauth2 and spring-security-jwt libraries can be included in the application's build file.

Implementing JWT authentication involves creating a custom ReactiveAuthenticationManager, defining a ServerAuthenticationConverter to parse JWTs from incoming requests, and configuring the SecurityWebFilterChain to use these components.

Role-Based Access Control

Spring Security simplifies the implementation of role-based access control (RBAC) to protect application endpoints. Access control can be declaratively defined within the SecurityConfig class using the hasRole, hasAuthority, or access methods.

```
1   http
2       .authorizeExchange()
3       .pathMatchers("/admin/**").hasRole("ADMIN")
4       .pathMatchers("/user/**").hasRole("USER")
5       .anyExchange().authenticated()
6       .and()
7       .httpBasic();
```

In this configuration, only users with the ADMIN role can access resources under the /admin/ path, while those with the USER role have access to resources under the /user/ path.

Integrating Spring Security into reactive applications developed with Spring Boot and WebFlux enables developers to implement robust security mechanisms, including authentication and authorization. By utilizing Spring Security's support for Basic Authentication, JWT, and role-based access control, developers can protect application endpoints and ensure that sensitive information remains secure.

Furthermore, Spring Security's reactive support ensures that security contexts are efficiently managed across asynchronous and non-blocking application flows, making it an ideal choice for securing reactive applications.

3.8 Event-Driven Microservices with Spring Boot

Event-driven architecture (EDA) is a paradigm that promotes the production, detection, consumption, and reaction to events. Microservices adopting an event-driven approach benefit from elevated levels of scalability, flexibility, and resilience, which are essential characteristics for modern distributed systems. Spring Boot, with its comprehensive ecosystem, offers invaluable support for developing event-driven microservices, facilitating seamless integration with messaging systems and providing annotations and starters for various event-driven components. This section will discuss leveraging Spring Boot to architect, implement, and deploy event-driven microservices.

In an event-driven microservices architecture, services communicate through events. An event is a significant change in state or an update that a service wants to announce to the rest of the system. Spring Boot enables such communication through its integration with Spring Cloud Stream, an event-streaming library that abstracts away the specifics of message brokers, such as Apache Kafka or RabbitMQ. By adopting Spring Cloud Stream, developers focus on core business logic rather than the complexities of the underlying messaging infrastructure.

To effectively implement an event-driven microservices architecture using Spring Boot, begin by including the Spring Cloud Stream dependency in the project's build configuration. For Maven users, this involves adding the following dependency in the pom.xml file:

```
1  <dependency>
2     <groupId>org.springframework.cloud</groupId>
3     <artifactId>spring-cloud-starter-stream-kafka</artifactId>
4  </dependency>
```

This dependency includes everything needed to connect a Spring Boot application to a Kafka message broker, though you can replace Kafka with RabbitMQ or any other supported messaging system by simply changing the artifact ID.

With the dependency in place, Spring Boot simplifies the configuration of event publishers and listeners. The `@EnableBinding` annotation is used to signify the interfaces that define channels for inbound and outbound messaging:

```
1   @EnableBinding(Source.class)
2   public class EventPublisher {
3       @Autowired
4       private MessageChannel output;
5
6       public void publishEvent(DomainEvent event) {
7           output.send(MessageBuilder.withPayload(event).build());
8       }
9   }
```

In this example, `MessageChannel` is injected into the `EventPublisher` class, allowing it to send messages. `DomainEvent` represents a domain-specific event, which can be anything from a user creating an account to an order being placed.

On the listener side, Spring Cloud Stream simplifies the declaration of event handlers through the `@StreamListener` annotation:

```
1   @EnableBinding(Sink.class)
2   public class EventListener {
3
4       @StreamListener(target = Sink.INPUT)
5       public void handle(DomainEvent event) {
6           // Process event
7       }
8   }
```

Here, `Sink.INPUT` refers to the input channel from which the `EventListener` should consume messages. The system automatically converts incoming messages back into domain events, ready for processing.

Event-driven microservices also need to handle failure scenarios gracefully, ensuring that system-wide consistency is maintained. With Spring Cloud Stream, managing these scenarios is facilitated through consumer groups and dead letter queues, which allow for fine-tuned control over message consumption and error handling.

Moreover, when integrating multiple microservices, event-driven communication promotes loose coupling, as services do not directly depend on each other's APIs but rather react to events asynchronously. This approach significantly enhances system resilience, as the failure of a single service does not necessarily impact the entire system.

To monitor and manage event streams, Spring Boot actuator endpoints can be leveraged, providing real-time insights into message channels and helping identify bottlenecks or failures in the messaging infrastructure.

Building event-driven microservices with Spring Boot offers a pathway to creating distributed systems that are scalable, resilient, and maintainable. The abstraction provided by Spring Cloud Stream over messaging infrastructures, along with Spring Boot's simplicity in configuration and operational insight, empowers developers to focus on business logic and adds value to their applications without getting bogged down by the complexity of inter-service communication. Through the careful design of events and handling of asynchronous communication patterns, developers can architect systems that are not only efficient and reliable but also capable of evolving over time as new services are added or existing ones are modified.

3.9 Testing Reactive Applications with Spring Boot

Testing Reactive Applications with Spring Boot requires an understanding of both the reactive programming model and the testing facilities provided by Spring Boot. The reactive model introduces non-blocking operations, which can lead to challenges in testing because traditional testing approaches may not apply. Spring Boot, however, offers tools and libraries specifically designed to address these challenges, allowing developers to create comprehensive test suites for their reactive applications. This section will discuss strategies for unit testing, integration testing, and end-to-end testing of reactive applications using Spring Boot's testing capabilities.

First, let's start with unit testing. In a reactive application, components such as controllers, services, and repositories are often designed to return reactive types like Mono or Flux. To test these components effectively, one must utilize the StepVerifier API provided by Project Reactor. The StepVerifier provides a declarative way to assert the events produced by a reactive stream. For instance, to verify that a service method returns the expected value, one would use:

```
1  StepVerifier.create(myReactiveService.findById(1))
2      .expectNext(expectedResult)
3      .verifyComplete();
```

This code snippet creates a `StepVerifier` to test the `findById` method of `myReactiveService`. It asserts that the service method returns a single expected result followed by the completion signal.

Integration testing in a reactive Spring Boot application often involves the use of the `@WebFluxTest` annotation. This annotation enables auto-configuration of the WebFlux infrastructure and provides a way to mock other components within the application context. For instance, when testing a reactive controller, one might use the `WebTestClient` to perform and verify web requests as follows:

```
1   @Autowired
2   private WebTestClient webTestClient;
3
4   @Test
5   public void testGetEndpoint() {
6       webTestClient.get().uri("/data/{id}", 1)
7           .exchange()
8           .expectStatus().isOk()
9           .expectBody(String.class).isEqualTo("data");
10  }
```

In this example, `WebTestClient` is used to simulate a GET request to the '/data/1' endpoint, expecting a 200 OK response with a specific body content.

For end-to-end testing, Spring Boot provides the `@SpringBootTest` annotation with WebFlux support. This annotation loads the full application context and is useful for testing the application as a whole. Using the `WebTestClient.bindToServer()` method, you can create a `WebTestClient` that makes requests to the actual running application. For example:

```
1   @Test
2   public void testApplicationEndToEnd() {
3       WebTestClient
4           .bindToServer()
5           .baseUrl("http://localhost:" + port)
6           .build()
7           .get().uri("/data")
8           .exchange()
9           .expectStatus().isOk()
10          .expectBodyList(String.class)
11          .hasSize(1)
12          .contains("data");
13  }
```

This test initiates a real HTTP request to the '/data' endpoint and verifies the response. Such tests are valuable for verifying the interaction between different parts of the application and its overall behavior.

- Understand the specificities of testing reactive code and the non-blocking nature of the operations.

- Utilize `StepVerifier` for testing reactive streams and asserting the results.

- Apply `@WebFluxTest` for integration testing of web layers, utilizing `WebTestClient` for mock web requests.

- Execute end-to-end tests using `@SpringBootTest` with real web requests to test the application in a more integrated environment.

Testing a reactive application with Spring Boot involves a nuanced understanding of both the reactive paradigm and the testing facilities of Spring Boot, which are designed to cater to reactive applications specifically. By leveraging these tools effectively, developers can ensure their reactive applications are robust, reliable, and perform as expected.

3.10 Monitoring and Managing Reactive Spring Boot Applications

Ensuring the optimal performance and reliability of reactive applications developed with Spring Boot necessitates effective monitoring and management strategies. These strategies enable developers and system administrators to gain insights into the application's behavior, resource utilization, and to detect issues before they affect users. This section will detail methodologies and tools recommended for monitoring and managing reactive Spring Boot applications.

Spring Boot Actuator is a vital tool for achieving this goal. It is a sub-project of Spring Boot that provides a series of built-in endpoints enabling monitoring and interaction with the application. To incorporate Spring Boot Actuator into a project, it is necessary to include its dependency in the pom.xml or build.gradle file, depending on the project's build system.

```
1  <dependency>
2      <groupId>org.springframework.boot</groupId>
3      <artifactId>spring-boot-starter-actuator</artifactId>
4  </dependency>
```

Once integrated, Spring Boot Actuator exposes numerous endpoints, such as /health, /info, and /metrics, each serving a distinct purpose.

The /health endpoint, for example, provides basic application health information, indicating whether the application is running correctly. The /metrics endpoint offers a wealth of information about the application's performance, including details about system memory, processor usage, and thread statistics, which are critically important for reactive applications. To access these endpoints securely, it's advisable to adjust their access permissions using Spring Security, ensuring that sensitive data remains protected.

Monitoring system metrics is a vital part of understanding an application's performance. Actuator's metrics capture a wide range of data, but to visualize and analyze this data effectively, integration with an external monitoring system like Prometheus and Grafana is often recommended. Prometheus can scrape metrics exposed by Spring Boot Actuator, store them efficiently, and allow for customizable alerts based on predefined conditions. Grafana can then be used to create dynamic dashboards that visualize the collected data, offering insights into the application's performance and health over time.

```
# Configuration for Prometheus to scrape Spring Boot Actuator metrics
scrape_configs:
  - job_name: 'spring-actuator'
    metrics_path: '/actuator/prometheus'
    static_configs:
      - targets: ['<application-IP>:<application-port>']
```

Furthermore, effective management of reactive applications also involves dealing with the data streams efficiently and ensuring that the resources are optimized for non-blocking operations. Spring WebFlux, used for creating reactive applications within Spring Boot, supports back-pressure and efficient data handling, which must be monitored to avoid common pitfalls such as resource starvation or overwhelming back-end services.

One method for detecting such issues is to use the log() operator provided by Project Reactor, which Spring WebFlux is built upon. This operator allows developers to gain insights into the reactive streams, including subscription, data flow, and error events, making it easier to locate and resolve issues.

```
flux.log().subscribe(System.out::println);
```

Monitoring and managing reactive Spring Boot applications is a multi-faceted task that requires an understanding of the tools and techniques available. By leveraging Spring Boot Actuator, integrating with external monitoring solutions like Prometheus and Grafana, and having a deep understanding of reactive streams, developers can ensure that their applications are not only performing optimally but are also maintainable and scalable. The operational insights gained through effective monitoring enable teams to make informed decisions about their applications, enhancing their resilience and reliability.

3.11 Optimizing Spring Boot Application Performance

Optimizing the performance of a Spring Boot application is crucial for ensuring that it operates efficiently, especially in a reactive context where scalability and responsiveness are paramount. This section will discuss various strategies for enhancing the performance of Spring Boot applications, focusing on aspects such as JVM options, database interactions, caching, and code profiling.

The first aspect to consider is the configuration of the Java Virtual Machine (JVM). The JVM plays a critical role in the performance of any Java application. For Spring Boot applications, it is essential to fine-tune JVM options to optimize for throughput and latency. One common approach is to adjust the garbage collection (GC) strategy. For instance, using the -XX:+UseG1GC option enables the G1 Garbage Collector, which is designed for applications requiring large heaps while maintaining low pause times.

```
1  # Example JVM options for a Spring Boot application
2  java -jar -XX:+UseG1GC -Xms512m -Xmx2048m myapp.jar
```

Next, optimizing database interactions is fundamental. Reactive applications often face the challenge of efficiently managing non-blocking I/O operations. Spring Data R2DBC offers a solution by providing reactive database access. However, optimizing query performance and effectively using database indexes become even more critical. Employing strategies such as query optimization, proper indexing, and connection pooling can significantly improve the performance of database operations.

Caching is another powerful technique for optimizing performance. Caching frequently requested data reduces the load on the database

83

and decreases latency. Spring Boot supports various caching mechanisms, including in-memory and distributed caching. Utilizing the @Cacheable annotation on methods can enable caching with minimal code changes.

```
1  @Cacheable(value = "books", key = "#isbn")
2  public Book findBookByIsbn(String isbn) {
3      // Method implementation goes here
4  }
```

Additionally, leveraging reactive streams for backpressure management is crucial. In reactive applications, it's essential to control the flow of data and prevent downstream services from being overwhelmed. Spring WebFlux integrates reactive streams and provides mechanisms for handling backpressure efficiently, ensuring that the system remains responsive under varying loads.

Code profiling and monitoring are essential practices for performance optimization. Tools such as VisualVM, JProfiler, or Spring Boot Actuator can be utilized to identify bottlenecks and monitor application metrics. Profiling an application exposes inefficiencies, such as slow service calls, memory leaks, or excessive GC activity.

Finally, adhering to best practices in reactive programming is imperative for optimizing performance. Techniques such as avoiding blocking calls in the event loop, favoring functional programming paradigms, and decomposing the application into smaller, composable services can greatly enhance the scalability and efficiency of a Spring Boot application.

Optimizing a Spring Boot application for high performance in a reactive context involves a multifaceted approach. By fine-tuning the JVM, optimizing database interactions, employing caching, managing backpressure with reactive streams, conducting thorough code profiling, and adhering to reactive programming best practices, developers can ensure that their applications are scalable, responsive, and efficient. Continuous monitoring and profiling are key to maintaining optimal performance throughout the application's lifecycle.

3.12 Deploying Reactive Spring Boot Applications

Deploying reactive Spring Boot applications involves several key steps that ensure the application is correctly configured and optimized for the target environment. Deployment strategies vary depending on the hosting environment, such as cloud platforms, virtual or physical servers. This section explores essential considerations and practices for deploying reactive Spring Boot applications effectively.

First, it is vital to package the application appropriately. Spring Boot applications can be packaged as jar files, which include all necessary dependencies. The Spring Boot Maven or Gradle plugins simplify this process by providing a dedicated goal to package the application. The `spring-boot:repackage` Maven goal or the `bootJar` Gradle task handles this. Below is an example using Maven:

```
1  <build>
2     <plugins>
3        <plugin>
4           <groupId>org.springframework.boot</groupId>
5           <artifactId>spring-boot-maven-plugin</artifactId>
6        </plugin>
7     </plugins>
8  </build>
```

Once packaged, the application jar can be deployed to the target environment. However, before deployment, configuring the application's environment-specific settings is critical. Application profiles and externalized configuration allow specifying environment-specific properties without changing the code. For instance, database URLs, credentials, and other environment-dependent settings should be externalized:

```
1  spring:
2    profiles: prod
3    datasource:
4      url: jdbc:postgresql://<production-db-url>:5432/mydatabase
5      username: dbuser
6      password: dbpass
```

Containerization has become a standard practice for deploying applications, offering benefits such as consistency across environments, scalability, and isolation. Docker is a popular choice for containerizing Spring Boot applications. A `Dockerfile` specifies the build steps and can leverage the layered jar structure that Spring Boot's build plugins create. Below is a simplified `Dockerfile` example:

```
1  FROM openjdk:11-jre-slim
2  ARG JAR_FILE=target/*.jar
3  COPY ${JAR_FILE} app.jar
4  ENTRYPOINT ["java","-jar","/app.jar"]
```

Deployment also requires careful consideration of the application's resource requirements and performance tuning. For reactive applications, configuring the number of event loop threads to match the server's CPU resources is crucial. This can significantly impact the application's scalability and responsiveness. Application properties or environment variables can accomplish this configuration:

```
1  -Dreactor.netty.ioWorkerCount=4
```

Monitoring and managing deployed applications are also crucial aspects. Spring Boot Actuator provides production-ready features to monitor application health, metrics, info, and audit events. These endpoints facilitate real-time monitoring and are essential tools in identifying issues early:

```
/actuator/health
/actuator/metrics
/actuator/info
```

Finally, deploying applications to cloud platforms such as AWS, Azure, or GCP usually involves additional considerations like computing resources, managed databases, and cloud-specific deployment tools. For example, deploying to a Kubernetes cluster might require creating a deployment configuration that specifies the docker images, replicas, and resources:

```
1   apiVersion: apps/v1
2   kind: Deployment
3   metadata:
4     name: my-reactive-app
5   spec:
6     replicas: 3
7     selector:
8       matchLabels:
9         app: my-reactive-app
10    template:
11      metadata:
12        labels:
13          app: my-reactive-app
14      spec:
15        containers:
16        - name: my-reactive-app
17          image: mydockerhub/my-reactive-app:latest
18          ports:
19          - containerPort: 8080
20          resources:
```

```
21      limits:
22        memory: "512Mi"
23        cpu: "500m"
```

To summarize, deploying reactive Spring Boot applications involves multiple crucial steps, such as packaging, environment-specific configuration, containerization, resource considerations, monitoring, and cloud or server deployment. By paying close attention to these steps and optimizing based on the target environment, developers can ensure their reactive applications are well-prepared for production, offering scalability, resilience, and efficient resource utilization.

Chapter 4

Combining RxJava and Spring Boot

The integration of RxJava with Spring Boot represents a powerful synergy for developing reactive applications, combining the asynchronous programming model of RxJava with the enterprise-level capabilities of Spring Boot. This conjunction allows for crafting applications that can efficiently manage streams of data with ease, providing a responsive and resilient service architecture. This chapter explores the practicalities of melding RxJava and Spring Boot, detailing how to harness these technologies together to craft sophisticated, non-blocking, and event-driven applications that stand up to the demands of modern software development.

4.1   Setting Up the Development Environment

Setting up the development environment is the foundational step for starting any project that combines RxJava and Spring Boot. This environment includes the necessary tools, frameworks, and dependencies required to build, test, and run the applications. The configuration must ensure compatibility between different components used in development. The process involves several steps, starting from installing Java, to setting up an Integrated Development Environment (IDE), and configuring the project with appropriate dependencies.

Installing Java

Spring Boot and RxJava are built on top of the Java ecosystem. Hence, the first step is to install a Java Development Kit (JDK). As of the writing of this book, Spring Boot 2.x requires JDK 8 or newer. It is recommended to use JDK 11, which is a long-term support (LTS) version, for the best compatibility and extended support. To install JDK, one can download it from the official Oracle website or adopt open JDK versions available at AdoptOpenJDK or similar repositories.

Choosing an Integrated Development Environment

The choice of an Integrated Development Environment (IDE) is crucial for productivity and ease of development. Popular IDEs for Spring Boot and Java development include IntelliJ IDEA, Eclipse, and Spring Tool Suite (STS). IntelliJ IDEA, with its Spring Boot support, provides comprehensive assistance for development, including intelligent code completion, refactoring, and integration with version control systems. Eclipse and STS, being open source, are also viable options with extensive support for Java and Spring Boot development.

Project Initialization

Spring Boot projects can be easily initialized using the Spring Initializr web tool, which provides a user-friendly interface for generating boilerplate project configurations. It allows specifying project metadata, selecting the version of Spring Boot, and adding project dependencies, such as RxJava. The generated project can then be imported into the chosen IDE.

Dependencies Management

Dependency management is handled by build tools such as Maven or Gradle. These tools aid in declaring, resolving, and managing library dependencies required by the project. For integrating RxJava with a Spring Boot project, the following dependencies must be included in the 'pom.xml' or 'build.gradle' file, based on the chosen build tool.

For Maven:

```
1  <dependency>
2      <groupId>io.reactivex.rxjava3</groupId>
```

```
3      <artifactId>rxjava</artifactId>
4      <version>3.x.x</version> <!-- Use the latest version -->
5  </dependency>
6  <dependency>
7      <groupId>org.springframework.boot</groupId>
8      <artifactId>spring-boot-starter-webflux</artifactId>
9      <version>2.x.x</version> <!-- Use the Spring Boot compatible version -->
10 </dependency>
```

For Gradle:

```
1  implementation 'io.reactivex.rxjava3:rxjava:3.x.x' // Use the latest version
2
3  implementation 'org.springframework.boot:spring-boot-starter-webflux:2.x.x' // Use
       the Spring Boot compatible version
```

IDE Configuration

After setting up Java, selecting an IDE, initializing a project, and configuring dependencies, the next step is to ensure that the IDE is configured correctly for Spring Boot and RxJava development. This includes setting up the JDK, configuring the build tool, and ensuring that the IDE recognizes the project structure. Additionally, it is beneficial to install any plugins or extensions that enhance support for Spring Boot, RxJava, or the chosen build tool.

With the development environment set up, developers are now ready to start building applications using RxJava and Spring Boot. The correctly configured environment simplifies the development process, aids in faster application development, and helps in avoiding compatibility issues. It sets a solid foundation for building sophisticated, non-blocking, and event-driven applications using the powerful combination of RxJava and Spring Boot.

4.2 Creating a Reactive Spring Boot Application with RxJava

Let's start with the fundamental steps to set up a reactive application using Spring Boot and RxJava. This involves the initial setup of the development environment, followed by creating a new Spring Boot project that leverages RxJava to handle data streams asynchronously.

Initially, ensure that you have Java 8 or later installed on your system as both Spring Boot and RxJava require it. Next, the Spring Boot CLI or

Spring Initializr can be used to generate a new project. For this example, we will use Spring Initializr, which is available online, to create our project. Choose a project with Maven as the build tool, and add 'Spring Webflux' and 'RxJava2' as dependencies. 'Spring Webflux' is pivotal as it provides the reactive web framework necessary to build non-blocking and event-driven web applications with Spring Boot. RxJava2 is required for handling asynchronous data streams.

After generating the project, import it into your IDE and begin by creating a new Class named `ReactiveController`. This controller will hold our reactive endpoints. Below is a basic example of a reactive endpoint using Spring WebFlux and RxJava:

```
1  @RestController
2  public class ReactiveController {
3
4      @GetMapping("/reactive")
5      public Flowable<String> reactiveEndpoint() {
6          return Flowable.just("This is a reactive response!");
7      }
8  }
```

In this example, `Flowable` is an RxJava 2 type that represents a reactive data stream that can emit 0 or multiple items. `@RestController` and `@GetMapping` are Spring Boot annotations that define this class and method as a controller and handler for HTTP GET requests, respectively.

To demonstrate the asynchronicity, let's enhance our controller by introducing a delay in the emission of the data stream. This is simulated as follows:

```
1  @GetMapping("/delayed-reactive")
2  public Flowable<String> delayedReactiveEndpoint() {
3      return Flowable.just("Delayed reactive response")
4                  .delay(2, TimeUnit.SECONDS);
5  }
```

In the enhanced example, `.delay(2, TimeUnit.SECONDS)` artificially introduces a two-second delay before emitting the response. This illustrates the non-blocking nature of a Spring WebFlux and RxJava application, as the server does not need to hold the thread while waiting to emit the response.

The next step in creating a reactive application involves the integration of data access mechanisms. Spring Data offers support for reactive data access through the Repository abstraction. We can define a Reactive CRUD repository as follows:

```
1  public interface ReactiveSampleEntityRepository
2      extends ReactiveCrudRepository<SampleEntity, String> {
3  }
```

The ReactiveCrudRepository interface is part of Spring Data and supports reactive operations on the data source. SampleEntity would be a domain object annotated with @Document or @Entity depending on whether you are connecting to a NoSQL or SQL database, respectively.

Data retrieval operations in the repository can then be utilized within the web controller via Spring's dependency injection:

```
1  @Autowired
2  private ReactiveSampleEntityRepository repository;
3
4  @GetMapping("/entities")
5  public Flowable<SampleEntity> findAllEntities() {
6      return repository.findAll();
7  }
```

The repository.findAll() method returns a Flowable<SampleEntity> representing a reactive data stream of SampleEntity objects. Thus, integrating reactive data access into the web layer seamlessly.

Correct error handling in a reactive application is crucial for resilience and robustness. Spring WebFlux provides several mechanisms for handling errors in a non-blocking way. For instance, when an error occurs during a database operation, you can handle it reactively as follows:

```
1  @GetMapping("/error-handling")
2  public Flowable<SampleEntity> errorHandlingEndpoint() {
3      return repository.findAll()
4              .onErrorReturnItem(new SampleEntity("Default", "Default Value"));
5  }
```

In this example, .onErrorReturnItem(new SampleEntity("Default", "Default Value")) ensures that in case of any error during the findAll() operation, a default SampleEntity is emitted rather than propagating the error. This pattern enhances the user experience by providing fallback behavior.

To summarize, creating a reactive Spring Boot application with RxJava involves setting up the project with necessary dependencies, defining a reactive controller to handle web requests, integrating reactive data access with Spring Data, and implementing robust error handling.

93

This foundation enables the development of efficient, scalable, non-blocking, and event-driven applications that can meet the modern demands of software development.

4.3 Integrating RxJava with Spring WebFlux

Integrating RxJava with Spring WebFlux extends the reactive programming capabilities of a Spring Boot application by leveraging the asynchronous and non-blocking features of both technologies. This synergy enables the development of highly scalable and efficient web applications.

Spring WebFlux is a non-blocking web framework for building reactive applications on the Spring ecosystem. It provides support for back pressure and offers scalability under load. RxJava complements this by providing a rich library for composing asynchronous and event-based programs using observable sequences.

To begin the integration, it is essential to add the required dependencies in the project's build configuration file. For a Maven project, the following dependencies should be included:

```
1  <dependency>
2      <groupId>org.springframework.boot</groupId>
3      <artifactId>spring-boot-starter-webflux</artifactId>
4  </dependency>
5  <dependency>
6      <groupId>io.reactivex.rxjava3</groupId>
7      <artifactId>rxjava</artifactId>
8      <version>3.0.0</version>
9  </dependency>
```

Having configured the project with the necessary dependencies, the next step involves creating a reactive controller using Spring WebFlux. Consider the following example:

```
1  @RestController
2  @RequestMapping("/api/reactive")
3  public class ReactiveController {
4
5      @GetMapping("/data")
6      public Mono<String> getData() {
7          return Mono.just("Hello, Reactive World with RxJava and WebFlux!");
8      }
9  }
```

In this example, a RESTful endpoint is defined that returns a reactive Mono<String> type. Mono is a reactive stream component from Project

Reactor (the reactive library used by Spring WebFlux) that emits at most one item.

To integrate RxJava into this setup, data operations can be wrapped and manipulated using RxJava's observable sequences. RxJava's Observable, Single, Maybe, and Flowable types can be converted to and from Spring Reactor's Mono and Flux types.

The following example demonstrates converting an RxJava Observable to a Spring Reactor Flux, which is then returned from a Spring WebFlux controller:

```
1  @GetMapping("/rxdata")
2  public Flux<String> getRxData() {
3      Observable<String> observable = Observable.just("One", "Two", "Three");
4      return Flux.from(observable.toFlowable(BackpressureStrategy.BUFFER));
5  }
```

In this scenario, RxJava's Observable is created with a list of strings. Given that Observable does not support back pressure directly, it is converted to Flowable with a specified back pressure strategy before being converted to Flux.

Integrating RxJava with Spring WebFlux not only involves returning data but also handling data streams from request bodies. For instance, processing POST request payloads reactively can be achieved as follows:

```
1  @PostMapping("/post")
2  public Mono<Void> postRxData(@RequestBody Flux<String> dataFlux) {
3      return dataFlux
4              .map(String::toUpperCase)
5              .doOnNext(System.out::println)
6              .then();
7  }
```

This method accepts a Flux<String> as a request body, transforms each string to uppercase, and prints it. The then() method is called to return a Mono<Void>, indicating the end of the processing.

To proficiently handle errors in a reactive chain, Spring WebFlux and RxJava provide mechanisms to deal with exceptions in a non-blocking and functional style. For example, fallback methods or default values can be provided in case of errors:

```
1  @GetMapping("/fallback")
2  public Mono<String> getFallbackData() {
3      return Mono.just("default")
4              .flatMap(data -> riskyOperation(data))
5              .onErrorResume(e -> Mono.just("fallback"));
6  }
7
```

```
8   private Mono<String> riskyOperation(String data) {
9       // Simulate an operation that may fail
10      return Mono.error(new RuntimeException("Operation fails"));
11  }
```

In getFallbackData, a default value is initially provided, followed by a risky operation simulated by riskyOperation method. If an error occurs, onErrorResume provides a fallback Mono with a safe value.

The integration of RxJava with Spring WebFlux facilitates the development of robust, scalable, and responsive web applications. By combining the strengths of both libraries, developers can harness reactive programming models to build non-blocking, event-driven applications that efficiently handle streams of data and provide exceptional performance under high loads.

4.4   Implementing Reactive Data Access with RxJava and Spring Data

In this section, we will discuss the integration of RxJava with Spring Data for creating reactive data access layers in your applications. This combination facilitates an efficient, non-blocking data access strategy, which is crucial for developing responsive applications capable of handling a large volume of concurrent data operations.

Spring Data provides a comprehensive abstraction for data access layers in Spring applications, simplifying the complexity of database operations. When combined with RxJava, it enables the development of reactive repositories that can handle data operations asynchronously, improving the overall performance and scalability of applications.

First, to leverage RxJava within a Spring Data context, it's imperative to understand the reactive repositories support provided by Spring Data. Reactive Repositories are an extension of Spring Data's repository support, allowing for the creation of repository interfaces that return types like RxJava's Observable, Single, or Maybe instead of traditional synchronous types.

To set up a project to use RxJava with Spring Data, you need to include the 'spring-boot-starter-data-mongodb-reactive' or similar starter dependency for reactive support in your build configuration. This starter includes the necessary dependencies for reactive data access with Spring Data. Here is an example dependency configuration in Maven:

```
1  <dependency>
2      <groupId>org.springframework.boot</groupId>
3      <artifactId>spring-boot-starter-data-mongodb-reactive</artifactId>
4  </dependency>
```

Next, define a reactive repository interface. For instance, to work with an entity named `Person`, your repository interface might look like this:

```
1  public interface PersonRepository extends ReactiveCrudRepository<Person, String> {
2
3      Flux<Person> findByLastName(String lastName);
4
5      @Query("{ 'age' : { \$gt: ?0 } }")
6      Flux<Person> findOlderThan(int age);
7
8  }
```

In the example above, `Flux` and `Mono` from Project Reactor are used, which are the reactive types that Spring Data repositories typically work with for streaming and single or empty values, respectively. However, RxJava types can easily be adapted to and from these Reactor types, allowing for seamless integration of RxJava into the repository layer.

To bridge RxJava with Spring Data's Reactor types, you can use the `RxJava2Adapter` class. For instance, converting a `Flux<Person>` to an RxJava `Observable<Person>` can be done as follows:

```
1  Flux<Person> flux = personRepository.findByLastName("Doe");
2  Observable<Person> observable = RxJava2Adapter.fluxToObservable(flux);
```

In the context of integrating RxJava with Spring Data, it's essential to understand how to perform asynchronous database operations. For example, saving an entity asynchronously using RxJava's `Single` could look like this:

```
1  Single<Person> personSingle = RxJava2Adapter.monoToSingle(personRepository.save(
       person));
```

This approach ensures that database operations do not block the application's execution thread, thereby improving the efficiency and responsiveness of the application.

Implementing custom queries in a reactive manner requires attention to detail. For operations that do not directly translate to simple CRUD operations, use the `@Query` annotation to define custom query methods within your repository interface. It's important to return reactive types (`Flux` or `Mono`) for these custom queries to maintain the non-blocking behavior throughout your data access layer.

Error handling in a reactive data access layer is accomplished by leveraging the error handling mechanisms provided by RxJava. For example, to handle a possible error during a database operation, you can use the onErrorReturn method provided by RxJava's Observable type:

```
observable.onErrorReturn(throwable -> {
    // Log error or perform fallback operation
    return new Person("Fallback", "Person");
});
```

Integrating RxJava with Spring Data enhances the reactive capabilities of your data access layer, allowing for more scalable and efficient applications. By defining reactive repository interfaces, converting between Reactor and RxJava types, and handling errors in a reactive manner, you can build a robust data access layer that leverages the best of both RxJava and Spring Data. This integration is key to developing non-blocking, event-driven applications that can gracefully handle a high volume of concurrent data operations.

4.5   Building a Reactive RESTful API with RxJava and Spring Boot

Building a Reactive RESTful API with RxJava and Spring Boot involves leveraging the strengths of both frameworks to create highly responsive and resilient web services. This process encompasses setting up the development environment, defining the data model, creating service components, and crafting controller endpoints that subscribe to RxJava observables or singles for data handling. This chapter delineates the methodology for constructing such an API.

Firstly, ensure that the development environment is properly configured with the necessary dependencies for Spring Boot and RxJava. The implementation of RxJava in a Spring Boot project requires the addition of RxJava and Spring Boot starter web flux libraries in the pom.xml or build.gradle file. The inclusion of these dependencies enables the seamless integration of reactive programming concepts within a Spring Boot application, thereby facilitating the creation of non-blocking, event-driven services.

```
<dependency>
    <groupId>org.springframework.boot</groupId>
    <artifactId>spring-boot-starter-webflux</artifactId>
</dependency>
```

```
7   <dependency>
8       <groupId>io.reactivex.rxjava3</groupId>
9       <artifactId>rxjava</artifactId>
10      <version>3.0.0</version>
11  </dependency>
```

Upon configuring the environment, the next step involves defining the data model. In this context, a data model typically consists of domain entities that represent the data structure. For instance, considering a RESTful API designed to manage a library of books, a Book class can be defined as follows:

```
1
2   public class Book {
3       private String id;
4       private String title;
5       private String author;
6
7       // Constructors, Getters, and Setters
8   }
```

Following the data model setup, creating service components constitutes the next phase. Service components are responsible for the business logic and interact with the database or other services. In a reactive setup with RxJava, services return observables or singles. For instance, a service method to retrieve all books can be fashioned as follows:

```
1
2   public Observable<Book> findAllBooks() {
3       // Implementation to fetch all books
4   }
```

The final and crucial aspect of building a Reactive RESTful API involves crafting the controller endpoints. Spring Framework's support for reactive programming through the Spring WebFlux module allows for handling asynchronous streams of data from the service layer. As such, controller endpoints subscribe to the observables or singles returned by service methods. Here's an example of a controller that retrieves all books using a GET request:

```
1
2   @RestController
3   @RequestMapping("/books")
4   public class BookController {
5
6       private final BookService bookService;
7
8       @GetMapping
9       public Flux<Book> getAllBooks() {
10          return bookService.findAllBooks().toFlux();
11      }
12  }
```

In this example, the `BookService` method `findAllBooks` returns an Observable of `Book`. The controller converts this Observable to a `Flux` using the `toFlux` method, to be compatible with Spring WebFlux. `Flux` is a part of Project Reactor and is used for handling streams of 0 to N elements. It is essential to perform the conversion to match the reactive types expected by Spring WebFlux.

Incorporating error handling in reactive applications is paramount for maintaining the reliability and resilience of the service. Reactive error handling can be approached by utilizing the error handling operators provided by RxJava, such as `onErrorReturn`, `onErrorResume`, and `onErrorMap`, enabling fine-grained control over how errors are handled and propagated through the observable stream.

To illustrate, here's an example of utilizing `onErrorResume` to handle database connectivity issues gracefully:

```
public Observable<Book> findAllBooks() {
    return databaseClient.query("SELECT * FROM books")
            .map(...)
            .onErrorResume(e -> {
                log.error("Database connection error", e);
                return Observable.empty();
            });
}
```

This segment demonstrates that in the event of a database connectivity issue, the observable stream does not terminate abruptly. Instead, it logs the error and resumes with an empty observable, thus preventing the entire application from becoming unresponsive due to a single point of failure.

Crafting a Reactive RESTful API with RxJava and Spring Boot requires a meticulous integration of both frameworks aimed at achieving non-blocking, event-driven application behavior. By following the steps outlined—from setting up the environment and defining the data model to creating service components and controller endpoints—a powerful and resilient reactive system can be constructed. Additionally, incorporating robust error handling mechanisms ensures the application's reliability, enhancing its ability to meet the demands of modern software development environments.

4.6 Reactive Error Handling in Spring Boot and RxJava

Error handling is an integral part of developing reactive applications, especially when combining RxJava with Spring Boot. Reactive programming paradigms introduce unique challenges and opportunities in managing exceptions and errors that might occur during asynchronous data streams processing. This section will discuss the strategies and practices for effective error handling within a reactive application developed using RxJava and Spring Boot.

In RxJava, errors are considered as first-class data items that can be propagated through the observable streams. When an error occurs, it is wrapped into an OnErrorNotImplementedException and transmitted down the stream to be handled by the subscriber. It is crucial to handle these errors to prevent the application from terminating unpredictably.

The first step in reactive error handling is understanding how to catch and handle exceptions within RxJava observables. RxJava provides several operators for this purpose, such as onErrorReturn, onErrorResumeNext, and onErrorMap. These operators allow developers to intercept errors, transform them, recover from them, or replace the error with a default value. For instance:

```
1  Observable
2      .fromCallable(() -> { throw new RuntimeException("Exception"); })
3      .onErrorReturnItem("Default Value")
4      .subscribe(System.out::println, Throwable::printStackTrace);
```

In this example, onErrorReturnItem is used to emit a default value when an error is encountered, preventing the application from crashing and allowing it to continue its operation.

Spring WebFlux integrates seamlessly with RxJava, providing mechanisms to handle errors in a non-blocking and reactive manner. One method is to use the onErrorMap operator within the controller to catch exceptions and transform them into an appropriate HTTP response:

```
1  @GetMapping(value = "/data")
2  public Mono<ResponseEntity> getData() {
3      return reactiveService.retrieveData()
4          .map(data -> ResponseEntity.ok(data))
5          .onErrorMap(ex -> new ResponseStatusException(HttpStatus.
                  INTERNAL_SERVER_ERROR, ex.getMessage()));
6  }
```

Here, onErrorMap catches any exceptions thrown during the execution of retrieveData() and transforms them into a ResponseStatusException with a 500 status code, allowing Spring WebFlux to handle it accordingly.

Implementing global error handling in Spring Boot with RxJava can be achieved by extending the WebExceptionHandler interface. This approach enables centralized error handling across the application, allowing for a consistent method of managing exceptions:

```
@Component
public class GlobalErrorHandler implements WebExceptionHandler {
    @Override
    public Mono<Void> handle(ServerWebExchange exchange, Throwable ex) {
        ...
        return exchange.getResponse().setComplete();
    }
}
```

In this global error handler, you can inspect the exception, log it, and modify the HTTP response accordingly. This provides a robust method to manage errors across the entire application.

Furthermore, reactive applications benefit from applying backpressure strategies and implementing custom exception types to encapsulate specific error states, which can be particularly useful in complex data processing scenarios. By leveraging RxJava's and Spring Boot's reactive features, one can construct a resilient and responsive application capable of handling errors gracefully and efficiently.

Error handling in reactive applications requires a paradigm shift from traditional imperative error handling methods. By utilizing RxJava's error handling operators and Spring Boot's WebFlux error handling mechanisms, developers can implement effective and seamless error handling strategies. These practices not only improve the application's resilience and robustness but also enhance the overall user experience by providing clear and informative responses to exceptional situations.

4.7 Achieving Concurrency and Parallelism

Concurrency and parallelism are pivotal in enhancing the performance and responsiveness of reactive applications developed using RxJava and Spring Boot. Concurrency involves the decomposition of tasks that can be executed out-of-order or in partial order, without affecting the final outcome, thereby enabling multitasking within a single processor. Parallelism, on the other hand, refers to the simultaneous execution of multiple tasks across different processors or cores, exploiting multiple resources to improve computational speed.

In the context of RxJava and Spring Boot, achieving concurrency and parallelism involves a judicious use of schedulers and threading models that RxJava provides, as well as understanding how these integrate with the underlying execution model of Spring Boot.

Schedulers in RxJava: Schedulers in RxJava are responsible for controlling the threads on which Observable operations are executed. By default, RxJava operations are executed on the immediate thread, but by leveraging different types of schedulers, one can alter this behavior to achieve asynchronous execution and parallelism.

Here are the primary schedulers available in RxJava:

- `Schedulers.io()` - Optimized for I/O-bound operations. It creates a pool of threads that dynamically adjusts according to the workload.

- `Schedulers.computation()` - Designed for CPU-intensive computations. It is bounded by the number of available CPU cores.

- `Schedulers.newThread()` - Creates a new thread for each unit of work.

- `Schedulers.single()` - Provides a single-threaded environment for operations that need to be executed sequentially.

To utilize these schedulers, one can use the `subscribeOn()` and `observeOn()` operators in RxJava. The `subscribeOn()` operator specifies the scheduler on which the Observable will operate, while the `observeOn()` operator alters the scheduler midway through the operator chain, allowing subsequent operations to switch threads.

Integrating with Spring Boot: Spring Boot's reactive stack, including WebFlux, is designed to work with non-blocking servers and provides its own mechanisms for managing concurrency and resource utilization. When integrating RxJava with Spring Boot, it is essential to understand how these mechanisms interact.

Spring WebFlux, for instance, uses Reactor's `Schedulers.parallel()` for running tasks on parallel threads, which works well with RxJava's schedulers. By default, WebFlux configures a number of threads equal to the number of available CPU cores, aiming to effectively utilize system resources without overwhelming the CPU with excessive context switching.

Example of Achieving Parallelism:

Consider a scenario where you have a list of user IDs, and for each ID, you need to perform a resource-intensive operation, such as fetching user details from a remote API.

```
1  Observable.fromIterable(userIds)
2      .flatMap(id ->
3          Observable.fromCallable(() -> fetchUserDetails(id))
4              .subscribeOn(Schedulers.io()))
5      .toList()
6      .subscribe(users -> /* Process the list of users */);
```

In this example, `flatMap()` combined with `subscribeOn(Schedulers.io())` allows each `fetchUserDetails` call to be executed in parallel on the I/O scheduler, which is optimized for such operations. Thus, rather than executing the network requests sequentially, the application can handle them concurrently, substantially reducing the total execution time.

:

Achieving concurrency and parallelism in RxJava and Spring Boot applications requires a comprehensive understanding of RxJava's scheduling capabilities and how they integrate with Spring Boot's reactive paradigm. By judiciously choosing the appropriate schedulers and understanding the execution model of Spring Boot, developers can harness the full power of reactive programming to build highly responsive and efficient applications.

4.8 Implementing Backpressure with RxJava in Spring Boot Applications

Implementing backpressure is paramount in creating responsive and resilient Spring Boot applications that leverage RxJava. Backpressure is a mechanism to prevent overwhelming a consumer with data from a producer that emits values at a higher rate than the consumer can process. This section will discuss implementing backpressure in Spring Boot applications that use RxJava, focusing on the techniques and best practices for managing data flows effectively.

In RxJava, backpressure support is elegantly integrated into the library, offering strategies and operators to control the flow of data. However, integrating these capabilities within Spring Boot requires understanding how RxJava's backpressure mechanisms can complement Spring's reactive stack.

First, let's examine how to detect and handle backpressure scenarios. RxJava provides the Flowable type as the primary means of supporting backpressure. Unlike the Observable type, Flowable is designed to handle large or infinite streams of data with backpressure. When integrating RxJava with Spring Boot, especially with Spring WebFlux, you may often find yourself returning Flux or Mono instances from your controllers. To leverage RxJava's backpressure, these can be converted from and to Flowable instances.

```
1  Flowable<String> flowable = Flowable.just("value1", "value2", "value3");
2  Flux<String> flux = Flux.from(flowable);
```

The conversion enables seamless integration, allowing Spring Boot applications to benefit from RxJava's sophisticated backpressure support while working with Spring WebFlux's reactive types.

Implementing backpressure effectively requires understanding the available strategies in RxJava. The library provides several policies such as BUFFER, DROP, LATEST, and ERROR, each suited to different scenarios.

```
1  Flowable<Integer> source = Flowable.range(1, 1000);
2  source.onBackpressureBuffer().subscribe(System.out::println);
```

In the example above, the onBackpressureBuffer strategy buffers all emissions until the downstream can consume them, preventing a MissingBackpressureException. Choosing the right strategy requires assessing the application's data flow characteristics and consumer capacity.

Integrating backpressure with Spring Data involves the use of reactive repositories. When dealing with I/O bound operations, such as database access, leveraging Spring Data's support for reactive types together with RxJava's backpressure is crucial. This integration ensures that database operations do not become a bottleneck and are efficiently managed.

```
1  Flowable<User> users = userRepository.findAll()
2      .toFlowable()
3      .onBackpressureBuffer();
```

In this scenario, the `findAll` method, typically returning a `Flux<User>`, is converted to a `Flowable` allowing the application of backpressure strategies. This pattern is particularly useful when dealing with large datasets that must be consumed at a controlled pace to prevent memory issues or sluggish UIs in client applications.

For error handling in backpressure scenarios, RxJava provides mechanisms to gracefully degrade performance or alert the system to prevent catastrophic failures. Utilizing the `onBackpressureError` strategy can be a method to signal when the consumer cannot keep up with the producer, allowing the application to respond appropriately, such as by shedding load or informing users of degraded performance.

Moreover, achieving concurrency and parallelism while maintaining backpressure integrity is achievable through RxJava's `flatMap` and `parallel` operators, among others. These operators are designed to respect backpressure, ensuring that even when operations are performed in parallel, the overall system remains responsive and stable.

```
1  Flowable.range(1, 10)
2    .flatMap(v ->
3      Flowable.just(v)
4        .subscribeOn(Schedulers.computation())
5        .map(w -> w * w)
6    )
7    .blockingSubscribe(System.out::println);
```

In this example, the `flatMap` operator is used to perform calculations in parallel while `subscribeOn` introduces concurrency. The `blockingSubscribe` method is then used to consume the flowable, respecting backpressure throughout the process.

Implementing backpressure in Spring Boot applications that utilize RxJava is vital for maintaining a responsive and resilient system. By carefully employing RxJava's backpressure strategies and integrating them within Spring's reactive ecosystem, developers can create applications capable of handling high volumes of data efficiently. Understanding the principles of backpressure, selecting the appropriate strategies, and leveraging the integration points between RxJava and Spring Boot are critical steps in architecting modern, reactive applications.

4.9 Reactive Caching Strategies

Caching is a crucial component in the architecture of highly responsive and scalable reactive applications. It significantly reduces the latency of data retrieval operations and alleviates the load on the system's resources by avoiding redundant data processing or database queries. When combining RxJava and Spring Boot in a reactive application, implementing effective caching strategies is pivotal for maximizing performance and ensuring the swift delivery of content to the user. This section delves into the methodologies and configurations necessary for integrating reactive caching mechanisms in applications leveraging RxJava and Spring Boot.

To commence with the practical implementation of reactive caching strategies, it is essential to understand the concept of caching in the realm of reactive programming. Caching in a reactive application involves temporarily storing the results of expensive operations (such as database queries or remote service calls) in a readily accessible location. This allows subsequent requests for the same data to be served quickly from the cache rather than recomputing them, thus significantly enhancing the application's performance.

The integration of RxJava with Spring Boot provides a suite of tools and frameworks that facilitate the implementation of reactive caching. One such tool is the Spring Cache abstraction, which offers a transparent approach to adding caching to an application. To utilize reactive caching with RxJava and Spring Boot, it is recommended to adhere to the following strategies:

- **Selecting the Appropriate Cache Provider:** Spring Boot supports various caching providers such as Caffeine, EhCache, and Redis. For reactive applications, choosing a non-blocking cache provider such as Redis is crucial to maintain the non-blocking behavior and ensure that all operations are performed in a non-blocking manner.

- **Cache Configuration:** Configuring the cache involves defining cache names, specifying the data retention policy, and setting the maximum size of the cache. These configurations can be accomplished through the application.properties or application.yml files in a Spring Boot application.

```
spring.cache.cache-names=users,transactions
spring.cache.caffeine.spec=maximumSize=500,expireAfterAccess=600s
```

- **Implementing Cacheable Operations:** To leverage the caching mechanism, methods in the application services that perform expensive operations can be annotated with @Cacheable. This annotation tells Spring to cache the method's result. When a method annotated with @Cacheable is called, Spring checks if the result is present in the cache. If a cache hit occurs, the cached result is returned; otherwise, the method is executed, and its result is stored in the cache.

```
1  @Cacheable(value = "users", key = "#userId")
2  public Mono<User> getUserById(String userId) {
3      return userRepository.findById(userId);
4  }
```

- **Cache Invalidation and Eviction:** To ensure the cache's consistency, it is essential to invalidate or evict stale entries when the underlying data changes. Spring provides the @CacheEvict annotation to automate cache eviction upon the execution of methods that modify the cached data.

```
1  @CacheEvict(value = "users", key = "#user.id")
2  public Mono<User> updateUser(User user) {
3      return userRepository.save(user);
4  }
```

- **Dynamic Caching Strategies:** Depending on the application's requirements, it may be beneficial to implement dynamic caching strategies. This involves programmatically manipulating the cache, such as dynamically changing the cache configuration or selectively caching data based on specific conditions.

Integrating reactive caching in applications that combine RxJava and Spring Boot not only boosts performance but also improves the scalability and responsiveness of the service. By judiciously selecting the caching strategy and meticulously configuring the cache properties, developers can effectively manage data latency and resource utilization, ensuring that the application consistently delivers superior performance.

Finally, it is worth noting that monitoring and managing the cache's health is essential to prevent cache-related issues from impacting the application's performance. Utilizing management endpoints exposed by Spring Boot Actuator can aid in monitoring cache metrics and performing administrative operations, thus maintaining the health and efficiency of the caching layer.

4.10 Securing your Reactive Application

Securing a reactive application is paramount to safeguarding the data and functionalities from unauthorized access and potential threats. This entails protecting the endpoints, data stream integrity, and ensuring that the communication between the client and the server is secure. When combining RxJava with Spring Boot, security measures become both essential and intricate due to the nature of reactive programming and the asynchronous data flows it involves.

Spring Security offers a comprehensive security framework that integrates well with Spring Boot, including support for reactive applications through its reactive security context. This framework allows for declarative security configuration, simplifying the process of securing your reactive application. The primary focus is on Authentication and Authorization, protecting sensitive endpoints, encrypting sensitive data, and securing the data stream.

Authentication and Authorization: Authentication verifies a user's identity, while authorization determines the level of access or permissions that the authenticated user has. In the context of a reactive Spring Boot application, this involves configuring a chain of security filters that process authentication and authorization asynchronously.

```
1  @EnableWebFluxSecurity
2  public class SecurityConfig {
3
4      @Bean
5      public SecurityWebFilterChain springSecurityFilterChain(ServerHttpSecurity http
           ) {
6          http
7              .authorizeExchange()
8              .pathMatchers("/public/**").permitAll()
9              .anyExchange().authenticated()
10             .and().formLogin();
11         return http.build();
12     }
13 }
```

This configuration example demonstrates how to permit unauthenticated access to endpoints prefixed with '/public' and require authentication for any other requests. It leverages Spring Security's DSL to configure the security filter chain in a reactive application context.

Data Encryption: Ensuring the confidentiality and integrity of the data as it flows between the client and the server is critical. SSL/TLS encryption is the standard for secure data transmission over the internet. Configuring SSL with Spring Boot is straightforward, requiring minimal properties set in the application's configuration file.

```
1  server:
2    ssl:
3      key-store: keystore.p12
4      key-store-password: secret
5      keyStoreType: PKCS12
6      keyAlias: springboot
```

This YAML configuration specifies the key store file, its type, password, and the alias under which the application's key is stored. It ensures that all data transmitted between the client and server is encrypted, providing a secure communication channel.

Data Stream Security: Securing the data stream in a reactive application involves protecting the data as it moves between publishers and subscribers. Applying security at this level must consider the non-blocking nature of reactive streams. Implementing authentication and authorization logic as part of the data processing pipeline ensures that only authenticated users can access specific data streams, and are authorized to perform certain operations.

```
1   Flux<User> secureUserStream(Flux<User> users) {
2       return users.flatMap(user -> {
3           Mono<Boolean> isAuthenticated = checkAuthentication(user);
4           return isAuthenticated.flatMap(authenticated -> {
5               if (authenticated) {
6                   return Mono.just(user);
7               } else {
8                   return Mono.empty();
9               }
10          });
11      });
12  }
```

This code snippet demonstrates how to secure a reactive data stream by integrating authentication logic directly into the processing pipeline. It checks whether each user in a stream is authenticated and filters out unauthenticated users, ensuring that the downstream subscribers only receive data they are authorized to access.

: Securing a reactive application built with RxJava and Spring Boot requires a holistic approach that covers authentication, authorization, data encryption, and the security of the data streams. By leveraging the features provided by Spring Security in a reactive context, developers can effectively protect their applications against common security threats. Understanding and correctly implementing these security controls is crucial for building resilient, secure reactive applications.

4.11 Monitoring and Metrics for RxJava and Spring Boot Applications

Monitoring and metrics play an indispensable role in the development and maintenance of reactive applications using RxJava and Spring Boot. The inherently asynchronous nature of these applications necessitates a robust strategy for insights into their performance and behavior. This section will discuss the mechanisms and tools available for effectively monitoring RxJava and Spring Boot applications, focusing on gathering, visualizing, and analyzing performance metrics to ensure optimal application health and responsiveness.

Firstly, it's vital to understand the types of metrics relevant to reactive applications. These include but are not limited to, throughput (the number of requests processed per unit of time), latency (the time taken to process a request), error rates, and backpressure-related metrics. Collecting these metrics provides insights into the application's performance under various conditions and helps in identifying bottlenecks, inefficiencies, and potential failures.

Spring Boot Actuator is an essential tool in the Spring ecosystem for application monitoring and management. It exposes various endpoints for monitoring application health, metrics, and environment properties. When integrated with RxJava applications, the Actuator makes it easier to monitor the behavior of asynchronous streams and scheduled tasks. To enable Spring Boot Actuator in a reactive application, the following dependency should be added to the project's build configuration:

```
1  <dependency>
2      <groupId>org.springframework.boot</groupId>
3      <artifactId>spring-boot-starter-actuator</artifactId>
4  </dependency>
```

Once the Actuator is included, application metrics can be accessed via predefined endpoints, such as '/actuator/metrics' for metrics and '/actuator/health' for health status. These endpoints can be customized and extended to include custom metrics specific to the application's requirements.

For a more granular view into the reactive streams powered by RxJava, integrating with a monitoring tool such as Micrometer is recommended. Micrometer acts as an application metrics facade that supports numerous monitoring systems, including Prometheus, Graphite, and InfluxDB. By binding Micrometer with Spring Boot and RxJava, developers can capture detailed metrics about the operation of their reactive pipelines:

```
1  <dependency>
2      <groupId>io.micrometer</groupId>
3      <artifactId>micrometer-core</artifactId>
4  </dependency>
```

With Micrometer configured, custom metrics can be created to track the behavior of RxJava components. For example, measuring the latency of database queries executed within a reactive stream or the rate of emissions in an Observable:

```
1  Flux<String> flux = Flux.fromIterable(data)
2      .name("myFlux") // Naming the sequence for identification in metrics
3      .metrics(); // Enabling metrics collection
```

Visualizing the collected metrics is a critical aspect of monitoring. Tools such as Grafana can be used to create dashboards that display real-time data about the application's performance. Configuring Grafana to consume metrics exposed by Spring Boot Actuator or Micrometer enables developers and operations teams to monitor application health, visualize trends, and set up alerts based on predefined thresholds.

Effective monitoring also requires attention to error handling and back-pressure management in reactive streams. Utilizing the features of RxJava and Spring Boot to handle errors gracefully and manage back-pressure is crucial for maintaining application stability. These mechanisms should be monitored to ensure they function as expected under stress conditions. For example, tracking the rate at which backpressure signals are emitted can help in identifying issues with the flow of data within the application.

Lastly, application logs provide invaluable insights into the operational aspects of the application and should not be overlooked. Integrating a logging framework such as Logback or Log4J2, configured to include detailed information about the reactive flows, will enhance the monitoring and troubleshooting capabilities.

Effective monitoring and metrics collection for RxJava and Spring Boot applications involves a multi-faceted approach that includes leveraging tools and frameworks such as Spring Boot Actuator, Micrometer, and Grafana, along with careful attention to the application's error handling and backpressure strategies. By systematically collecting, visualizing, and analyzing metrics, developers can ensure their reactive applications remain performant, scalable, and reliable.

4.12   Best Practices for Combining RxJava and Spring Boot

When combining RxJava with Spring Boot for developing reactive applications, adhering to best practices ensures that the integration is both effective and efficient. This section will discuss these practices in detail, outlining strategies for maximizing the strengths of both frameworks and avoiding common pitfalls.

First and foremost, understanding the execution model of RxJava is crucial. RxJava operates on a scheduler-based execution model, which means that operations can be offloaded to different threads, thereby enabling non-blocking I/O operations. When integrating RxJava with Spring Boot, especially with Spring WebFlux for handling HTTP requests in a non-blocking manner, it is important to make effective use of RxJava's subscribeOn and observeOn methods to control the execution context of your reactive streams.

```
1  Flux<String> flux = Flux.just("A", "B", "C")
2                     .map(String::toLowerCase)
3                     .subscribeOn(Schedulers.boundedElastic());
```

This code snippet demonstrates the use of the subscribeOn method with the Schedulers.boundedElastic() scheduler, which is suitable for I/O bound tasks. Utilizing appropriate schedulers ensures that the application remains responsive, by not blocking the main thread for I/O operations.

Error handling in a reactive stack is another critical area that demands careful attention. RxJava provides a comprehensive API for dealing with errors in a non-blocking manner. Utilizing operators like onErrorReturn, onErrorResumeNext, and retry can help in gracefully handling errors and ensuring that the application remains resilient.

```
1  Flux<String> fluxWithErrorHandling = flux.onErrorResume(e -> Flux.just("default"));
```

This example demonstrates the use of onErrorResume, which allows for providing a fallback method in the event of an error, thus ensuring that the application can continue to operate under adverse conditions.

When working with Spring Data in a reactive application, it is advisable to use reactive repositories. Spring Data provides support for reactive data access through project Reactor types like Mono and Flux. This allows for non-blocking data access, which is essential for maintaining the responsiveness of the application.

113

```
@Repository
public interface ReactiveUserRepository extends ReactiveCrudRepository<User, String> {}
```

Utilizing reactive repositories enables the application to perform database operations in a non-blocking manner, leveraging the full capabilities of the reactive programming model.

Another important practice is the efficient management of backpressure. Backpressure is a mechanism to prevent overwhelming a consumer with data from a producer. RxJava provides various strategies to deal with backpressure, such as buffer, drop, and latest. Understanding and applying these strategies appropriately is key to building resilient reactive applications.

```
1   Flux<String> fluxWithBackpressure = flux.onBackpressureBuffer();
```

This snippet demonstrates the use of onBackpressureBuffer, which buffers elements if the downstream cannot keep up, preventing an overflow of data and potential application failure.

Monitoring and metrics are integral to maintaining and optimizing a reactive application. Spring Boot Actuator, in conjunction with Micrometer, provides a robust set of tools for monitoring application health, performance, and behavior in production environments. It is essential to instrument your application with these tools to gain insights into its operation and identify potential bottlenecks or issues.

Combining RxJava with Spring Boot for reactive programming requires a deep understanding of both frameworks' principles and best practices. By following the strategies outlined above—controlling execution context, handling errors gracefully, using reactive data access patterns, managing backpressure effectively, and monitoring application performance—a high-performing, resilient, and responsive application can be built to meet the challenges of modern software development.

Chapter 5

Data Streams and Back-Pressure

The concepts of data streams and back-pressure are pivotal in reactive programming, ensuring that applications can handle data flows efficiently without overwhelming consumers. Data streams encapsulate the idea of processing series of data items reactively, while back-pressure provides a mechanism to control the flow of data to prevent bottlenecks and system crashes. This chapter delves into the intricacies of implementing and managing data streams alongside strategies for effectively applying back-pressure within reactive systems, highlighting the tools and techniques critical to maintaining stability and performance in reactive applications.

5.1 Understanding Data Streams in Reactive Programming

Data streams in reactive programming represent the concept of handling data that is produced and consumed asynchronously over time. This approach allows applications to react to new data items as they arrive, processing each item in turn without blocking the execution thread. Unlike imperative programming, where operations are executed in a sequential and synchronous manner, reactive programming is built around the asynchronous and non-blocking manipulation of data streams, enabling a more efficient handling of I/O-bound tasks and real-time updates.

At the core of reactive programming are Observables and Observers. An Observable is a data source that emits items to be processed, while an Observer subscribes to an Observable to receive and react to the emitted items. This interaction is the foundation upon which reactive programming constructs its asynchronous data flow control.

```
1  Observable<String> observable = Observable.fromArray("Item1", "Item2", "Item3");
2  observable.subscribe(item -> System.out.println(item),
3     error -> error.printStackTrace(),
4     () -> System.out.println("Completed"));
```

The above example illustrates the basic structure of creating an Observable from an array of strings and subscribing an Observer to it. The Observer reacts to each emitted item by printing it out, handles any possible errors, and acknowledges the completion of the data stream.

In a reactive system, data streams can represent anything from variable values changing over time, user inputs, or more complex data flows such as database records or network packets. To effectively manage these streams, especially in high-throughput or real-time applications, it is essential to understand and implement back-pressure, a form of flow control.

Back-pressure is a technique used to prevent overwhelm by allowing downstream consumers (Observers) to signal upstream producers (Observables) when they are ready to process more data. This ensures that consumers are not forced to handle more data than they can process, which could lead to buffer overflow, memory issues, or degraded performance.

```
Subscriber -> requests 10 items
Publisher -> emits 10 items
Subscriber -> processes items
```

The sequence of actions outlined above demonstrates a simplistic model of back-pressure in action. The Subscriber specifies how many items it is capable of processing at a time, and the Publisher emits data accordingly. This request-emit pattern is a cornerstone of back-pressure handling, promoting a stable and responsive data stream flow within a reactive system.

Data streams are, therefore, not just a way of structuring asynchronous data delivery but also a methodology for ensuring that data flows through a system in a controlled, efficient manner. Reactive Programming requires developers to think in terms of data streams and back-pressure, viewing applications as networks of reactive components that communicate and collaborate through these streams.

In summary, the understanding of data streams in reactive programming is paramount for the development of responsive, resilient, and scalable applications. By modeling data as streams that can be observed and manipulated reactively, and by effectively implementing back-pressure, developers can harness the full potential of reactive programming paradigms to construct complex, data-centric applications that can handle high volumes of data in real-time, with minimal resource consumption and maximal efficiency.

5.2 The Concept of Back-Pressure Explained

Back-pressure is a critical concept in the realm of reactive programming, particularly concerning how systems handle varying loads of data efficiently. It is a feedback mechanism that allows a data consumer to communicate to the data producer about how much data it can process at a given time, effectively controlling the flow of data and preventing the consumer from being overwhelmed. This communication is vital in scenarios where the data producer is capable of emitting data at a faster rate than the consumer can process, leading to potential bottlenecks or system failures due to resource exhaustion.

In essence, back-pressure aims to ensure that the pace of data production aligns with the consumer's capacity for processing. Without an effective back-pressure strategy, systems may encounter issues such as out-of-memory errors, decreased performance, and unresponsive services. These are symptoms of a system being overwhelmed with data, unable to process incoming requests efficiently.

The implementation of back-pressure involves two primary roles: the producer and the consumer. The producer is responsible for generating data, while the consumer processes this data. In reactive systems, both parties negotiate the rate of data flow based on the consumer's ability to handle the data. This negotiation is often facilitated by a protocol or standard, with Reactive Streams being a prominent example in the Java ecosystem. Reactive Streams define a standard for asynchronous stream processing with non-blocking back-pressure.

117

Implementing back-pressure correctly requires understanding the Reactive Streams API, which comprises four main interfaces: Publisher, Subscriber, Subscription, and Processor. The Publisher emits data items, while the Subscriber receives them. The Subscription acts as a contract between the Publisher and Subscriber for delivering a specific number of items, allowing the Subscriber to request an amount of data it can handle, which is the essence of back-pressure. Finally, the Processor acts as both a Subscriber and a Publisher, enabling transformation and forwarding of data.

Consider the following example, which demonstrates a simple interaction between a Publisher and a Subscriber utilizing back-pressure:

```
import org.reactivestreams.Publisher;
import org.reactivestreams.Subscriber;
import org.reactivestreams.Subscription;

public class SimplePublisher implements Publisher<Integer> {
    @Override
    public void subscribe(Subscriber<? super Integer> subscriber) {
        subscriber.onSubscribe(new Subscription() {
            private int count = 0;

            @Override
            public void request(long n) {
                for (int i = 0; i < n; i++) {
                    subscriber.onNext(count++);
                }
            }

            @Override
            public void cancel() {
                // Handle cancellation
            }
        });
    }
}
```

In this example, the SimplePublisher provides integers to its subscribers. The Subscription within the subscribe method allows the Subscriber to request a specific number of items it is capable of handling by calling the request method, embodying the principle of back-pressure.

Understanding and implementing back-pressure effectively can significantly impact the responsiveness and resilience of reactive systems. By managing data flow precisely, reactive applications can maintain high levels of performance and stability, even under varying loads or in resource-constrained environments.

Through the proactive application of back-pressure, developers can create systems that are not only efficient and responsive but also robust and scalable. This aspect is particularly important in today's data-driven world, where applications must manage large volumes of data in real-time, making back-pressure an indispensable technique in the toolkit of modern software development.

5.3 Creating Responsive Data Streams

In this section, we discuss how to create responsive data streams by employing various techniques and utilizing the capabilities of the RxJava and Project Reactor libraries. Responsive data streams are an essential component of reactive programming, enabling applications to process large volumes of data efficiently and reliably. The goal of this section is to provide a comprehensive overview of the methods used to construct these data streams, ensuring that they can handle varying data loads while maintaining high performance and responsiveness.

Let's start with the foundational step of creating a data stream in RxJava. The creation of a data stream in RxJava typically involves the use of the Observable class or its cousin, the Flowable class. The choice between these two often depends on the expected data volume and the necessity for back-pressure support. For example, to create a simple data stream that emits a sequence of integers, one might use the following code snippet:

```
Observable<Integer> observable = Observable.range(1, 10);
```

This code creates an Observable that emits integers from 1 to 10. However, for streams that might emit a large number of items or infinite sequences, Flowable is a more appropriate choice because it supports back-pressure, helping to prevent memory overflows:

```
Flowable<Integer> flowable = Flowable.range(1, 1000);
```

Creating responsive data streams not only involves emitting data but also processing it efficiently. This is where operators come into play. RxJava and Project Reactor provide a vast set of operators that can filter, transform, combine, and control the data flow. For instance, to filter out even numbers from a stream of integers, one could use the filter operator as follows:

```
Flowable<Integer> evenNumbers = flowable.filter(x -> x % 2 == 0);
```

119

Transforming items emitted by a stream can be achieved using the map operator. For example, to square each number in a stream of integers:

```
Flowable<Integer> squared = flowable.map(x -> x * x);
```

Combining multiple data streams is another crucial aspect of creating responsive data streams. The zip operator can be used to combine the emissions of two or more streams by applying a function to each combination of items:

```
Flowable<Integer> firstStream = Flowable.just(1, 2, 3);
Flowable<Integer> secondStream = Flowable.just(4, 5, 6);
Flowable<Integer> zipped = Flowable.zip(firstStream, secondStream, (a, b) -> a + b)
    ;
```

The above zip operator combines the corresponding elements of firstStream and secondStream by summing them.

Error handling is a critical feature of responsive data streams, ensuring they can gracefully handle exceptional conditions. In RxJava, the onError method allows specifying an action to be taken when an error occurs:

```
observable.subscribe(
    item -> System.out.println(item),
    error -> error.printStackTrace()
);
```

This ensures that if an error occurs within the stream, it does not crash the application but instead is handled in a controlled manner.

Lastly, controlling the rate of data processing is crucial for creating responsive data streams, which is where back-pressure management and flow control strategies come into play. The Flowable class in RxJava is designed to handle back-pressure explicitly. For example, applying back-pressure can be achieved using the onBackpressureDrop operator:

```
Flowable<Integer> protectedFlowable = flowable.onBackpressureDrop();
```

This operator prevents back-pressure related issues by dropping emissions that cannot be processed in time, ensuring the responsiveness of the data stream under high load conditions.

Creating responsive data streams in reactive programming involves a careful combination of choosing the right data types, applying operators for data processing, handling errors gracefully, and managing back-pressure effectively. By employing these strategies within the context of RxJava and Project Reactor, developers can construct robust and efficient reactive systems capable of handling diverse and demanding data processing tasks.

5.4 Flow Control Strategies in Reactive Programming

Flow control in reactive programming is critical to maintaining the stability and performance of reactive systems. It ensures that a consumer does not get overwhelmed with too many data items emitted by a publisher. This balance is especially crucial in systems where the data-producing component can emit data at a much faster rate than the consuming component can process. In this section, we will discuss various strategies employed in reactive programming to manage flow control effectively.

One fundamental concept in reactive programming for managing flow control is back-pressure. Back-pressure allows consumers to signal publishers how much data they are ready to process, thereby preventing the consumer from being overloaded. Effective application of back-pressure requires a comprehensive understanding of the reactive streams specification, which defines a standard for asynchronous stream processing with non-blocking back-pressure.

Buffering

Buffering is a common flow control strategy where data emitted by a publisher that cannot be immediately consumed is temporarily stored in a buffer. By implementing buffering, a system can smooth out short-term discrepancies in processing rates between publishers and subscribers. However, while buffering can mitigate issues related to bursty traffic patterns, it introduces new considerations such as buffer size management and the potential for buffer overflow. Careful attention must be paid to buffer configuration to prevent memory issues.

```
Flux<Integer> dataStream = Flux.range(1, 100)
  .onBackpressureBuffer(10); // Buffer up to 10 items
```

Dropping

Dropping is another strategy where items emitted by the publisher are simply discarded if the consumer is not ready to process them. This approach is suitable for scenarios where real-time processing is more critical than complete data processing, and missing some data does not compromise the application's integrity. Dropping helps in maintaining the system's responsiveness by ensuring that slow consumers do not cause the system to become unresponsive.

```
1  Flux<Integer> dataStream = Flux.range(1, 100)
2      .onBackpressureDrop(); // Drop items that cannot be processed
```

Latest

Similar to dropping, the latest strategy ensures that the consumer always processes the most recent items. When the consumer is ready, it receives the latest emitted item, with all previous unprocessed items being discarded. This strategy is particularly useful in situations where the latest data is more valuable than older data, such as in real-time monitoring or dashboard applications.

```
1  Flux<Integer> dataStream = Flux.range(1, 100)
2      .onBackpressureLatest(); // Keep only the latest item
```

Windowing

Windowing is a more sophisticated flow control strategy that groups emitted items into windows based on time or size and processes each window as a batch. This approach is useful for reducing the overhead associated with processing each item individually and can be particularly effective when combined with aggregation operations.

```
1  Flux<Long> dataStream = Flux.interval(Duration.ofMillis(100))
2      .window(Duration.ofSeconds(1)); // Window items into 1-second windows
```

Throttling

Throttling limits the rate at which items are processed, allowing a system to cap the processing rate to a level that the consumer can handle. This can be achieved through various techniques such as delaying the processing of items or limiting the processing to a fixed rate. Throttling is beneficial in scenarios where it's crucial to limit the consumption of resources such as CPU or network bandwidth.

```
1  Flux<Integer> dataStream = Flux.range(1, 100)
2      .sample(Duration.ofSeconds(1)); // Process at most one item per second
```

Each of these strategies offers a different approach to managing flow control in reactive systems, and the choice of strategy should be guided by the specific requirements of the application. A thoughtful application of flow control can significantly enhance the responsiveness, resilience, and scalability of reactive applications.

Mastering flow control strategies is indispensable for developing efficient and robust reactive systems. By judiciously applying concepts such as buffering, dropping, windowing, and throttling, developers can ensure that their reactive systems remain responsive and stable under varying load conditions. The key lies in understanding the nature of the data and the processing capabilities of the system components to select the most appropriate flow control strategy.

5.5 Implementing Back-Pressure with Reactive Streams

In the context of reactive programming, back-pressure is a critical concept that enables managing the flow of data through asynchronous streams, ensuring that faster producers do not overwhelm slower consumers. Reactive Streams, an initiative and a set of interfaces that guide asynchronous stream processing with non-blocking back pressure, provide the foundation for implementing back-pressure in applications. This section will discuss the principles of Reactive Streams and how they facilitate the implementation of back-pressure in a reactive system.

Reactive Streams define four key interfaces: Publisher, Subscriber, Subscription, and Processor. Each plays a vital role in establishing and managing the flow of data within a stream, adhering to the back-pressure strategy.

The Publisher interface is responsible for producing data. When a Subscriber expresses an interest in receiving data, the Publisher subscribes them to the data stream. However, it is the Subscriber's responsibility to request data from the Publisher, controlling the flow of data by specifying the volume of data it can handle. This is where back-pressure inherently comes into play.

The interaction between `Publisher` and `Subscriber` is mediated by the `Subscription` object. A `Subscription` is created when a `Subscriber` subscribes to a `Publisher`. It acts as a contract between the two, allowing the `Subscriber` to request or cancel data flow. The method `request(long n)` defined in the `Subscription` interface is where the back-pressure mechanism is explicitly realized. The `Subscriber` uses this method to request a specific number of items from the `Publisher`, allowing it to control the pace at which data is consumed.

The `Processor` interface inherits from both `Publisher` and `Subscriber`, combining the production and consumption of data streams. This allows for creating components that both receive data, apply some processing, and emit the result downstream, all the while respecting back-pressure signals.

Implementing back-pressure effectively requires understanding the balance between production and consumption rates within your system. Below is a simplified example demonstrating how a `Subscriber` might request data from a `Publisher`:

```java
public class SampleSubscriber<T> implements Subscriber<T> {
    private Subscription subscription;

    @Override
    public void onSubscribe(Subscription subscription) {
        this.subscription = subscription;
        subscription.request(1); // Request the first item
    }

    @Override
    public void onNext(T item) {
        processItem(item);
        subscription.request(1); // Request the next item
    }

    @Override
    public void onError(Throwable t) {
        // Handle error
    }

    @Override
    public void onComplete() {
        // Handle stream completion
    }

    private void processItem(T item) {
        // Implement item processing logic
    }
}
```

In this example, the `SampleSubscriber` requests one item at a time from the `Publisher`. This simplistic strategy demonstrates how a `Subscriber` can control the flow of data, ensuring it only receives as much data as it can process at a time, embodying the essence of back-pressure.

It is important to note that the implementation of back-pressure is both a responsibility and a challenge. Developers must make judicious use of the `request` method, requesting enough data to maintain throughput without overloading the system. Over-requesting can diminish the benefits of back-pressure by leading to potential memory issues, while under-requesting can result in underutilized resources and reduced overall system throughput.

Reactive Streams offer a robust framework for implementing back-pressure in asynchronous data streams, ensuring that the flow of data between producers and consumers is managed efficiently. By understanding and leveraging the interfaces and patterns provided by Reactive Streams, developers can create responsive and resilient reactive systems capable of handling varying loads and preventing system overload.

5.6   Back-Pressure in RxJava Explained

Back-pressure, a term often encountered in the context of reactive programming, is a critical concept to understand for effective application development using RxJava. This mechanism is designed to prevent scenarios where data producers overwhelm data consumers, potentially leading to system instability or failure. In RxJava, back-pressure is particularly relevant due to the library's emphasis on processing asynchronous data streams. This section will explore how RxJava handles back-pressure, elucidate its importance in reactive systems, and present techniques to apply it correctly.

RxJava, a prominent library in the Java ecosystem for composing asynchronous and event-based programs by using observable sequences, provides comprehensive support for back-pressure through its 'Flowable' class. Unlike the 'Observable' class, which does not inherently support back-pressure, 'Flowable' is designed to handle streams of data that can be controlled to prevent the overwhelming of consumers. The distinction between 'Observable' and 'Flowable' is fundamental in RxJava's approach to back-pressure.

```
1   Flowable<Integer> flowable = Flowable.range(1, 1000);
2   flowable.observeOn(Schedulers.io())
3       .subscribe(data -> {
4           System.out.println(data);
5           try {
6               Thread.sleep(100); // Simulated work
7           } catch (InterruptedException e) {
8               Thread.currentThread().interrupt();
9           }
10      });
```

In the example above, a 'Flowable' is created that emits a range of integers from 1 to 1000. The 'observeOn' method directs the 'Flowable' to emit items on the I/O scheduler, a common scenario in applications where data is generated quickly but consumed slowly. The 'subscribe' method includes a consumer that simulates work by sleeping for 100 milliseconds. Due to RxJava's back-pressure support, the 'Flowable' will not overwhelm the consumer; instead, it will adjust the flow of data emitted to match the consumer's capacity.

Back-pressure in RxJava is not automatically applied to all 'Flowable' instances. It requires the developers to strategically apply it based on the specific scenario. One such strategy involves specifying a back-pressure strategy when creating 'Flowable' instances.

```
1   Flowable<Integer> flowable = Flowable.create(emitter -> {
2       for (int i = 0; i < 1000; i++) {
3           if (emitter.isCancelled()) {
4               return;
5           }
6           emitter.onNext(i);
7       }
8       emitter.onComplete();
9   }, BackpressureStrategy.BUFFER);
```

In the code snippet above, a 'Flowable' is created with a custom source that emits integers. The 'BackpressureStrategy.BUFFER' strategy is specified, which tells RxJava to buffer all emitted items until the downstream can consume them. Other strategies include 'DROP', which drops the most recent item if the downstream can't keep up, and 'LATEST', which only retains the latest value.

Understanding and applying back-pressure correctly is crucial for preventing common pitfalls in reactive programming, such as 'MissingBackpressureException'. This exception indicates that a situation has occurred where the data producer is emitting items at a rate faster than the consumer can handle, and no back-pressure strategy has been applied to mitigate the issue.

```
io.reactivex.exceptions.MissingBackpressureException
```

Back-pressure is an essential concept in RxJava for developing responsive and resilient reactive applications. By leveraging the 'Flowable' class and thoughtful application of back-pressure strategies, developers can ensure that their applications remain stable and efficient under varying conditions of data flow. Additionally, understanding the nuances of back-pressure in RxJava empowers developers to prevent common issues associated with unmanaged data streams, enhancing the overall robustness of reactive systems.

5.7   Dealing with Back-Pressure in Project Reactor

Project Reactor is a fully non-blocking foundation with efficient demand management, or back-pressure, built into the library. It operates on the principle that data streams, or Flux and Mono in Reactor terms, should be manageable and responsive under a variety of system loads. This necessity arises from the reality of modern applications where the rate of data production can significantly outpace consumption. In this framework, back-pressure is an inherent characteristic allowing downstream consumers to signal upstream producers about how much data they are ready to process, reducing the risk of overwhelming consumer capacity and potentially leading to system failures.

A fundamental understanding of Flux and Mono is imperative. Mono represents a single or empty asynchronous value, while Flux is used for an asynchronous sequence of 0 to N values. Both support back-pressure inherently and offer various methods to control the flow of data.

The Project Reactor provides several strategies to manage back-pressure effectively:

- onBackpressureDrop(): This approach simply drops the values that exceed the downstream's demand. While it prevents system overload, it risks losing data.

- onBackpressureBuffer(): Buffers all the surplus values until the downstream can process them. This method can potentially lead to OutOfMemoryError if the producer continuously outpaces consumption and the buffer size grows unbounded.

- onBackpressureLatest(): Caches only the latest value, discarding any previously buffered values when a new item is emitted. This method balances between buffering and dropping strategies, ensuring at least the latest data is processed.

- onBackpressureError(): Throws an error if the downstream can't keep up, providing a clear signal that the flow control needs reevaluation.

To manage the complexity around back-pressure and ensure that data flows smoothly between producers and consumers, Reactor also offers the flatMap method, which is essential for maintaining a high level of performance and responsiveness. It does so by concurrently subscribing to multiple Mono or Flux, effectively managing downstream requests across these streams with back-pressure in mind.

Consider the following example that demonstrates the use of flatMap in combination with back-pressure control methods:

```
Flux.range(1, 100)
    .flatMap(value ->
        Mono.just(value)
            .delayElement(Duration.ofMillis(100))
            .onBackpressureDrop())
    .subscribe(System.out::println);
```

In this scenario, values exceeding the downstream capability are dropped, ensuring that the application remains responsive under heavy loads by not allowing the queue to build up indefinitely. Such a mechanism is critical in scenarios where timely response to new data is more valuable than complete data integrity.

Testing and debugging play crucial roles in understanding how back-pressure manifests under real-world conditions. Project Reactor provides tools and hooks to diagnose and visualize back-pressure behavior. For instance, reactor-tools library offers a graphical representation of your reactive pipelines, including how back-pressure is being applied at each stage, unveiling the dynamics of your data flow management.

Another critical aspect of dealing with back-pressure in Project Reactor is understanding the signals between producers and consumers. These signals manage the demand and supply of data, ensuring a responsive and resilient system. Leveraging Reactor's built-in mechanisms for dealing with back-pressure allows developers to create non-blocking, highly responsive applications capable of handling surges in data without degrading performance.

In summary, effectively dealing with back-pressure in Project Reactor requires a sound understanding of its foundational principles, a thoughtful application of strategies to balance data flow, and a commitment to testing and fine-tuning. Reactor's comprehensive suite of tools and methods for managing back-pressure ensures that developers can build resilient, scalable, and responsive applications, testament to the strength of reactive programming paradigms.

5.8 Strategies for Handling Overflow in Reactive Systems

Handling overflow in reactive systems is paramount to ensure stability and responsiveness. Reactive systems are designed to process streams of data asynchronously and non-blocking, promoting better resource utilization and performance. However, this design introduces the challenge of managing data overflow—a situation where the data producer generates data at a faster rate than the consumer can process. This section will discuss strategies to manage overflow effectively, ensuring that reactive systems can maintain their resilience and responsiveness under varying load conditions.

Buffering is one of the primary strategies to handle overflow in reactive systems. It involves temporarily storing data in memory until the consumer is ready to process it. Buffering can be implemented in various ways, each with its trade-offs regarding memory usage and latency. A fixed-size buffer can prevent out-of-memory errors by limiting the amount of data stored. However, when the buffer is full, new data must be dropped, or back-pressure must be applied to slow down the producer. The code example below demonstrates how to implement a fixed-size buffer:

```
1  Flowable<Integer> flowable = Flowable.range(1, 1000)
2     .onBackpressureBuffer(100); //Buffer size of 100
```

This code snippet creates a data stream that can buffer up to 100 items. If the buffer is exceeded, the excess data will be dropped, or back-pressure is applied.

Dropping data is another strategy to manage overflow, sacrificing data fidelity for system stability. Dropping strategies can range from dropping the oldest or newest data in the buffer to more sophisticated algorithms that only drop data deemed less important or redundant.

This approach is useful in scenarios where real-time data processing is more critical than processing every piece of data. Below is an example of implementing a dropping strategy:

```
Flowable<Integer> droppingFlowable = Flowable.range(1, 1000)
    .onBackpressureDrop();
```

The above code will drop incoming data items if the downstream cannot keep up, ensuring that the system does not crash due to memory overload.

Alternatively, back-pressure strategies can be more adaptive, dynamically adjusting the rate of data processing based on current system load and consumer capacity. Reactive Streams specification provides a mechanism called 'request(n)' for consumers to signal demand to producers, indicating how many more data items they can handle at that moment. This allows for a more sophisticated and adaptive approach to data flow control. See the following code snippet for an adaptive back-pressure usage:

```
Flowable<Integer> adaptiveFlowable = Flowable.range(1, 1000)
    .onBackpressureLatest();
```

The 'onBackpressureLatest()' operator makes the Flowable emit only the latest item to the downstream if it cannot keep up, combining both buffering and dropping strategies dynamically based on the situation.

Furthermore, implementing custom back-pressure mechanisms can offer tailored solutions for specific use cases. This can involve creating a custom operator that leverages existing reactive library features or directly implementing the Reactive Streams interfaces to gain fine-grained control over data flow. Such custom implementations require a deep understanding of reactive principles and the specific requirements of the application.

Finally, reactive systems should be designed with overflow strategies in mind from the outset. This means considering the strategies for handling overflow during architecture design, selecting the appropriate techniques based on system requirements, and continuously monitoring and adjusting these strategies as the system evolves.

In summary, managing overflow in reactive systems is a crucial aspect of maintaining their performance, stability, and responsiveness. By effectively employing strategies such as buffering, dropping, adaptive back-pressure, and custom mechanisms, developers can ensure that their reactive systems are resilient under high load conditions. Each strategy has its trade-offs and must be selected based on the specific requirements of the system being developed.

5.9 Implementing Custom Back-Pressure Mechanisms

Implementing custom back-pressure mechanisms in reactive systems requires a nuanced understanding of the existing flow control strategies and the peculiarities of the system's data streams. This section will discuss the process of developing bespoke back-pressure strategies, tailored to specific reactive applications. The goal is to ensure that these strategies enhance the system's responsiveness, resilience, and stability by effectively managing the data flow rate.

To begin with, it is essential to grasp the nature of the data streams in the application. Data streams can vary widely in terms of volume, velocity, and volatility. Understanding these characteristics will enable the identification of potential bottlenecks and points at which back-pressure may be required. This analysis is vital for determining the appropriate back-pressure strategy to implement.

Once the need for custom back-pressure has been identified, the next step involves the explicit signaling between the producer and the consumer components. In reactive systems, this signaling is crucial for indicating when the consumer is ready to process more data or when it needs the producer to slow down. The implementation of signaling mechanisms can be achieved through several approaches, including leveraging existing reactive libraries' facilities or developing a custom signaling protocol.

```
1   // Example of a custom signaling mechanism
2   public interface BackpressureSignal {
3       void request(long n);
4       void cancel();
5   }
6
7   public class CustomBackpressureMechanism implements BackpressureSignal {
8       private final AtomicLong requested = new AtomicLong(0);
9
10      @Override
11      public void request(long n) {
12          requested.addAndGet(n);
13      }
14
15      @Override
16      public void cancel() {
17          requested.set(0);
```

```
18      }
19    }
```

This example outlines a simple signaling mechanism where the consumer can request a specific number of data items or cancel the request. The use of `AtomicLong` ensures thread safety, which is crucial in concurrent environments common in reactive systems.

In addition to signaling, implementing custom back-pressure mechanisms often involves managing queues or buffers to hold data items temporarily when the downstream cannot keep up. The management strategy for these buffers is critical, as improper handling can lead to memory issues or data loss.

- Employing fixed-size buffers to limit memory usage but potentially dropping data when the buffer is full.

- Using dynamic buffers that grow as needed, which avoids data loss but increases the risk of memory leaks.

- Implementing strategies such as buffering with dropping, buffering with back-off, or sample-and-hold to manage overflow in a controlled manner.

Following the integration of signaling and buffering mechanisms, it is imperative to incorporate mechanisms to monitor and adjust the flow dynamically. This could involve analyzing the rate of data production and consumption, monitoring the system's health, and adjusting the rate of data flow accordingly.

In practice, implementing custom back-pressure mechanisms is a process of continuous refinement. It requires monitoring the system's performance, identifying issues related to back-pressure, and adjusting the strategy as necessary. Testing and debugging play a crucial role in this process, allowing for the identification and remediation of potential issues.

```
Output example:
Consumer capacity exceeded. Dropping incoming data.
Adjusting data flow rate to match consumer capability.
```

The implementation of custom back-pressure mechanisms enhances the resilience and responsiveness of reactive systems. By carefully designing these mechanisms, developers can ensure that their applications are capable of handling varying loads efficiently, maintaining stability even under challenging conditions.

5.10 Testing and Debugging Back-Pressure Issues

Testing and debugging back-pressure issues in reactive programming require a nuanced understanding of both the conceptual and practical aspects of reactive systems. These tasks are critical for maintaining the stability and performance of applications that employ reactive programming models, such as RxJava or Project Reactor. This section will discuss methods and practices for identifying, diagnosing, and resolving back-pressure problems in reactive streams.

Back-pressure issues often manifest as errors or degraded performance in reactive systems. Symptoms can include unbounded memory usage, slow consumer performance, or even system crashes. Identifying these symptoms early is key to maintaining system health.

To effectively test for back-pressure issues, developers must first understand the normal behavior and performance metrics of their application under various load conditions. Performance testing, using tools such as JMeter or Gatling, can simulate varying levels of traffic and help identify thresholds at which the system begins to exhibit back-pressure related symptoms.

```
1   // Example of a simple load test in Gatling
2   class BasicSimulation extends Simulation {
3     val scn = scenario("Basic Test")
4       .exec(http("Request")
5       .get("/"))
6
7     setUp(
8       scn.inject(atOnceUsers(1000))
9     ).protocols(http.baseUrl("http://yourapplication.com"))
10  }
```

Upon identifying that the system is experiencing back-pressure issues, the next step is to isolate the component or operation within the data stream causing these issues. This involves detailed logging and monitoring of the reactive pipeline. Tools such as Micrometer or Prometheus can be instrumental in providing insights into system behavior by tracking metrics like subscriber demand, processing time, and queue sizes.

```
Example log: Subscriber demand exceeds production rate, causing buffer overflow.
```

Debugging back-pressure issues effectively often requires examining the flow of data through the reactive streams in real-time. Utilizing debuggers that are aware of reactive constructs is crucial. IDEs like IntelliJ IDEA provide advanced debugging tools that allow developers to set breakpoints and inspect reactive streams during execution.

Once the problematic components or operations have been identified, developers can employ various strategies to resolve back-pressure issues. These may include:

- Adjusting the size of the buffer or windowing operations to better match the producer and consumer rates.

- Implementing or modifying back-pressure strategies such as onBackpressureDrop(), onBackpressureBuffer(), or onBackpressureLatest() in RxJava, which determine how excess items in the stream are handled.

- Redesigning parts of the reactive pipeline to introduce more efficient processing or parallelism, thereby reducing bottlenecks.

In cases where standard back-pressure strategies do not suffice, developers might need to implement custom mechanisms. This could involve creating bespoke operators that more closely match the application's unique requirements.

```
1   // Example of implementing a custom back-pressure strategy in RxJava
2   Flowable<Integer> source = Flowable.range(1, 1000);
3
4   source
5       .observeOn(Schedulers.computation(), false, 100) // Custom buffer size
6       .subscribe(number -> {
7           // Simulate heavy computation
8           Thread.sleep(100);
9           System.out.println("Processed " + number);
10      });
```

To ensure the longevity and reliability of back-pressure solutions, thorough testing is paramount. This includes unit testing of individual components and integration testing of the entire reactive stream. Reactive testing libraries such as StepVerifier in Project Reactor can aid in this process by allowing developers to assert specific expectations about the behavior of a reactive stream.

Finally, documenting the behavior and limitations of the system under different load conditions is crucial for future maintenance and scalability planning. This documentation should detail the testing methodologies used, the results obtained, and the rationale behind the chosen solutions to back-pressure issues.

134

In summary, testing and debugging back-pressure issues in reactive systems is a multifaceted process that involves understanding normal system behavior, identifying and isolating problems, and implementing effective solutions. Through diligent testing, monitoring, and debugging, developers can ensure their reactive applications remain robust and performant under a wide range of conditions.

5.11 Back-Pressure and Resilience Patterns

Back-pressure and resilience patterns are fundamental in designing reactive systems that are both robust and reliable. This section will discuss the conceptual design and practical implementation of these patterns in the context of reactive programming, particularly focusing on RxJava and Spring Boot.

Back-pressure, as previously elaborated, is a system's ability to control the pace of data flow to prevent overwhelming the consumer or processing service. In a reactive system, where data streams can potentially emit items at a rate higher than the consumer can process, back-pressure mechanisms are crucial. Without back-pressure, systems are prone to crashing or losing data, undermining the system's reliability and performance.

Resilience patterns, on the other hand, are strategies employed to ensure that the system can gracefully handle and recover from failures. These patterns are essential in maintaining system stability under adverse conditions, enhancing the overall fault tolerance of the system. When combined with back-pressure, resilience patterns ensure that reactive systems can manage data efficiently and reliably, even under high load or in the case of component failures.

In reactive programming with RxJava and Spring Boot, several back-pressure and resilience patterns stand out:

- **Bounded Queue**: This pattern involves limiting the memory footprint of the system by using queues of a fixed size for buffering data streams. When the queue is full, the system can adopt a strategy such as dropping data, blocking further emissions until there's more room, or signaling back-pressure upstream.

- **Rate Limiting**: This involves dynamically adjusting the rate of data flow based on the current system load or preset thresholds.

Rate limiting can be implemented using various algorithms, including leaky bucket and token bucket, to smooth out bursts in the data stream.

- **Bulkheads**: Inspired by the compartments in a ship, this pattern isolates elements of the system into separate pools. If one component fails or is overwhelmed, it does not affect the entire system, enhancing resilience.

- **Circuit Breaker**: This pattern prevents a failure in one part of the system from cascading through to other parts. By monitoring for failures and temporarily disabling functionality, the system can avoid operations that are likely to fail, providing time for recovery and reducing the strain on resources.

- **Retry Patterns**: In scenarios where operations may intermittently fail due to temporary issues, applying retry patterns with exponential backoff can enhance resilience by giving the system multiple opportunities to succeed without immediately escalating failures.

- **Timeouts**: Implementing timeouts for operations ensures that the system can recover from stalls or long-running processes that may hold up resources, allowing the system to maintain responsiveness even in adverse conditions.

Implementing back-pressure and resilience patterns requires careful consideration of the system's characteristics, including the nature of the data streams, the processing capabilities of the consumer, and the requirements for data integrity and availability.

For instance, when applying the bounded queue pattern in RxJava, one can use the `onBackpressureBuffer` operator, which buffers emitted items into a queue of a specified size. Here's a simple example:

```
Flowable<Integer> flowable = Flowable.range(1, 1000)
    .onBackpressureBuffer(100); // Buffer size of 100

flowable.subscribe(new Subscriber<Integer>() {
    @Override
    public void onSubscribe(Subscription s) {
        s.request(Long.MAX_VALUE); // Requests essentially unbounded
    }

    @Override
    public void onNext(Integer t) {
        // Process the item
    }

```

```
15    @Override
16    public void onError(Throwable t) {
17        // Handle any errors
18    }
19
20    @Override
21    public void onComplete() {
22        // Completion logic
23    }
24 });
```

In Spring Boot, employing a resilience pattern like the circuit breaker can be facilitated by the use of libraries such as Resilience4j. Annotating a service method with @CircuitBreaker ensures that, in the face of failures, the system can trip the circuit breaker and redirect or temporarily halt operations, thus preventing cascading failures:

```
1  @CircuitBreaker(name = "exampleService", fallbackMethod = "fallback")
2  public String exampleServiceMethod() {
3      // Implementation that might fail
4  }
5
6  public String fallback(Throwable t) {
7      // Fallback method to execute when the primary method fails
8      return "Fallback response";
9  }
```

Back-pressure and resilience patterns are essential components of modern reactive systems, ensuring that applications remain responsive and reliable under a wide range of conditions. By understanding and implementing these patterns, developers can build reactive applications that are both robust and scalable, leveraging the full power of RxJava and Spring Boot in creating high-performance, resilient systems.

5.12 Real-World Examples of Back-Pressure Management

Back-pressure management plays a crucial role in the design and operation of highly responsive and resilient systems in real-world scenarios. This section discusses several practical examples where back-pressure mechanisms are effectively applied to ensure system stability and performance in the face of varying data loads.

In the context of financial trading platforms, data streams consist of price updates, trade executions, and order book changes that occur at an extremely high frequency. These platforms utilize back-pressure to dynamically adjust the flow of data. This ensures that downstream systems, such as trading algorithms and risk management systems, can process incoming data without the risk of overload and potential failure. Implementing back-pressure in this scenario often involves using reactive streams that can signal upstream producers to throttle data emission rates based on the current processing capacity of consumer services.

Another compelling case is found within telecommunications infrastructure. Telecom services deal with vast amounts of data in the form of voice calls, text messages, and internet data packets. To manage these data flows efficiently, especially during peak traffic periods, back-pressure mechanisms are employed. These mechanisms balance the load on network nodes and prevent service degradation by regulating the data flow based on the processing capabilities of each node. The application of back-pressure in this context ensures high availability and quality of service for end-users, preventing potential system failures from overwhelming data influx.

In IoT (Internet of Things), devices generate large volumes of data, including sensor readings, state changes, and control messages. The challenge lies in processing and analyzing this data in real-time, often necessitating the use of back-pressure. For instance, a centralized data processing hub may apply back-pressure by informing IoT devices to reduce data transmission rates during high load conditions. This mechanism enables the system to maintain data integrity and prevents loss of critical information, thus ensuring efficient processing and timely response to significant events.

Social media platforms offer yet another example. These platforms experience enormous and highly variable data volumes, driven by user interactions such as posts, likes, and comments. To manage this, back-pressure techniques dynamically adjust the processing of user-generated content based on current system load, maintaining system responsiveness and preventing overload. This might involve prioritizing content processing or temporarily reducing the feed update frequency under heavy load conditions, thereby ensuring a continuous and smooth user experience.

The implementation of back-pressure across these examples leverages a variety of techniques and technologies, including reactive streams and custom back-pressure mechanisms. This underscores the flexibility and importance of back-pressure in designing systems that are both highly responsive and resilient in the face of dynamic and unpredictable data flows. Understanding these real-world applications highlights the practical significance of back-pressure management in contemporary software engineering and system design practices.

Chapter 6

Reacting to Data with RxJava Operators

RxJava operators play a crucial role in reacting to data, allowing for the transformation, filtering, combination, and handling of observable data streams. These operators provide the building blocks for composing asynchronous and event-driven programs that can efficiently manage complex data transformations and flow control. This chapter focuses on introducing and demonstrating the use of RxJava operators, offering insights into their practical applications for manipulating data streams, error handling, and implementing concurrency within RxJava applications. Through these operators, developers can craft more readable, robust, and reactive code.

6.1 Operators Overview: The Building Blocks of RxJava

Operators in RxJava are fundamental entities that serve as the building blocks for composing and manipulating data streams in reactive programming. They provide a comprehensive toolkit for transforming, filtering, combining, and otherwise manipulating observable sequences. This section will discuss the pivotal role these operators play in crafting reactive applications, elaborating on their categorization, utility, and how they facilitate the creation of complex, asynchronous, and event-driven programs.

Operators are essentially functions that enable the modification of data emitted by Observables. They can modify the data, change the structure of Observables, filter or combine multiple Observables, and much more. The power of RxJava lies in its operators, which allow developers to solve complex asynchronous tasks with simple and readable code.

To understand the role of operators, consider an example where data from a network request is observed. The data might need to be transformed or filtered before being displayed to the user. RxJava operators enable these operations to be performed in a declarative manner, where the focus is on the what and not the how.

```
1  Observable<String> dataObservable = getDataFromNetwork();
2  dataObservable
3      .map(data -> transformData(data))
4      .filter(transformedData -> transformedData.isNotEmpty())
5      .subscribe(transformedData -> displayData(transformedData));
```

In the code above, the `map` and `filter` operators are used to transform and filter the data emitted by the observable `dataObservable`. The transformed and filtered data is then consumed by the `subscribe` method, which displays it to the user. This exemplifies the declarative nature of RxJava, where the data flow and transformations are defined upfront, and the library takes care of executing them in the correct order and manner.

Operators in RxJava can be broadly categorized into a few types based on their purpose and functionality:

- **Creation Operators:** These operators are used to create Observables from scratch or from existing data structures like arrays or collections. Examples include `just`, `fromArray`, and `create`.

- **Transformation Operators:** Operators that transform items emitted by an Observable into other forms or shapes. This includes operators like `map`, `flatMap`, and `buffer`.

- **Filtering Operators:** These operators are utilized to filter the data stream, allowing only the items that satisfy a certain condition to pass through. Examples are `filter`, `distinct`, and `take`.

142

- **Combination Operators:** They are used to combine multiple Observables into a single Observable. Operators like `merge`, `concat`, and `zip` fall into this category.

- **Error Handling Operators:** Essential for handling errors in RxJava, these operators allow for the graceful handling and recovery from errors that occur during the data stream processing. `onErrorReturn`, `retry`, and `catch` are examples.

- **Utility Operators:** These operators serve various auxiliary purposes, such as subscribing to Observables or logging debug information. `subscribe`, `observeOn`, and `doOnNext` are examples of utility operators.

- **Conditional and Boolean Operators:** Operators that evaluate the emitted items and terminate or alter the Observable sequence based on certain conditions. `all`, `contains`, and `isEmpty` are examples of such operators.

- **Mathematical and Aggregate Operators:** These operators perform mathematical or aggregating operations on the items of an Observable. `reduce` and `scan` are examples that fall into this category.

The composition of these operators allows for highly expressive and concise programming. By chaining together multiple operators, developers can define complex data transformations and control flows succinctly and elegantly. Moreover, since RxJava is designed with concurrency in mind, these operators inherently manage threading and synchronization, liberating developers from the intricacies of manual thread management and synchronization primitives.

Operators are the quintessence of RxJava, providing an extensive and versatile toolkit for processing asynchronous data streams. Their ability to compose, transform, and control asynchronous computations offers an unparalleled advantage in developing responsive, resilient, and efficient applications. Understanding and leveraging the full potential of RxJava operators is pivotal for mastering reactive programming in the Java ecosystem.

6.2 Creating Observables with Creation Operators

Creating Observables in RxJava is foundational for working with any reactive programming model. Observables represent data sources that emit items, which observers then consume. The creation operators in RxJava simplify the process of creating these observables from various data sources, including individual items, collections, and even non-reactive data structures. This part will delve into the prominent creation operators provided by RxJava, such as just, fromIterable, create, and range, to illustrate their usage and applicability in building reactive applications.

just is one of the most straightforward operators for creating observables. It is capable of taking up to ten arguments, which can be of any type, and emits them sequentially. This operator is particularly useful when you have a fixed set of known items that you wish to emit.

```
1  Observable<String> observable = Observable.just("Item1", "Item2", "Item3");
```

The fromIterable operator allows creating an Observable from any iterable object (e.g., a list or a set). This operator iterates over the iterable and emits each item individually. It is useful for integrating existing collections into your reactive flow.

```
1  List<String> list = Arrays.asList("Item1", "Item2", "Item3");
2  Observable<String> observable = Observable.fromIterable(list);
```

The create operator provides a powerful but more complex way to generate observables. It offers total control over the emission of items, including the ability to emit an arbitrary number of items, handle backpressure, and manage resources. The create operator requires a ObservableOnSubscribe action, where you call the appropriate methods on the ObservableEmitter to emit items or signals.

```
1  Observable<Integer> observable = Observable.create(emitter -> {
2      try {
3          for (int i = 0; i < 5; i++) {
4              emitter.onNext(i);
5          }
6          emitter.onComplete();
7      } catch (Throwable e) {
8          emitter.onError(e);
9      }
10 });
```

The range operator generates an Observable that emits a sequence of integers within a specified range. The first parameter is the start value, and the second is the count of sequential numbers to generate. This operator is invaluable when you need a simple way to produce a series of numbers without manually iterating.

```
Observable<Integer> observable = Observable.range(1, 5);
```

To demonstrate the practical application of these operators in a real-world scenario, consider an application that requires asynchronous data retrieval from a database and then processes the data reactively. You could use fromIterable to create an Observable from the list of data retrieved from the database. For operations that require generating a series for pagination purposes, range could be highly useful.

One of the key advantages of using creation operators in RxJava is their expressive power combined with simplicity. They abstract away the complexities involved in manual Observable creation and handling, allowing developers to focus on the reactive logic of their applications.

- just - Best for emitting a fixed number of elements.

- fromIterable - Ideal for integrating with collections.

- create - Offers complete control for complex scenarios.

- range - Simplifies generating a sequence of numbers.

In summary, creation operators in RxJava offer a versatile set of tools for creating observables. By selecting the appropriate operator for the task at hand, developers can efficiently create data streams that are the foundation of any RxJava-based reactive application. As you progress through the subsequent sections, the importance of understanding these operators and their correct application will become increasingly apparent, underscoring their role in facilitating effective reactive programming.

6.3 Transforming Data with Transformation Operators

Transforming data streams is an essential capability in reactive programming, particularly when dealing with RxJava. Transformation operators allow developers to modify, reshape, and manipulate the emitted items from Observables into a form more suitable for the given requirements. This section will discuss the key transformation operators available in RxJava, how they operate, and provide examples to demonstrate their application in real-world scenarios.

The map operator is fundamental in data transformation. It applies a function to each item emitted by an Observable and emits the transformed items. The function provided to the map operator can perform a variety of operations, such as converting values, extracting information, or applying calculations.

```
Observable.just("1", "2", "3")
    .map(item -> Integer.parseInt(item))
    .subscribe(item -> System.out.println(item));
```

```
1
2
3
```

This example demonstrates converting String items to Integer items. The map operator processes each emitted item, applying the parsing function, and the resultant integers are emitted onwards.

Next is the flatMap operator, which is used for handling nested Observables, effectively flattening them into a single Observable. This operator is helpful in scenarios where each item in an Observable is itself capable of generating multiple items, possibly asynchronously.

```
Observable.just("reactive", "programming")
    .flatMap(s -> Observable.fromArray(s.split("")))
    .subscribe(letter -> System.out.println(letter));
```

```
r
e
a
c
t
i
v
e
p
r
o
g
r
a
m
m
i
n
g
```

In the above code, each string emitted by the Observable is split into an array of its letters, and flatMap seamlessly merges these arrays into a single stream of letters.

The buffer operator collects items from an Observable and bundles them into lists of a specified size. This operator is particularly useful for handling large streams of data in batches rather than one item at a time.

```
1  Observable.range(1, 10)
2      .buffer(3)
3      .subscribe(System.out::println);
```

```
[1, 2, 3]
[4, 5, 6]
[7, 8, 9]
[10]
```

This example demonstrates the buffer operator collecting items emitted by an Observable into lists of three items. The final list might be smaller if the total number of items does not divide evenly by the buffer size.

The scan operator is similar to reduce found in many programming languages but instead of emitting only the final aggregated result, it emits the intermediate results as well. This feature makes scan especially useful for real-time data aggregation and analysis.

```
1  Observable.range(1, 5)
2      .scan((accumulator, currentItem) -> accumulator + currentItem)
3      .subscribe(System.out::println);
```

```
1
3
6
10
15
```

In this code snippet, the scan operator emits the sum of the current item and the accumulator, effectively outputting the running total of the numbers emitted by the source Observable.

Lastly, the groupBy operator categorizes items emitted by an Observable into separate Observables based on a specified criterion. This operator is instrumental in organizing and segregating data streams dynamically.

```
1  Observable.fromArray(1, 2, 3, 4, 5, 6)
2      .groupBy(item -> item % 2 == 0 ? "Even" : "Odd")
```

```
3        .subscribe(groupedObservable ->
4            groupedObservable.subscribe(item ->
5                System.out.println(groupedObservable.getKey() + ": " + item)));
```

```
Odd: 1
Even: 2
Odd: 3
Even: 4
Odd: 5
Even: 6
```

This example demonstrates using groupBy to divide numbers into "Odd" and "Even" categories, where each category is represented as an Observable. By subscribing to these grouped Observables, we can handle each category separately.

In summary, RxJava provides an extensive set of transformation operators which are pivotal in processing and manipulating data streams. Understanding and applying these operators enable developers to easily perform complex data transformations, ultimately leading to more efficient and concise code. Exceptions and edge cases need to be considered while applying these operators to ensure robust and error-free applications.

6.4 Filtering Data Stream with Filtering Operators

Filtering operators in RxJava are specialized tools designed to process an Observable stream by allowing only certain elements to pass through based on specific criteria. These operators provide a way to selectively listen to items that are of interest while ignoring others, making them particularly useful for managing large or complex data streams where not all data points are relevant to the current operation or requirement.

filter() is among the most straightforward and commonly used filtering operators. It applies a predicate to each item emitted by an Observable and emits only those items for which the predicate evaluates to true. The syntax and usage of *filter()* can be demonstrated as follows:

```
1  Observable<Integer> observable = Observable.fromIterable(Arrays.asList(1, 2, 3, 4,
       5));
2  observable.filter(item -> item % 2 == 0)
3      .subscribe(System.out::println);
```

148

In this example, the `filter()` operator is used to select only even numbers from the list. The output of this code would be:

```
2
4
```

Another important operator is *distinct()*, which ensures that only unique items are emitted by an Observable sequence, effectively removing any duplicates. This operator is especially useful when dealing with data streams that may contain repeated elements and where the uniqueness of each item is required.

```
1  Observable<Integer> observable = Observable.just(1, 2, 2, 3, 4, 4, 5);
2  observable.distinct()
3     .subscribe(System.out::println);
```

The code above would produce an output where each number appears only once:

```
1
2
3
4
5
```

The *take()* operator is another filtering operator, which allows a specified number of the first items from an Observable sequence to be emitted and then completes the sequence. For example:

```
1  Observable<Integer> observable = Observable.range(1, 10);
2  observable.take(5)
3     .subscribe(System.out::println);
```

This will limit the output to the first five items:

```
1
2
3
4
5
```

Conversely, *skip()* is used to ignore the first N items in an Observable sequence, emitting the rest. This is particularly useful when the initial items are not needed or are to be discarded.

```
1  Observable<Integer> observable = Observable.range(1, 5);
2  observable.skip(2)
3     .subscribe(System.out::println);
```

Here, the first two items are skipped, and the output is:

```
3
4
5
```

For scenarios where the data stream may be large or infinite, operators like *takeWhile()* and *skipWhile()* provide more dynamic filtering capabilities. *takeWhile()* will emit items until a specified condition becomes false. Meanwhile, *skipWhile()* will skip items until a condition becomes true, at which point it will start emitting items.

These filtering operators in RxJava are powerful tools that enhance the handling of Observable streams. By selectively allowing data through, they enable developers to focus on the relevant data, reduce noise, and potentially improve the efficiency and performance of applications. Understanding and effectively applying these operators is fundamental for developers aiming to implement responsive, data-driven applications using RxJava.

6.5 Combining Observables with Combination Operators

Combination operators in RxJava play a pivotal role in developing complex and responsive applications by allowing multiple data streams to be merged, concatenated, or combined in various meaningful ways. These operators are essential for scenarios where data from different sources or observables need to be operated upon as a single stream. The ability to combine observables adds a layer of flexibility and power to the application design, enabling developers to implement intricate reactive systems efficiently. In this section, we will discuss the various combination operators provided by RxJava, such as merge, concat, zip, and combineLatest, showcasing their unique characteristics and practical applications through code examples.

The merge operator is used to merge multiple Observables into one by interleaving their emissions. When dealing with data streams that are independent of each other but need to be handled in a unified manner, merge is an ideal choice. However, it's important to note that the merged stream does not guarantee the sequential order of items from the source observables.

```
1  Observable<String> observable1 = Observable.just("A", "B", "C");
2  Observable<String> observable2 = Observable.just("1", "2", "3");
3  Observable.merge(observable1, observable2)
```

```
4        .subscribe(System.out::println);
```

```
A
B
C
1
2
3
```

Contrastingly, the concat operator combines multiple Observables by emitting all items from the first observable followed by all items from the subsequent observables, preserving the order. This operator is particularly useful when the order of emissions must be maintained across the combined streams.

```
1   Observable<String> observable1 = Observable.just("A", "B", "C");
2   Observable<String> observable2 = Observable.just("1", "2", "3");
3   Observable.concat(observable1, observable2)
4       .subscribe(System.out::println);
```

```
A
B
C
1
2
3
```

The zip operator is a powerful tool for combining items from multiple observables together based on their order, emitting combined items only when each of the observables has emitted a new item. This is useful for cases where there is a clear one-to-one relationship between items across streams and combined data is required.

```
1   Observable<String> observable1 = Observable.just("A", "B");
2   Observable<Integer> observable2 = Observable.just(1, 2);
3   Observable.zip(observable1, observable2, (s, n) -> s + n)
4       .subscribe(System.out::println);
```

```
A1
B2
```

Lastly, combineLatest combines the latest item emitted by each observable via a specified function at the time of each emission, producing a new value. This is ideal for scenarios where the latest state from multiple streams is required to evaluate or produce a new state.

```
1   Observable<Long> observable1 = Observable.interval(1, TimeUnit.SECONDS).take(2);
2   Observable<Long> observable2 = Observable.interval(500, TimeUnit.MILLISECONDS).take
        (4);
```

151

```
3  Observable.combineLatest(observable1, observable2, (o1, o2) -> "o1: " + o1 + " o2:
       " + o2)
4      .subscribe(System.out::println);
```

This code snippet illustrates `combineLatest` by combining items from two time-based observables. The output demonstrates how the operator reacts to each new emission by either observable, combining it with the latest emitted item from the other stream.

Combining observables using RxJava's combination operators offers a flexible approach to handling multiple data streams in a unified manner. Whether preserving the order of emissions, combining related data, or managing the latest states from various sources, these operators provide the necessary tools to implement complex data handling scenarios effectively. Understanding and applying these operators correctly is crucial for leveraging the full potential of reactive programming with RxJava.

6.6 Managing Time with Time-Based Operators

Time-based operators in RxJava are pivotal for manipulating observable sequences in relation to time. These operators allow for the performance of time-based operations on streams, including delaying emissions, sampling periodic data points, and timing out operations. Through these time-based mechanisms, developers can fine-tune the reactivity of applications, handling latency, debouncing user input, or creating windows of time for batch processing. This section will elucidate the use of key time-based operators, demonstrating their application with examples for enhancing the development of reactive applications.

`delay` is a fundamental time-based operator that postpones the emission of items from an Observable by a specified duration. This operator is instrumental when an operation needs to be delayed as part of the flow. For example, delaying user interactions or network requests. The utilization of `delay` can be demonstrated as follows:

```
1  Observable.just("RxJava")
2      .delay(1, TimeUnit.SECONDS)
3      .subscribe(System.out::println);
```

This code snippet will delay the emission of the string "RxJava" by one second. The output will be as shown:

```
RxJava
```

`throttleFirst` and `throttleLast` are operators designed to filter out items emitted by an Observable within a specified time frame. `throttleFirst` emits the first item in a window duration, discarding the rest, whereas `throttleLast` (also known as `sample`) emits the last item within the specified duration. These operators are particularly useful for handling rapid bursts of events or inputs, such as multiple button clicks or sensor data, where only the first or last event in a given time frame is relevant.

An example of using `throttleFirst` to ignore multiple clicks that occur within a 500-millisecond window would look like this:

```
1  Observable.just("click1", "click2", "click3")
2      .throttleFirst(500, TimeUnit.MILLISECONDS)
3      .subscribe(System.out::println);
```

If "click1", "click2", and "click3" happen within 500 milliseconds of each other, only "click1" will be emitted.

`window` operator groups items emitted by an Observable into Observable windows based on time criteria. This operator is adept at dividing an Observable stream into slices or windows of time and processing each window separately.

Here is an example of using `window`:

```
1  Observable.interval(1, TimeUnit.SECONDS)
2      .window(5, TimeUnit.SECONDS)
3      .flatMapSingle(obs -> obs.count())
4      .subscribe(System.out::println);
```

In this example, items emitted by an interval Observable are grouped into windows of 5 seconds. The `count` operation is then applied to each window, resulting in the count of emitted items in each 5-second window.

`timeout` operator is crucial for specifying a maximum duration for the completion of the Observable sequence. If the specified duration elapses without the Observable emitting any items, it will terminate with an error. This is particularly useful for preventing endless waiting periods for observables that fail to emit, effectively implementing a timeout policy.

For instance:

```
1  Observable.just("item1")
2     .delay(2, TimeUnit.SECONDS)
3     .timeout(1, TimeUnit.SECONDS)
4     .subscribe(System.out::println, Throwable::printStackTrace);
```

Here, timeout is set to 1 second, but the item is delayed for 2 seconds, resulting in a timeout error.

Utilizing these time-based operators effectively allows the construction of responsive, resilient, and user-friendly reactive applications. By manipulating observable sequences in relation to time, RxJava developers can implement complex temporal logic effortlessly, enhancing the functionality and reliability of applications.

6.7   Error Handling Operators

Error handling is a critical aspect of building resilient Reactive systems. RxJava provides a comprehensive suite of operators designed specifically for error handling in reactive streams. These operators allow developers to manage exceptions methodically, ensuring the application remains responsive even in the face of errors.

In the RxJava context, when an Observable encounters an error, it typically terminates the data stream and notifies its subscribers of the error. This behavior can be altered using error-handling operators to resume the data stream or perform specific actions when an error occurs.

The onErrorReturn operator allows an Observable to emit a predefined item when an error occurs, effectively preventing the error from terminating the data stream. It provides a straightforward mechanism for returning a fallback value.

```
1   Observable<Integer> source = Observable.create(emitter -> {
2       emitter.onNext(1);
3       emitter.onError(new RuntimeException("Unexpected error"));
4       emitter.onNext(2);
5       emitter.onComplete();
6   });
7
8   Observable<Integer> withFallback = source.onErrorReturn(error -> 0);
9
10  withFallback.subscribe(
11      item -> System.out.println(item),
12      Throwable::printStackTrace,
13      () -> System.out.println("Completed successfully")
14  );
```

154

This would result in the following output:

```
1
0
Completed successfully
```

The onErrorResumeNext operator provides more flexibility than onErrorReturn by allowing the substitution of another Observable when an error occurs. This can be useful for retrying operations or switching to a different data source in case of failure.

```
1   Observable<String> source = Observable.create(emitter -> {
2       emitter.onNext("Hello");
3       emitter.onError(new Exception("Failed!"));
4   });
5
6   Observable<String> fallback = Observable.just("World");
7
8   Observable<String> resilient = source.onErrorResumeNext(fallback);
9
10  resilient.subscribe(
11      item -> System.out.println(item),
12      Throwable::printStackTrace,
13      () -> System.out.println("Completed successfully")
14  );
```

The output is:

```
Hello
World
Completed successfully
```

The retry operator enables an Observable to resubscribe to the source after an error occurs, with an optional limit on the number of retries. This can be particularly useful for transient errors that might succeed upon retrying.

```
1   Observable<Integer> source = Observable.create(emitter -> {
2       emitter.onNext(1);
3       emitter.onNext(2);
4       emitter.onError(new IOException("Network error"));
5   }).retry(2);
6
7   source.subscribe(
8       item -> System.out.println(item),
9       Throwable::printStackTrace,
10      () -> System.out.println("Completed successfully")
11  );
```

Given the non-deterministic nature of errors in this example, the output will vary based on whether the error occurs again upon retrying.

Understanding and effectively leveraging these error handling operators is vital for developing robust RxJava applications. They empower

155

developers to gracefully handle errors, ensuring that reactive streams can continue operating or terminate in a controlled manner, thereby enhancing the overall resilience and user experience of applications.

6.8 Controlling Back-Pressure with Reactive Operators

Controlling back-pressure is a critical aspect of building scalable and responsive applications using RxJava. It entails managing the scenario where the data emit rate by an Observable is higher than the rate at which its Observers can consume the data. Without effective back-pressure strategies, such applications face the risk of running out of memory, which can lead to crashes or a degraded user experience. This section discusses reactive operators provided by RxJava that specifically address back-pressure, ensuring a smooth data flow between producers and consumers.

Back-pressure in RxJava can be managed using a specific type of observable: `Flowable`. Unlike `Observable`, `Flowable` supports back-pressure directly, allowing it to cope with scenarios where observables emit items more rapidly than subscribers can consume them.

The conversion from an `Observable` to a `Flowable` can be achieved with the `toFlowable` method. Similarly, `Flowable` can be converted back to an `Observable` using the `toObservable` method. These conversions facilitate the smooth integration of back-pressure support into the existing RxJava applications.

One of the foundational strategies for managing back-pressure is to control the volume of the data stream. This can be done using the `onBackpressureDrop` or `onBackpressureBuffer` operators. The `onBackpressureDrop` operator discards items that cannot be immediately processed by the subscriber, effectively reducing the pressure on the system's resources. On the other hand, the `onBackpressureBuffer` operator buffers these excessive emissions until the subscriber is ready to process them, ensuring that no data is lost.

Another vital operator in controlling back-pressure is `onBackpressureLatest`. This operator ensures that only the most recent item is retained and delivered to the subscriber once it's ready to process further emissions. This approach is particularly useful in scenarios where only the latest data point is relevant, making it unnecessary to process outdated items.

Below is a simple code example demonstrating the use of the onBackpressureDrop operator:

```
Flowable<Integer> source = Flowable.range(1, 1000);
source
    .onBackpressureDrop()
    .observeOn(Schedulers.io())
    .subscribe(System.out::println, Throwable::printStackTrace);
```

In this code, a `Flowable` emits a range of integers from 1 to 1000. The `onBackpressureDrop` operator is applied to drop emitted items that cannot be immediately consumed, preventing potential memory issues.

Back-pressure can also be managed by adjusting the subscriber's request rate. The `Flowable` class provides the `request` method, which allows subscribers to specify the number of items they are ready to receive. This manual control mechanism helps in fine-tuning the data flow according to the application's current capacity and prevents overwhelming the subscriber.

Implementing back-pressure effectively requires a deep understanding of the application's data flow and the potential bottlenecks. The reactive operators discussed in this section provide a robust toolkit for managing back-pressure, but they should be applied judiciously to avoid unintended consequences such as data loss or unnecessary resource utilization. Correctly employed, these operators empower developers to build resilient, responsive, and scalable applications using RxJava.

6.9 Conditional and Boolean Operators

Conditional and Boolean operators in RxJava serve a crucial purpose in controlling the flow of data based on specific conditions. These operators allow developers to perform logical operations on the data streams, enabling decision-making processes within the stream's flow. This section will discuss several significant operators in this category, including `all`, `contains`, `defaultIfEmpty`, `sequenceEqual`, and `takeUntil`. Through understanding and utilizing these operators, developers can add a layer of logic to their reactive programming paradigm, making their applications more dynamic and responsive to changing data conditions.

The all operator evaluates items emitted by an Observable against a specified predicate. This operator returns a Single that emits a single Boolean value, true, if all items meet the predicate condition; otherwise, it emits false. This can be particularly useful when a certain criterion must be met by every element in a data stream. For example, to check if all numbers emitted by an Observable are even, the following code snippet demonstrates the use of the all operator:

```
Observable.just(2, 4, 6)
    .all(num -> num % 2 == 0)
    .subscribe(System.out::println);
```

```
true
```

The contains operator checks whether the Observable emits a specific item. If the Observable emits the item, contains returns a Single that emits true; otherwise, it emits false. This operator enables efficient searches within a data stream. For instance, to determine if a data stream contains the number 5, the code below illustrates the contains operator:

```
Observable.just(1, 2, 3, 4, 5)
    .contains(5)
    .subscribe(System.out::println);
```

```
true
```

The defaultIfEmpty operator emits a default item if the source Observable is empty. This is useful for ensuring that subscribers always receive data, even if the original Observable does not emit any items. By providing a fallback value, applications can maintain continuity even when expected data is not available. Here is an example usage:

```
Observable.empty()
    .defaultIfEmpty("No data")
    .subscribe(System.out::println);
```

```
No data
```

The sequenceEqual operator compares two Observables to determine if they emit the same items in the same sequence. This operator is valuable for tasks that require validation or synchronization of sequences from different sources. The output is a Single that emits true if both sequences are identical. Consider the following example comparing two sequences:

```
1  Observable.sequenceEqual(Observable.just(1, 2, 3), Observable.just(1, 2, 3))
2    .subscribe(System.out::println);
```

```
true
```

Lastly, the `takeUntil` operator discards items emitted by an Observable after a second Observable emits an item or terminates. This allows developers to halt the data flow based on external triggers or conditions. For illustration, to take values from the source until a condition is met:

```
1  Observable<Long> source = Observable.interval(1, TimeUnit.SECONDS);
2  Observable<Long> stopper = Observable.timer(5, TimeUnit.SECONDS);
3  source.takeUntil(stopper)
4    .subscribe(System.out::println);
```

This code will emit the values from the source Observable every second until the stopper Observable emits an item after 5 seconds, effectively controlling the flow of data based on temporal conditions.

In summary, Conditional and Boolean operators provide essential tools for injecting logical control into reactive streams. By leveraging these operators, developers can build more sophisticated, context-aware data processing pipelines that respond dynamically to the conditions of the data they manipulate. Whether ensuring data meets certain criteria, providing default values, synchronizing data streams, or controlling the lifespan of subscriptions, these operators extend the power and flexibility of RxJava, enabling the creation of robust, reactive applications.

6.10   Mathematical and Aggregate Operators

In RxJava, mathematical and aggregate operators assume a pivotal role in synthesizing data points spread across an observable stream into succinct, comprehensible results. These operators facilitate the performance of arithmetic operations and the aggregation of data streams into a single outcome, making them indispensable for scenarios requiring summarization or statistical analysis of collected data points. This section will delve into the core mathematical and aggregate operators provided by RxJava, including their syntax, operational dynamics, and practical examples to elucidate their applications.

The count operator emits the total number of items emitted by the source Observable as a single item. This operator is instrumental when the total item count of an Observable is required for further processing or logging purposes.

```
1  Observable.just("Alpha", "Beta", "Gamma")
2      .count()
3      .subscribe(count -> System.out.println("Total items: " + count));
```

```
Total items: 3
```

The reduce operator applies a function to the first item emitted by the source Observable, then feeds the result of the function along with the second item into the same function, and continues this process until all items have been emitted by the source Observable. The final output is then emitted as a single item. This operator is particularly useful for accumulating a single result from a series of items, such as calculating sums or products.

```
1  Observable.just(1, 2, 3, 4)
2      .reduce((total, next) -> total + next)
3      .subscribe(sum -> System.out.println("Sum: " + sum));
```

```
Sum: 10
```

The sum, max, and min operators are commonly used aggregate functions in many programming paradigms, but RxJava does not provide these operators out of the box. However, their functionality can be easily replicated using the reduce operator for summation and comparison purposes.

For maximum and minimum operations, the reduce operator can be employed as follows:

```
1  Observable.just(5, 3, 10, 6)
2      .reduce((max, next) -> next > max ? next : max)
3      .subscribe(max -> System.out.println("Max: " + max));
4
5  Observable.just(5, 3, 10, 6)
6      .reduce((min, next) -> next < min ? next : min)
7      .subscribe(min -> System.out.println("Min: " + min));
```

```
Max: 10
Min: 3
```

The scan operator, akin to the reduce operator, applies a function to the first item emitted and emits the resulting value. Unlike reduce, scan

160

emits the accumulating value after each application of the function, providing a running total or accumulation of the values emitted thus far.

```
1  Observable.just(1, 2, 3, 4)
2      .scan((total, next) -> total + next)
3      .subscribe(partialSum -> System.out.println("Partial Sum: " + partialSum));
```

```
Partial Sum: 1
Partial Sum: 3
Partial Sum: 6
Partial Sum: 10
```

In summary, mathematical and aggregate operators in RxJava serve as powerful tools for data aggregation and summary statistic computation. By applying operations like count, reduce, and scan, developers can perform complex data analysis and transformation pipelines with succinct, expressive code. Through practical application and understanding of these operators' mechanics, RxJava users can leverage the library's full potential to efficiently process and manage data streams in reactive programming paradigms.

6.11 Converting Observables with Conversion Operators

Converting Observables with Conversion Operators involves changing the form of an Observable sequence to another type or data structure, making it compatible or more suitable for certain operations. This conversion is critical in scenarios where the downstream operators or subscribers expect a specific type or form of data. RxJava provides a set of operators designed specifically for this purpose.

The toList() and toSortedList() operators are perhaps the most frequently used conversion operators. They convert an Observable into a single emission of a list containing all the items emitted by the source Observable. The key difference between the two is that toSortedList() also sorts the items before emitting them. These operators are particularly useful when an operation requires knowledge of all items at once, such as aggregating values or batch processing.

```
1  Observable.just(3, 5, 1, 2, 6)
2      .toList()
3      .subscribe(System.out::println);
4
```

```
5  Observable.just(3, 5, 1, 2, 6)
6      .toSortedList()
7      .subscribe(System.out::println);
```

The above code snippets illustrate the use of toList() and toSortedList() operators. The output will be:

```
[3, 5, 1, 2, 6]
[1, 2, 3, 5, 6]
```

Another crucial operator for conversion is toMap(). This operator converts the emissions of an Observable into Map entries. Each emitted item is associated with a key generated by a specified key selector function. This is particularly useful for categorizing emitted items or when the application logic requires a dictionary-like structure for fast data lookup.

```
1  Observable.just("Alpha", "Beta", "Gamma")
2      .toMap(item -> item.length())
3      .subscribe(System.out::println);
```

In this example, strings are mapped to their length, producing output that resembles a map where lengths are keys and strings are values. The expected output might look like:

```
{5=Gamma, 4=Beta, 3=Alpha}
```

Furthermore, the toMultimap() operator allows for the collection of items emitted by the Observable into a map where each key may correspond to multiple values. This operator is effectively an extension of toMap() for cases where items can be categorized under multiple keys, providing a versatile tool for data organization.

```
1  Observable.just("Alpha", "Beta", "Gamma", "Delta")
2      .toMultimap(item -> item.length())
3      .subscribe(System.out::println);
```

This will collect the items into a map where the keys are the lengths of the strings, and the values are collections of strings with those lengths, resulting in:

```
{5=[Gamma, Delta], 4=[Beta], 3=[Alpha]}
```

Additionally, RxJava provides to operator that allows for more customized conversions by accepting a function that transforms the Observable sequence into an arbitrary type. This operator caters to cases

162

not covered by the standard conversion operators and offers significant flexibility in handling Observable conversions to fit specific requirements.

```
1  Observable.just(1, 2, 3, 4, 5)
2      .to(Collections::singletonList)
3      .subscribe(System.out::println);
```

This code demonstrates the conversion of an Observable into a singleton list containing all the emitted items as a single collection, showcasing the versatility of the to operator.

Conversion Operators in RxJava provide a powerful set of tools for transforming Observable sequences into different forms or data structures. These operators enhance the capabilities of RxJava, allowing developers to adapt Observable sequences to the requirements of downstream operations, thereby enabling more efficient and effective data handling within reactive programming paradigms.

6.12 Utility Operators to Debug and Test

Utility operators in RxJava provide an essential toolkit for debugging and testing reactive streams. They allow developers to gain insight into the behavior of their observables, helping to identify and resolve issues more efficiently. This section will discuss various utility operators that can be used to debug and test RxJava applications.

Operators such as doOnNext, doOnError, doOnComplete, and doOnSubscribe are invaluable for understanding how data flows through an observable chain and for detecting where errors occur. Each of these operators allows you to perform side-effect actions without altering the stream's data.

```
1  Observable<Integer> observable = Observable.range(1, 5);
2
3  observable
4    .doOnSubscribe(disposable -> System.out.println("Subscribed"))
5    .doOnNext(item -> System.out.println("Processing item: " + item))
6    .doOnComplete(() -> System.out.println("Completed"))
7    .doOnError(throwable -> System.out.println("Error: " + throwable.getMessage()))
8    .subscribe();
```

```
Subscribed
Processing item: 1
Processing item: 2
Processing item: 3
Processing item: 4
```

163

```
Processing item: 5
Completed
```

The doOnNext operator is particularly useful for logging or performing actions with each emitted item without impacting the subsequent processing of these items. doOnError and doOnComplete offer hooks into the error handling and successful completion stages of an observable's lifecycle, respectively.

Beyond logging and side-effect actions, RxJava provides the TestObserver and TestScheduler classes for more structured testing scenarios. TestObserver can be attached to any Observable, Flowable, Single, Maybe, or Completable and offers a variety of assertion methods to verify expected outcomes.

```
1  TestObserver<Integer> testObserver = new TestObserver<>();
2
3  Observable<Integer> observable = Observable.range(1, 3);
4  observable.subscribe(testObserver);
5
6  testObserver.assertComplete();
7  testObserver.assertNoErrors();
8  testObserver.assertValues(1, 2, 3);
```

TestScheduler is a specialized scheduler that allows precise control over the timing of tasks. This is especially useful in unit tests where you need to simulate the passage of time or test time-dependent operations without actual delay.

```
1   TestScheduler testScheduler = new TestScheduler();
2   Observable<Long> observable = Observable.interval(1, TimeUnit.SECONDS,
        testScheduler);
3
4   TestObserver<Long> testObserver = new TestObserver<>();
5   observable.subscribe(testObserver);
6
7   testScheduler.advanceTimeBy(1, TimeUnit.SECONDS);
8   testObserver.assertValueCount(1);
9
10  testScheduler.advanceTimeBy(1, TimeUnit.SECONDS);
11  testObserver.assertValueCount(2);
```

In summary, utility operators, alongside TestObserver and TestScheduler, form a powerful set of tools for debugging and testing RxJava applications. They not only facilitate understanding how observables behave and interact but also offer a structured and effective approach to verifying application logic under various conditions.

Chapter 7

Handling Errors in Reactive Streams

Error handling within reactive streams is integral to building resilient and fault-tolerant applications. It involves strategies and practices for detecting, logging, and reacting to errors that occur during
the asynchronous processing of data streams. This chapter explores
the mechanisms and patterns available in reactive programming for
handling errors gracefully, ensuring that applications can recover or
degrade functionality smoothly in the face of failures. Emphasis
is placed on understanding how errors propagate through reactive
pipelines and how to apply effective strategies to mitigate their impact, thereby enhancing the reliability and robustness of reactive
applications.

7.1 Understanding Error Handling in Reactive Streams

Error handling is a fundamental aspect of software development, especially in systems designed around reactive programming principles.
Reactive streams, being inherently asynchronous and non-blocking,
compound the complexity of error management due to their nature of

data processing across different execution contexts. This intricate environment necessitates a robust error-handling mechanism to maintain system resilience and reliability.

In reactive systems, errors are considered as first-class data, similar to the emitted items in a stream. This design philosophy allows errors to be propagated through reactive pipelines just like any other data element, enabling operators within the stream to react to errors in a declarative manner. However, the propagation of errors in reactive streams introduces unique challenges, as it can lead to the termination of the data flow, potentially resulting in unwanted behavior or system instability.

To understand how error handling works within reactive streams, it's crucial to recognize the distinction between two types of operations: synchronous and asynchronous. Synchronous operations occur in a single execution context, making error propagation and handling relatively straightforward, as the call stack can be unwound to find an appropriate catch block. Conversely, asynchronous operations, which are prevalent in reactive programming, complicate error handling due to the disconnection between the execution context where the error occurs and where it's handled.

Errors in reactive streams can be grouped into two main categories: transient errors and non-transient errors. Transient errors are temporary and often result from issues like network connectivity disruptions, timeouts, or temporary resource unavailability. In contrast, non-transient errors are more severe and typically indicate a flaw in the system's logic or an unrecoverable state.

Reactive programming frameworks, such as RxJava and Project Reactor, provide several mechanisms for addressing errors within reactive streams. These include:

- onErrorReturn: Allows specifying a fallback value that should be emitted when an error occurs, effectively replacing the error with a valid data item.

- onErrorResume: Enables the substitution of the error-containing stream with another stream, which could be used for retries or returning fallback values.

- retry: Facilitates the re-subscription to the source observable or publisher when an error occurs, offering a way to attempt operation execution again in the face of transient errors.

- `doOnError`: Provides a hook for executing side-effect logic when an error occurs, such as logging or metrics collection without altering the error handling behavior of the stream.

It's important to implement error handling strategically in a reactive system, focusing on resilience and graceful degradation of functionality. Strategies should be tailored based on the type of error (transient or non-transient) and the criticality of the operation being performed. For transient errors, retry mechanisms with exponential backoff can be effective, whereas for non-transient errors, more elaborate recovery or fallback logic may be required.

In summary, error handling in reactive streams demands a comprehensive understanding of the nature of errors and the available mechanisms for managing them. By leveraging the capabilities of reactive programming frameworks and adopting a thoughtful approach to error management, developers can build robust, resilient, and fault-tolerant applications that gracefully navigate the complexities of asynchronous data processing.

7.2 Error Propagation in Reactive Systems

Error propagation in reactive systems is a critical aspect that significantly impacts the overall resilience and stability of applications. Reactive programming, by its nature, involves dealing with data streams that are asynchronous and event-driven. This model enhances scalability and efficiency but introduces complexity in how errors are handled and communicated across different components of the system. It is imperative to understand the behavior of error propagation in such an environment to implement effective error handling strategies.

In reactive systems, errors are considered as first-class data items that can propagate through the data stream similar to regular data items. When an error occurs within a reactive pipeline, it immediately disrupts the normal data flow and initiates the propagation of the error down the stream. This propagation mechanism is intrinsic to the reactive streams specification, which defines a standardized approach for asynchronous stream processing, including error handling.

Upon encountering an error, the reactive stream adheres to a "stop-and-propagate" policy. This means that the error is propagated downstream to all subscribers, and the data stream is terminated. The termination of the stream signifies that no more data items will be processed or emitted post-error occurrence. This approach ensures that errors are not silently ignored or lost, promoting a model where failures are explicitly handled.

To illustrate how error propagation works within a reactive stream, consider the following example using RxJava:

```
Observable<String> source = Observable.create(emitter -> {
    emitter.onNext("value1");
    emitter.onError(new RuntimeException("Unexpected error"));
    emitter.onNext("value2");
    emitter.onComplete();
});

source.subscribe(
    value -> System.out.println("Received: " + value),
    error -> System.err.println("Error: " + error.getMessage()),
    () -> System.out.println("Stream completed")
);
```

In this example, an `Observable` is created that emits values and then encounters an error. As soon as the error is emitted using `emitter.onError`, the stream is terminated, and no subsequent values are emitted. The subscribers are notified of the error, and the following output is produced:

```
Received: value1
Error: Unexpected error
```

Notably, "value2" is not emitted, and the completion signal is not sent, illustrating the stop-and-propagate behavior.

Reactive systems provide several mechanisms to deal with the propagation of errors. These include catching and handling errors within the stream, recovering from errors by providing fallback data, retrying operations that have failed, and more sophisticated strategies such as implementing custom error handling operators. The choice of strategy depends on various factors including the nature of the application, the criticality of the operation, and the user experience goals.

Understanding the principles of error propagation in reactive systems is foundational to architecting applications that are resilient and capable of graceful error handling. It allows developers to anticipate how errors will impact their application flow and to design their reactive pipeline to ensure that errors are handled in a manner that aligns with the application's requirements for fault tolerance and user experience.

7.3 Catching and Handling Errors with RxJava

Error handling is a pivotal aspect of creating resilient reactive applications using RxJava. In RxJava, errors are considered first-class citizens, and the library provides a comprehensive API for catching and handling them effectively. This ensures that even when errors occur, the application can continue to operate or fail gracefully, enhancing the overall robustness and dependability of the system.

In RxJava, errors can be handled in several ways, including using the onErrorReturn, onErrorResumeNext, and retry operators.

- The onErrorReturn operator allows you to return a default value when an error occurs. It effectively switches the error notification with a success value, allowing the stream to terminate normally.

- The onErrorResumeNext operator provides more flexibility than onErrorReturn. It allows you to resume the stream with another Observable when an error occurs, thus providing an alternate data sequence that can take over in case of an error.

- The retry operator attempts to re-subscribe to the Observable when an error occurs, giving it another chance to complete successfully. This can be particularly useful when dealing with transient errors that may not reoccur on subsequent attempts.

When implementing error handling in RxJava, it's crucial to understand the difference between these operators and choose the one that fits the specific needs of your application.

```
1   // Example of onErrorReturn
2   Observable<String> observable = Observable.just("A", "B", "C")
3       .map(item -> {
4           if ("B".equals(item)) {
5               throw new RuntimeException("Error occurred");
6           }
7           return item;
8       })
9       .onErrorReturn(error -> "Default");
10
11  observable.subscribe(
12      item -> System.out.println(item),
13      error -> System.out.println("Error: " + error.getMessage()),
```

```
14    () -> System.out.println("Completed")
15 );
```

```
A
Default
Completed
```

The above example demonstrates the use of the onErrorReturn operator. It maps through a sequence of items and intentionally throws
an exception for the item "B". Instead of propagating the error and
terminating the sequence abruptly, the onErrorReturn operator allows
the sequence to emit a default value and complete normally.

```
1  // Example of onErrorResumeNext
2  Observable<String> originalObservable = Observable.just("1", "2", "3")
3      .map(item -> {
4          if ("2".equals(item)) {
5              throw new RuntimeException("Error on 2");
6          }
7          return item;
8      });
9
10 Observable<String> fallbackObservable = Observable.just("A", "B", "C");
11
12 Observable<String> resultObservable = originalObservable
13      .onErrorResumeNext(fallbackObservable);
14
15 resultObservable.subscribe(
16      item -> System.out.println(item),
17      error -> System.out.println("Error: " + error.getMessage()),
18      () -> System.out.println("Completed")
19 );
```

```
1
A
B
C
Completed
```

In the onErrorResumeNext example, when the error occurs for the
item "2", instead of terminating, the stream resumes with a fallback
Observable, seamlessly transitioning from the original data sequence
to an alternate one.

```
1  // Example of retry
2  Observable<String> sourceObservable = Observable.just("A", "B", "error trigger", "C
       ")
3      .map(item -> {
4          if ("error trigger".equals(item)) {
5              throw new RuntimeException("Forced error");
6          }
7          return item;
8      })
9      .retry(2);
```

```
10
11   sourceObservable.subscribe(
12       item -> System.out.println(item),
13       error -> System.out.println("Error: " + error.getMessage()),
14       () -> System.out.println("Completed")
15   );
```

```
A
B
A
B
Error: Forced error
```

The retry operator example attempts to process the sequence twice due to the forced error after emitting "B". After retrying the specified number of times (2 attempts in this case), if the error still persists, it's then propagated downstream.

Error handling in RxJava is an essential part of developing a resilient and robust reactive application. By choosing the appropriate operator and strategy to manage errors, developers can ensure that their applications can handle unexpected failures in a controlled and graceful manner, thus improving the overall user experience and reliability of the system.

7.4 Using onErrorReturn, onErrorResume, and retry Operators

Error handling in reactive programming requires a comprehensive understanding of the tools and operators provided by frameworks like RxJava. Among these, onErrorReturn, onErrorResume, and retry operators stand out for their effectiveness in managing errors within reactive streams. This section will discuss how to leverage these operators to implement resilient error handling strategies that significantly enhance the robustness of reactive applications.

onErrorReturn is designed to intercept exceptions and provide a fallback value, ensuring the stream does not terminate abruptly on encountering an error. This operator is particularly useful when maintaining a continuous data stream is critical, and default values can serve as an immediate, albeit temporary, solution to an error. The usage of onErrorReturn is straightforward:

```
1   Flux<String> source = Flux.just("key1", "key2")
2                   .map(key -> {
```

```
3        if ("key2".equals(key)) {
4            throw new RuntimeException("Error on " + key);
5        }
6        return "Value for " + key;
7    })
8    .onErrorReturn("Default Value");
```

In the above code snippet, a flux is created that maps each key to a value. However, if the key is "key2", an exception is thrown. The onErrorReturn operator catches this exception and emits "Default Value" instead, preventing the stream from terminating.

onErrorResume provides a more flexible approach compared to onErrorReturn. It allows for dynamic substitution of the errored stream with another stream based on the type of exception encountered. This contributes to more granular error handling where different fallback mechanisms can be implemented for specific exceptions. Consider the following example:

```
1  Flux<String> source = Flux.just("key1", "key2")
2                  .flatMap(key -> {
3                      if ("key2".equals(key)) {
4                          return Flux.error(new RuntimeException("Error on " +
                               key));
5                      }
6                      return Flux.just("Processed " + key);
7                  })
8                  .onErrorResume(e -> {
9                      if (e instanceof RuntimeException) {
10                         return Flux.just("Recovered from runtime exception");
11                     } else {
12                         return Flux.error(e);
13                     }
14                 });
```

Here, onErrorResume checks if the error is an instance of RuntimeException. If it is, it resumes the stream with a recovery flux. Otherwise, it propagates the error further, allowing for additional handling downstream or letting it terminate the stream if uncaught.

The retry operator takes a different approach to error handling by attempting to re-subscribe to the source Observable upon encountering an error. This is particularly useful when the error is expected to be transient or when an operation is likely to succeed upon retrying. The operator can be configured to retry a specific number of times before ultimately failing.

```
1  Flux<String> source = Flux.just("key1", "key2")
2                  .map(key -> {
3                      if ("key2".equals(key)) {
4                          throw new RuntimeException("Transient error on " + key
                               );
```

172

```
5          }
6              return "Value for " + key;
7          })
8          .retry(2);
```

In the example above, if an error occurs due to "key2", the stream will be re-subscribed up to two more times in an attempt to complete successfully before giving up and propagating the error.

Using onErrorReturn, onErrorResume, and retry operators efficiently can greatly contribute to the resilience of a reactive application. These operators enable developers to elegantly handle errors in reactive streams, ensuring that applications can continue to operate smoothly even in the face of unexpected failures. However, it's crucial to use these tools judiciously, keeping in mind the nature of the error and the implications of each error-handling strategy on the application's behavior and performance.

7.5 Error Handling Best Practices in Reactive Programming

Error handling in reactive programming requires a shift in perspective from traditional imperative error handling methods. Given the asynchronous and non-blocking nature of reactive streams, error handling must be integrated into the design of the application from the outset, ensuring that errors do not break the flow of data or cause unintended side effects. In this section, we will discuss several best practices for error handling in the context of reactive programming.

First, it is essential to understand that error handling in reactive streams is just as much a part of the data flow as the successful handling of data. Reactive libraries like RxJava and Project Reactor offer several operators for handling errors that can be used to declaratively specify how errors should be managed. These include, but are not limited to, onErrorReturn, onErrorResume, and retry.

- The onErrorReturn operator allows the stream to emit a default item when an error occurs, thereby preventing the error from propagating further.

- With onErrorResume, it's possible to switch to a new publisher when an error is encountered. This can be particularly useful for implementing fallback mechanisms.

173

- The retry operator attempts to re-subscribe to the source observable after an error has occurred, giving the application another chance to complete the operation successfully.

It is also crucial to encapsulate error details within domain-specific exceptions whenever possible. This encapsulation enables easier identification of error contexts and the application of specific error handling strategies. Furthermore, it is advisable to log errors comprehensively at the point of detection. Detailed logging will assist in diagnosing problems that may occur in production. However, be cautious not to expose sensitive information in logs.

Another key aspect of reactive error handling is the use of fallback methods. Fallback strategies can prevent an application from failing completely by providing an alternative way of completing an operation when a particular pathway fails. This is especially important in distributed systems where dependencies may not always be reliable. Implementing a fallback method could involve calling an alternative microservice, fetching cached data, or returning a default value to the end-user.

Timeouts are another vital consideration in reactive programming. Non-blocking operations should not wait indefinitely. Setting appropriate timeouts helps in avoiding potentially endless waits that can lead to resource exhaustion. Reactive libraries come equipped with timeout operators that can be used to specify a maximum duration for an operation before it is considered failed.

Below is an example of using the timeout operator in RxJava to apply a timeout to a stream:

```
Observable<String> sourceObservable = Observable.longOperation();
sourceObservable
    .timeout(1, TimeUnit.SECONDS)
    .subscribe(
        item -> System.out.println("Received: " + item),
        error -> System.out.println("Error: " + error)
    );
```

In this example, if the longOperation does not produce a value within 1 second, the timeout operator will emit a TimeoutException, which can then be handled appropriately.

Error handling in reactive programming also extends to the testing of reactive applications. It is important to include tests that simulate errors to guarantee that the error handling paths are correctly implemented and that the application behaves as expected when faced with failures.

Finally, it is worth noting that while reactive programming libraries provide a robust framework for error handling, each application's specific requirements will dictate the most suitable strategies to employ. Therefore, a deep understanding of both the reactive library in use and the application domain is essential for effective error handling.

In summary, error handling in reactive programming is a multifaceted issue that requires careful consideration and planning. By adhering to these best practices, developers can create more resilient and fault-tolerant applications that are capable of gracefully handling unavoidable errors.

7.6 Implementing Custom Error Handling Strategies

Implementing custom error handling strategies in reactive programming necessitates a comprehensive understanding of the behavioral dynamics of reactive streams. The objective is not only to catch and log errors but to formulate robust solutions that enhance the resilience of reactive systems. This involves crafting error handling mechanisms that are capable of gracefully managing unforeseen failures, thereby ensuring that the system remains stable and operational.

In reactive streams, errors are considered to be first-class data items that propagate downstream until they are explicitly handled or cause the stream to terminate. Leveraging this model, developers can implement custom error handling strategies that address specific business logic or system requirements. The methods discussed herein are applicable to RxJava and Project Reactor, two of the most prominent reactive libraries in the Java ecosystem.

Custom Exception Classes: The first step in formulating a custom error handling strategy is the definition of custom exception classes. These classes allow for the encapsulation of error-specific information, such as error codes, messages, or contextual data, making it easier to handle errors in a more granular and meaningful way.

```
1  public class CustomException extends RuntimeException {
2      private final String errorCode;
3
```

```
4    public CustomException(String message, String errorCode) {
5        super(message);
6        this.errorCode = errorCode;
7    }
8
9    public String getErrorCode() {
10       return errorCode;
11   }
12 }
```

Error Handling Operators: Both RxJava and Project Reactor provide several operators for intercepting and handling errors within a reactive pipeline. For custom error handling, operators such as onErrorResume, onErrorReturn, and retry are particularly useful. They allow the reactive stream to recover from errors by substituting the error with alternative data, returning a default value, or attempting to re-subscribe to the observable source, respectively.

```
1  Flux<Integer> flux = Flux.just(1, 2, 0)
2      .map(i -> 10 / i)
3      .onErrorResume(e -> Flux.just(-1)); // Substituting with -1 upon error
```

Using the onErrorResume operator, the stream is provided with a fall-back mechanism, ensuring continuity even in the presence of errors.

Global Error Handling: For applications that require a centralized approach to error handling, both RxJava and Project Reactor offer mechanisms to intercept and handle errors at a global level. This approach is beneficial for applying consistent error handling policies across the entire application.

```
1  Hooks.onOperatorError((error, signal) -> {
2      if (error instanceof CustomException) {
3          return new CustomException("Global handler: " + error.getMessage(), "
               GLOBAL_ERROR");
4      }
5      return error;
6  });
```

Composing Custom Error Handlers: Complex applications may necessitate a more nuanced error handling strategy that combines multiple techniques. By composing custom error handlers, it is possible to implement sophisticated error handling logic that can differentiate between various types of errors, apply specific handling policies, and integrate seamlessly with the application's error logging infrastructure.

Error Handling in Asynchronous Processes: In reactive systems, where operations often occur asynchronously, ensuring that errors are properly handled across different execution contexts is paramount. By employing the subscribeOn and publishOn operators, developers can control the execution context of the error handling logic, thereby safeguarding against potential issues related to thread confinement and concurrency.

Implementing custom error handling strategies in reactive systems is both an art and a science. It requires a deep understanding of the reactive programming paradigm, a clear grasp of the specific requirements of the application, and a creative approach to solving complex problems. By judiciously applying the techniques outlined above, developers can build reactive applications that are not only robust and reliable but also capable of gracefully managing failures, thereby enhancing the overall user experience.

7.7 Dealing with Timeout Errors

Timeout errors in reactive streams occur when an operation does not complete within a specified duration. These kinds of errors are significant because they can indicate underlying issues such as resource constraints, network latency, or unexpected system behavior. Managing timeout errors effectively is therefore paramount to maintaining the responsiveness and reliability of a reactive application.

In reactive programming, handling timeout scenarios involves specifying a duration after which, if a response is not received, the system can automatically trigger a fallback mechanism or an error handling routine. Both RxJava and Project Reactor provide operators to deal with timeout errors, each allowing developers to define how the system should behave when a timeout condition is met.

In RxJava, the `timeout` operator is used to specify a duration for waiting on an operation. If the operation does not complete within the given time frame, the `timeout` operator emits a `TimeoutException`. Let's consider an example where a data retrieval operation is expected to complete within 1 second:

```
Observable<String> source = Observable.create(emitter -> {
    // Simulate a long-running operation
    Thread.sleep(1500);
    emitter.onNext("Data");
    emitter.onComplete();
});

source.timeout(1, TimeUnit.SECONDS)
    .subscribe(System.out::println, Throwable::printStackTrace);
```

In this example, the `timeout` operator will emit a `TimeoutException` since the operation exceeds the specified 1-second duration. The error can then be caught and handled accordingly.

Project Reactor utilizes a similar approach with its `timeout` operator. The following example demonstrates handling a timeout in Project Reactor:

```
Flux<String> source = Flux.create(sink -> {
    // Simulate a long-running operation
    try {
        Thread.sleep(1500);
        sink.next("Data");
        sink.complete();
    } catch (InterruptedException e) {
        sink.error(e);
    }
});

source.timeout(Duration.ofSeconds(1))
    .subscribe(System.out::println, Throwable::printStackTrace);
```

In this scenario, if the operation does not emit any items within the specified 1-second duration, a `TimeoutException` is propagated downstream.

Handling timeout errors gracefully is crucial. One effective strategy is to implement fallback mechanisms using operators such as `onErrorReturn`, `onErrorResumeWith`, or `retry`. These operators allow the application to recover from timeout errors by providing alternative data sources, attempting to repeat the operation, or performing other custom error handling procedures.

For instance, the `onErrorResume` operator can be used to specify a fallback method in case of a timeout:

```
source.timeout(Duration.ofSeconds(1))
    .onErrorResume(e -> {
        if (e instanceof TimeoutException) {
            return Flux.just("Fallback data");
        }
        return Flux.error(e);
    })
    .subscribe(System.out::println);
```

This approach ensures that the application remains responsive, providing a path to recover or degrade gracefully in case of operational delays.

Dealing with timeout errors effectively is a critical aspect of building resilient reactive applications. Reactive programming frameworks such as RxJava and Project Reactor offer a variety of operators to manage these scenarios, enabling developers to implement sophisticated error handling and fallback strategies. By understanding and leveraging these tools, developers can enhance the robustness and reliability of their applications, ensuring a better user experience even in the face of unforeseen delays and errors.

7.8 Handling Errors in Project Reactor

Handling errors in Project Reactor, a reactive programming library for the JVM that integrates with the Spring ecosystem, requires an understanding of its operational dynamics. Project Reactor operates on the principles of reactive streams, where data flows in pipelines, and error handling is a critical aspect of creating a resilient and responsive application. This section will elucidate the mechanisms provided by Project Reactor for handling errors, ensuring graceful degradation, or recovery from failures during the data processing pipeline.

Firstly, it is imperative to comprehend how errors are communicated in a reactive stream. In Project Reactor, just like in any other implementation of reactive streams, errors are considered as data. When an error occurs, it is propagated downstream as an error signal, terminating the normal data flow. This mechanism ensures that errors do not go unnoticed and are addressed promptly. However, this also means that once an error signal is emitted, the stream cannot continue emitting regular data elements. Therefore, understanding how to react to these error signals is crucial for maintaining a robust reactive system.

One of the simplest ways to handle errors in Project Reactor is by using the onErrorResume function. This function intercepts an error and allows the developer to provide an alternative data stream in case of an error. The following example demonstrates its usage:

```
1   Flux<String> source = Flux.just("1", "2", "3", "four", "5")
2       .map(value -> {
3           try {
4               return Integer.parseInt(value);
5           } catch (NumberFormatException e) {
6               throw new RuntimeException(e);
7           }
8       })
9       .map(number -> "Number " + number)
10      .onErrorResume(e -> Flux.just("Error encountered, providing alternate data"));
11
12  source.subscribe(System.out::println);
```

In the example above, the map operation throws a RuntimeException when it attempts to parse a non-numeric string. The onErrorResume

179

function catches this error and provides an alternate data stream that indicates an error was encountered.

Another useful operator for error handling in Project Reactor is onErrorReturn. This operator allows specifying a single fallback value when an error occurs, making it particularly useful for simple defaults. For instance:

```
Flux<String> source = Flux.just("1", "2", "zero", "3")
    .map(value -> {
        try {
            return Integer.parseInt(value);
        } catch (NumberFormatException e) {
            throw new RuntimeException("Parsing error");
        }
    })
    .onErrorReturn("Fallback value");

source.subscribe(System.out::println);
```

The onErrorReturn clause intercepts the parsing error and instead of an error signal, the subscriber receives a pre-defined fallback value.

Project Reactor also provides the retry operator that can be used to re-subscribe to the original Publisher upon an error, hoping that the error is transient and the operation may complete successfully upon retry. The retry operator can be configured with a retry count to limit the number of retries. The following code snippet illustrates its usage:

```
Flux<String> source = Flux.<String>create(sink -> {
        sink.next("1");
        sink.next("2");
        sink.error(new RuntimeException("Connection error"));
    })
    .retry(2);

source.subscribe(System.out::println);
```

In the example, the source emits two elements before throwing a run-time exception. The retry operator attempts the entire sequence again, two more times, before finally propagating the error downstream if it persists.

Finally, for more complex error handling scenarios, Project Reactor allows the creation of custom error handling strategies. This is accomplished by implementing the doOnError method, which provides access to the error signal, enabling the execution of side-effect operations, such as logging, before propagating the error downstream or applying any of the recovery mechanisms discussed earlier.

```
Flux<String> source = Flux.just("1", "2", "three")
    .map(Integer::parseInt)
```

```
3      .doOnError(error -> System.err.println("Error encountered: " + error.getMessage
            ()))
4      .onErrorResume(e -> Flux.just("0")); // Providing a fallback value
5
6  source.subscribe(System.out::println);
```

The example above illustrates the doOnError usage, where it logs the encountered error, and subsequently, the onErrorResume provides a fallback value.

Project Reactor offers a comprehensive suite of operators and mechanisms for handling errors gracefully in reactive pipelines. Understanding how to employ onErrorResume, onErrorReturn, retry, and doOnError effectively allows developers to build resilient and fault-tolerant applications. It also emphasizes that anticipating and planning for errors as part of the data flow can enhance the reliability and robustness of applications built with Project Reactor.

7.9   Fallback Strategies for Resilient Systems

In reactive programming, employing fallback strategies is vital for maintaining system resilience and guaranteeing uninterrupted service despite encountering errors. Fallback strategies allow systems to provide alternative outcomes or simplified responses when the primary execution path fails. This approach is crucial in reactive systems where the asynchronous and non-blocking nature of operations lends itself to potential failure points across the data stream. This section will discuss various fallback mechanisms and how they contribute to building robust, resilient systems.

One commonly employed strategy is the usage of the onErrorReturn operator. This operator allows a reactive pipeline to return a default value when an error occurs. Instead of the error propagating downstream and possibly terminating the data flow, onErrorReturn provides a predetermined fallback value, ensuring continuity of operations. An illustrative example is shown below:

```
1  Flux<String> reactiveStream = Flux.just("data1", "data2")
2      .map(value -> {
3          if(value.equals("data2")) throw new RuntimeException("Error");
4          return value;
5      })
6      .onErrorReturn("fallback");
```

Another strategy involves the onErrorResume operator, which offers more flexibility than onErrorReturn by allowing the specification of an alternative data stream in the event of an error. This can be particularly beneficial when a fallback procedure involves complex or asynchronous operations. The following snippet exemplifies the onErrorResume usage:

```
1  Flux<String> reactiveStream = Flux.just("data1", "data2")
2      .map(value -> {
3          if(value.equals("data2")) throw new RuntimeException("Error");
4          return value;
5      })
6      .onErrorResume(e -> Flux.just("alternative1", "alternative2"));
```

The retry operator offers another dimension of resilience by reattempting the execution of a reactive stream when an error is encountered. This can be particularly useful for transient issues, such as network timeouts or temporary unavailability of an external service. The operator can be restricted to a specific number of retries or configured to apply complex logic to determine when to retry. An example of using retry is as follows:

```
1  Flux<String> reactiveStream = Flux.just("data1", "data2")
2      .map(value -> {
3          if(value.equals("data2")) throw new RuntimeException("Error");
4          return value;
5      })
6      .retry(3);
```

Beyond these predefined operators, designing custom error handling strategies is often necessary to accommodate the unique requirements of a system. Custom strategies can leverage the aforementioned operators in conjunction with other reactive programming constructs to devise sophisticated solutions to error handling.

Implementing timeout mechanisms is another cornerstone of fallback strategy. Timeout errors, often a symptom of downstream service degradation, can be mitigated by specifying a maximum duration for the operation and providing a fallback behavior if the operation does not complete in this timeframe. The timeout operator in reactive frameworks facilitates this approach, enabling developers to define explicit behavior when a timeout condition is met.

The realization of system resilience through fallback strategies extends to integrating error handling with higher-level frameworks like Spring WebFlux. In doing so, developers can uniformly apply these principles across the entirety of their reactive stack, from individual data processing operations to global exception handling in web controllers.

In summary, fallback strategies provide a safety net for reactive systems, enabling them to remain responsive and maintain a level of service even in the face of errors. By leveraging operators such as onErrorReturn, onErrorResume, and retry, along with custom and timeout-based strategies, developers can enhance the resilience and robustness of their reactive applications.

7.10 Integrating Error Handling with Spring WebFlux

Integrating error handling within the Spring WebFlux framework involves leveraging its rich set of features designed to handle various types of errors in a non-blocking and reactive manner. Spring WebFlux proposes a model where error handling is part of the functional programming paradigm, allowing developers to manage exceptions reactively. This section will discuss the implementation of error handling techniques in Spring WebFlux, focusing on the functional routing APIs, annotation-based controllers, and global error handling strategies.

Firstly, it is imperative to understand how Spring WebFlux differentiates itself from the traditional Servlet-based Spring MVC. In a reactive stack, the threading model is non-blocking, and as such, controlling the flow of errors requires a reactive approach. This is where Project Reactor, the foundational library for reactive programming in Spring, comes into play. Error handling in WebFlux, therefore, heavily relies on operators provided by Project Reactor, such as onErrorMap, onErrorResume, and onErrorReturn.

In the context of handling errors in routes defined by WebFlux's functional routing API, one can leverage these operators directly in the route handlers. Consider the following example:

```
RouterFunction<ServerResponse> route =
    RouterFunctions.route(RequestPredicates.GET("/data/{id}"),
        request -> repository.findById(request.pathVariable("id"))
                    .flatMap(data -> ServerResponse.ok().bodyValue(data))
                    .onErrorResume(Exception.class,
                                e -> ServerResponse.status(HttpStatus.
                                    INTERNAL_SERVER_ERROR).build()));
```

Here, onErrorResume is utilized to catch any exception that might be thrown during the execution of the reactive pipeline that fetches and returns the data. Instead of propagating the error, it provides a mechanism to return a fallback response, in this case, an Internal Server Error status.

For annotation-based controllers, error handling can be approached by annotating exception handling methods with @ExceptionHandler. This method will be invoked when the specified exception is thrown from any controller method within the same controller class:

```
1   @RestController
2   public class DataController {
3
4       @GetMapping("/data/{id}")
5       public Mono<Data> getData(@PathVariable String id) {
6           return repository.findById(id)
7                       .switchIfEmpty(Mono.error(new DataNotFoundException("Data not
                            found for id: " + id)));
8       }
9
10      @ExceptionHandler(DataNotFoundException.class)
11      public ResponseEntity<String> handleDataNotFoundException(DataNotFoundException
            e) {
12          return ResponseEntity.status(HttpStatus.NOT_FOUND).body(e.getMessage());
13      }
14  }
```

A more global approach to error handling in WebFlux applications can be achieved by implementing the WebExceptionHandler interface. This allows for centralized error handling that is applied across different routers or controllers. For example:

```
1   @Component
2   public class GlobalErrorHandler implements WebExceptionHandler {
3
4       @Override
5       public Mono<Void> handle(ServerWebExchange exchange, Throwable ex) {
6           if (ex instanceof DataNotFoundException) {
7               exchange.getResponse().setStatusCode(HttpStatus.NOT_FOUND);
8               return exchange.getResponse().setComplete();
9           }
10          exchange.getResponse().setStatusCode(HttpStatus.INTERNAL_SERVER_ERROR);
11          return exchange.getResponse().setComplete();
12      }
13  }
```

This technique ensures that irrespective of where the error occurs within the application, there's a unified strategy for handling it, thus promoting a cleaner and more maintainable codebase.

Understanding and implementing error handling in Spring WebFlux requires a different mindset from the imperative style of programming. Leveraging reactive operators for error handling directly in the data flow provides a powerful and flexible way to deal with exceptions. Additionally, Spring WebFlux offers tailored approaches for functional and annotation-based models, giving developers the tools to create robust, fault-tolerant reactive applications.

7.11 Testing Error Handling in Reactive Applications

Testing error handling in reactive applications is essential to ensure that the system behaves as expected under various failure scenarios. Effective testing verifies that the application can gracefully handle and recover from errors, thereby maintaining its reliability and robustness. This section will discuss the strategies and techniques for testing error handling within reactive streams, emphasizing the use of testing frameworks, designing test cases for error scenarios, and implementing custom error conditions.

To begin, it is vital to understand the importance of employing testing libraries that are designed to work with reactive programming models. Libraries such as 'StepVerifier' from Project Reactor, and the RxJava 'TestObserver', provide a fluent API for testing reactive streams. They allow developers to assert the expected state of a stream at various points in its lifecycle, including its completion or error states.

```
1  StepVerifier.create(myFlux)
2      .expectNextMatches(/* predicate */)
3      .expectError(MyCustomException.class)
4      .verify();
```

In the above example, 'StepVerifier' is used to test a Reactor 'Flux' instance. The test verifies that the 'Flux' emits items that match a given predicate, and then terminates with a specific error type, 'My-CustomException'.

When designing test cases for error handling, it is crucial to cover a broad range of scenarios that might cause the application to fail. This includes network timeouts, downstream service failures, data corruption, and invalid input scenarios. By simulating these conditions, developers can ensure that their error handling logic correctly identifies and addresses each scenario.

```
1  @Test
2  public void whenNetworkTimeout_thenExpectCustomTimeoutException() {
3      // Configure the reactive stream to simulate a network timeout
4      Flux<String> simulateNetworkTimeoutFlux = Flux.error(new TimeoutException());
5
6      StepVerifier.create(simulateNetworkTimeoutFlux)
```

```
7          .expectError(CustomTimeoutException.class)
8          .verify();
9    }
```

In this test case, the reactive stream is configured to simulate a network timeout scenario by emitting a 'TimeoutException'. The test then verifies that the stream's error handling logic correctly converts this into a 'CustomTimeoutException'.

Implementing custom error conditions is another crucial aspect of testing. It allows for the validation of error handling pathways that are specific to the application's business logic. For instance, testing can verify that certain input conditions trigger the appropriate validation errors, or that specific combinations of events lead to known error states.

```
1    @Test
2    public void whenInvalidInput_thenExpectValidationException() {
3        Mono<String> invalidInputMono = Mono.just("invalid_input")
4                                .flatMap(input -> {
5                                    if("invalid_input".equals(input)) {
6                                        return Mono.error(new ValidationException(
                                            "Invalid input"));
7                                    }
8                                    return Mono.just(input);
9                                });
10
11       StepVerifier.create(invalidInputMono)
12           .expectError(ValidationException.class)
13           .verify();
14   }
```

In this example, a 'Mono' is created that emits a validation exception when it receives an invalid input. The test case uses 'StepVerifier' to assert that the 'Mono' correctly identifies the invalid input and emits a 'ValidationException'.

Finally, testing error handling in reactive applications should also involve verifying the behaviour of fallback strategies. Fallback strategies ensure that the application can degrade gracefully under error conditions, providing alternate pathways for execution. Tests should validate that fallback methods are invoked as expected and that the resulting state of the application remains correct and consistent.

Testing error handling in reactive applications is a comprehensive task that involves verifying the application's resilience and robustness under failure conditions. By employing specialized testing libraries, designing thorough test cases for various error scenarios, and implementing custom error conditions, developers can ensure that their reactive applications are equipped to handle errors gracefully and maintain their reliability in production environments.

7.12 Real-World Scenarios and Solutions for Error Handling

Error handling in reactive applications is crucial for maintaining the reliability and performance of software systems. This section will explore several real-world scenarios where error handling is paramount, along with solutions to manage these errors effectively using RxJava and Spring Boot.

In reactive programming, errors can emanate from various sources such as external service failures, network latency, or even malformed data. Understanding how to navigate these failures gracefully is key to constructing resilient systems.

Scenario 1: External Service Failure

Consider an application that relies on external services for fetching critical data. These services might at times be unavailable or return erroneous responses due to various reasons such as server overload or maintenance windows.

```
Mono<String> fetchDataFromService(String endpointUrl) {
    return WebClient.create(endpointUrl)
            .get()
            .retrieve()
            .bodyToMono(String.class)
            .onErrorResume(e -> Mono.just("Fallback Data"));
}
```

In the code snippet above, we use the onErrorResume operator to provide a fallback mechanism. This ensures that even when the external service fails, our application can continue operating by resorting to predefined fallback data.

Scenario 2: Data Processing Errors

Another common scenario involves errors during the processing of data streams. For example, parsing JSON objects where the structure isn't as expected.

```
Flux<ProcessedData> processData(Flux<String> dataStream) {
    return dataStream.map(data -> {
        try {
            return new ObjectMapper().readValue(data, ProcessedData.class);
        } catch (JsonProcessingException e) {
```

```
 6              throw new RuntimeException("Processing error", e);
 7          }
 8      }).onErrorContinue((throwable, o) -> {
 9          // Log and skip the erroneous data
10          log.error("Failed to process data: "+ o, throwable);
11      });
12  }
```

Here, the onErrorContinue operator is used to log the error and skip over the problematic piece of data, allowing the rest of the stream to be processed without interruption.

Scenario 3: Handling Timeout Errors

In a reactive system, operations are often bounded by specific time frames to avoid indefinite waits. Handling timeout errors effectively is vital to keep the system responsive.

```
1  Mono<String> fetchWithTimeout(String endpointUrl) {
2      return WebClient.create(endpointUrl)
3              .get()
4              .retrieve()
5              .bodyToMono(String.class)
6              .timeout(Duration.ofSeconds(5))
7              .onErrorResume(TimeoutException.class, e -> Mono.just("Timeout Fallback
                   Data"));
8  }
```

In the example above, the timeout operator is utilized to specify that the operation should not exceed a duration of five seconds. The onErrorResume operator catches the TimeoutException and provides fallback data, ensuring the application remains resilient to delays in external services.

Scenario 4: Retry Strategies

Transient errors in external services or network glitches can often be resolved by simply retrying the failed operation after a brief delay.

```
1  Mono<String> resilientFetch(String endpointUrl) {
2      return WebClient.create(endpointUrl)
3              .get()
4              .retrieve()
5              .bodyToMono(String.class)
6              .retryBackoff(3, Duration.ofSeconds(1), Duration.ofSeconds(5))
7              .onErrorReturn("Final Fallback Data");
8  }
```

The retryBackoff operator in the snippet above initiates retries with an exponential backoff strategy, attempting up to three retries with delays between one and five seconds. The onErrorReturn operator provides a final layer of fallback if retries do not succeed.

By applying these error handling strategies, developers can ensure that reactive applications gracefully handle failures, maintaining robustness and delivering seamless user experiences even under adverse conditions. Incorporating such patterns into your error handling strategy is essential for building resilient and fault-tolerant applications with RxJava and Spring Boot.

Chapter 8

Building Reactive APIs with Spring WebFlux

Spring WebFlux represents a paradigm shift in building reactive and non-blocking API endpoints, catering to the modern needs of handling asynchronous stream processing. It enables developers to create scalable microservices and applications that can process large volumes of data with minimal latency. This chapter zeroes in on the fundamentals of Spring WebFlux, illustrating how to leverage its features to build reactive APIs effectively. From setting up a reactive environment to handling data streams and managing back-pressure, readers will gain insights into best practices for developing highly responsive and resilient APIs using Spring WebFlux, ensuring applications are future-ready and capable of handling evolving data demands.

8.1   Introduction to Spring WebFlux

Spring WebFlux is a reactive-stack web framework added to the Spring Framework 5.0, representing a significant shift towards building non-blocking, reactive applications. It supports the reactive streams paradigm and offers a way to build systems that are scalable, resilient, and responsive. Unlike Spring MVC, which is built on a servlet API,

Spring WebFlux is designed to work in an asynchronous and non-blocking environment. This allows it to handle a vast number of concurrent connections with a small number of threads.

The core of Spring WebFlux's reactive capabilities lies in its support for reactive programming, a programming paradigm oriented around data flows and the propagation of change. It means that when using Spring WebFlux, applications developed can process streams of data in a non-blocking fashion, leading to better utilization of resources and more scalable applications.

At the heart of Spring WebFlux are two types: Mono and Flux. Mono is used for representing a single or empty asynchronous value, while Flux represents a stream of 0 to N elements. Both types are part of Project Reactor, a reactive library which is the foundation of Spring WebFlux.

In order to understand how Spring WebFlux supports building reactive APIs, it is essential to grasp the concept of backpressure. Backpressure is a mechanism to ensure that the producer does not overwhelm the consumer. In a reactive system, the subscriber has the control to signal how much data it can process, effectively managing the flow of data and mitigating the risk of overloading the system.

Here is an example of creating a simple reactive endpoint using Spring WebFlux:

```
@GetMapping("/reactive")
public Mono<String> reactiveEndpoint() {
    return Mono.just("Hello, Reactive World!");
}
```

This example defines a @GetMapping with a URI of "/reactive". When accessing this endpoint, it returns a Mono<String> that emits "Hello, Reactive World!" asynchronously.

One of the advantages of using Spring WebFlux is its model for implementing asynchronous request handling, enabling the efficient execution of I/O operations. The non-blocking nature of I/O calls in WebFlux frees up threads to handle other requests, improving the application's overall throughput.

Spring WebFlux can be run on various servers such as Netty, Undertow, and the traditional Servlet 3.1+ containers. However, to fully leverage the non-blocking features, it is recommended to run WebFlux on servers that support non-blocking I/O operations. Netty is often the preferred choice due to its scalability and speed.

Integrating Spring WebFlux into projects encourages developers to adopt a more functional style of programming. This involves viewing application logic as a series of state transformations, which fits well with the reactive programming model. Functions become first-class citizens, and operations are represented as transformations applied to data streams.

In addition to its reactive features, Spring WebFlux includes support for Server-Sent Events (SSE) and WebSockets, allowing developers to build real-time, streaming applications. These features are essential for applications requiring high-performance, real-time data exchange, such as chat applications, live notifications, and streaming services.

Spring WebFlux represents a significant advancement in building reactive and non-blocking web applications. With its support for reactive programming, efficient handling of streams, and seamless integration with other reactive Spring projects, developers can create applications that are scalable, resilient, and responsive. As data volumes and system interactions continue to grow, adopting reactive programming with Spring WebFlux is becoming increasingly important for modern applications.

8.2 Setting Up a Spring WebFlux Project

Let's start with the foundational steps required to set up a Spring WebFlux project. To do this effectively, it is necessary to have the appropriate development tools installed on your system. The primary tools include Java Development Kit (JDK), Spring Tool Suite (STS) or an Integrated Development Environment (IDE) of your choice that supports Spring applications, and Maven or Gradle for managing dependencies. As of this writing, Spring WebFlux requires Java 8 or newer. Verify that the JDK is installed by running the command java -version in your terminal.

Following the verification of Java installation, the next step involves the creation of a new Spring Boot project that utilizes Spring WebFlux. This can be done easily using the Spring Initializr web interface accessible at https://start.spring.io/. On this website, you will select your project's parameters including the type of project (Maven Project or Gradle Project), language (Java, Kotlin, or Groovy), Spring Boot version, project metadata (such as Group, Artifact, Name, and Description), and dependencies.

For a Spring WebFlux project, it is essential to include the `Spring Reactive Web` dependency in your project. This dependency encapsulates the core functionalities of Spring WebFlux. Optionally, you might consider adding other dependencies relevant to your project at this stage, such as `Spring Data Reactive Repositories` for reactive database access, `Reactive Thymeleaf` for server-side HTML rendering in a reactive way, or `Reactive Security` for adding security features to your reactive applications.

After configuring your project's parameters and selecting the necessary dependencies, you can generate the project. Spring Initializr will create a zip file containing the project skeleton, which you can then import into your IDE. Upon importing the project, you will notice a typical Spring Boot project structure with a main application class annotated with `@SpringBootApplication`, and a `resources` directory containing application properties files.

In your main application class, Spring WebFlux is enabled by default through the `@SpringBootApplication` annotation. However, it is beneficial to understand that behind the scenes, if the Spring WebFlux dependency is present in the project, Spring Boot auto-configures the WebFlux framework using a Netty reactive web server by default. You can opt for another server, such as Tomcat or Jetty, by explicitly defining your choice in the application properties file. However, for optimal use of reactive features, Netty is recommended.

The initial setup concludes with the configuration of application properties. The `application.properties` file, located under the `resources` directory, is where you define properties specific to your application, such as server port, context path, database connection settings, and more. For instance, setting up the server port requires the following entry:

```
server.port=8080
```

This configuration instructs Spring Boot to run the application on port 8080. Various other configurations specific to WebFlux or any other integrated component can be specified here.

To verify the setup, create a simple reactive controller. The controller will demonstrate handling of a GET request in a non-blocking manner. This is accomplished by defining a method within a controller class, annotated with `@RestController` and `@RequestMapping` annotations. Below is an example of such a controller:

```
1    @RestController
2    @RequestMapping("/api")
3    public class SimpleController {
4
5        @GetMapping("/hello")
6        public Mono<String> sayHello() {
7            return Mono.just("Hello, Spring WebFlux!");
8        }
9    }
```

The Mono type represents a reactive type that either emits a single value or completes without emitting any value. This contrasts with traditional Spring MVC controllers that return values directly. In reactive programming, data is wrapped in reactive types like Mono and Flux to operate in a non-blocking fashion.

Finally, to run the Spring Boot application, execute the main method in the main application class, or use the Maven or Gradle command line interface with the command mvn spring-boot:run or gradle bootRun, respectively.

Upon successful application startup, test the /api/hello endpoint using a web browser or a tool like Postman. You should receive a response saying "Hello, Spring WebFlux!", confirming that your Spring WebFlux project setup is correct and operational.

This section has detailed the process of setting up a Spring WebFlux project from scratch, emphasizing the selection of relevant dependencies, project configuration, and a basic test to ensure the setup's correctness. Subsequent sections will delve into more advanced topics, building upon this foundational setup to explore the capabilities and features of Spring WebFlux in creating reactive APIs.

8.3   Creating Reactive Endpoints with Spring WebFlux

Creating reactive endpoints with Spring WebFlux involves understanding the core principles of reactive programming and how these principles are implemented within the Spring Framework. At its heart, reactive programming is about building systems that are asynchronous, non-blocking, and event-driven, capable of handling a large number of concurrent operations efficiently. This section will discuss how to set up and develop reactive endpoints using Spring WebFlux, providing concrete examples and highlighting best practices.

Spring WebFlux introduces a paradigm where data flow and the propagation of changes are the core concepts, as opposed to the traditional synchronous and blocking execution model. To leverage this, one must first become acquainted with a few key components: the Flux and Mono API types from Project Reactor, which are integral to Spring WebFlux. Flux represents a reactive sequence of 0..N items, while Mono represents a single or empty asynchronous value. Both are essential in defining reactive endpoints.

To begin, ensure the project is correctly set up to use Spring WebFlux. This typically involves including the reactive web dependency in your build configuration, which provides support for reactive HTTP and WebSocket clients and servers. With the required dependencies in place, one can start defining reactive endpoints.

Creating a basic reactive endpoint in Spring WebFlux is accomplished within a controller, annotated with @RestController. Within this controller, handler methods are annotated with @GetMapping, @PostMapping, or other relevant HTTP mapping annotations. These handler methods return Mono or Flux types, depending on whether they produce a single value or a stream of values, respectively.

Consider the following example, which defines a simple GET endpoint returning a stream of integers:

```
@RestController
public class NumberController {

    @GetMapping("/numbers")
    public Flux<Integer> getNumbers() {
        return Flux.just(1, 2, 3, 4);
    }
}
```

This endpoint utilizes Flux to return a sequence of integers. When accessed, it produces a non-blocking, asynchronous stream of data.

For endpoints that produce a single value, Mono is used. For example, retrieving a specific item by ID might be defined as follows:

```
@GetMapping("/item/{id}")
public Mono<Item> getItem(@PathVariable String id) {
    return repository.findById(id); // Assuming the repository returns a Mono<Item>
}
```

This reactive approach to defining endpoints facilitates handling a wide array of concurrent requests efficiently, without the overhead of blocking operations or thread context switches.

In addition to simple data retrieval, Spring WebFlux supports a multitude of operations for manipulating data streams, including filtering, transformation, and error handling. Combining these operations enables the development of sophisticated, highly responsive APIs.

For example, applying a transformation to a data stream might look like this:

```
1  @GetMapping("/items/uppercase")
2  public Flux<String> getUppercaseItemNames() {
3      return repository.findAll() // Assuming findAll returns Flux<Item>
4              .map(item -> item.getName().toUpperCase());
5  }
```

This approach of assembling logic through operators on Flux and Mono instances is a hallmark of reactive programming and allows for clear, declarative, and concise code.

Creating reactive endpoints with Spring WebFlux is grounded in leveraging the project Reactor's Flux and Mono to handle data streams reactively. This model facilitates building scalable, efficient, and responsive APIs by embracing an asynchronous, non-blocking execution mode throughout the application. As demonstrated through examples, the process of defining, transforming, and manipulating reactive streams with Spring WebFlux is both straightforward and powerful, showcasing its capability to meet modern application development demands.

8.4 Handling Requests with Server-Side Events (SSE)

Server-Side Events (SSE) represent a server push technology enabling a client to receive automatic updates from a server via HTTP connection. Unlike WebSockets, SSE is designed specifically for unidirectional communication from the server to the client, making it an excellent choice for applications where the server needs to update the web page without requiring any solicitation from the client. In this section, we will discuss implementing SSE with Spring WebFlux for building reactive and efficient applications.

Spring WebFlux provides comprehensive support for SSE through the Flux type of the Project Reactor, which is a key component in developing reactive applications with Spring. To understand how SSE works in

Spring WebFlux, it is essential to first establish how to define a reactive endpoint that produces a stream of events.

To define an SSE endpoint in a Spring WebFlux application, you can return a Flux<ServerSentEvent> from a controller method. Consider the following example:

```
@GetMapping(value = "/stream-events", produces = MediaType.TEXT_EVENT_STREAM_VALUE)
public Flux<ServerSentEvent<String>> streamEvents() {
    return Flux.interval(Duration.ofSeconds(1))
            .map(sequence -> ServerSentEvent.<String>builder()
                .id(String.valueOf(sequence))
                .event("periodic-event")
                .data("SSE - " + LocalTime.now().toString())
                .build());
}
```

In this example, the @GetMapping annotation specifies that this method handles GET requests for the /stream-events path and produces content of type MediaType.TEXT_EVENT_STREAM_VALUE. This media type is crucial for SSE, indicating that the server will send events in a special format understood by the client. The method returns a Flux<ServerSentEvent<String>>, which generates a new event every second. Each event contains a sequence ID, an event type, and the data payload formatted as a string with the current time.

To consume SSE in a client application, a common approach is to use the JavaScript EventSource API, which facilitates receiving events from a server in a web page:

```
var eventSource = new EventSource('/stream-events');
eventSource.onmessage = function(event) {
    console.log('Event: ', event.data);
};
eventSource.addEventListener('periodic-event', function(event) {
    console.log('Periodic Event: ', event.data);
});
```

The EventSource object is instantiated with the URL of the SSE endpoint. It listens for messages using the onmessage handler for generic messages and the addEventListener method for events of type periodic-event. This setup allows the client to perform actions, such as updating the UI, in response to events emitted by the server.

Handling back-pressure is an intrinsic part of building reactive applications, and SSE with Spring WebFlux is no exception. The reactive streams specification underlying Spring WebFlux ensures that the server dynamically adjusts how it generates events based on the client's capacity to consume them. This feature is crucial for ensuring that neither the server nor the client is overwhelmed with data, maintaining application responsiveness and efficiency even under high loads.

In summary, SSE is a powerful technique for implementing server push in reactive applications. Spring WebFlux simplifies the development of SSE endpoints through its support for the Project Reactor's Flux type, allowing developers to create scalable, efficient, and real-time applications. By leveraging SSE, developers can ensure that their applications remain responsive and can dynamically update clients with minimal latency, enhancing the overall user experience.

8.5 Implementing Reactive CRUD Operations

In this section, we will discuss the implementation of Create, Read, Update, and Delete (CRUD) operations using Spring WebFlux. These operations are fundamental for any application that interacts with a database, enabling the manipulation and retrieval of stored data. Spring WebFlux, with its non-blocking and reactive nature, offers a robust framework for handling these operations asynchronously, ensuring quick response times and efficient resource utilization.

To begin with, it's essential to set up a reactive repository interface for the entity class that operations will be performed on. This will leverage Spring Data's reactive support, which offers built-in reactive repository support through Project Reactor types like 'Mono' and 'Flux'.

```
import org.springframework.data.repository.reactive.ReactiveCrudRepository;
public interface ProductRepository extends ReactiveCrudRepository<Product, String>
    {
}
```

Here, 'Product' represents the entity class, and 'String' is the type of its identifier. The 'ReactiveCrudRepository' interface provides basic CRUD operations like save, delete, and find methods that return 'Mono' or 'Flux' types, enabling reactive composition.

Next, we create a service layer that encapsulates the business logic, calling the reactive repository methods. The service methods return 'Mono' or 'Flux' types, as well, providing a reactive API to the controllers.

```
import reactor.core.publisher.Flux;
import reactor.core.publisher.Mono;

public class ProductService {
    private final ProductRepository productRepository;
```

```
6
7    public ProductService(ProductRepository productRepository) {
8        this.productRepository = productRepository;
9    }
10
11   public Mono<Product> createProduct(Product product) {
12       return productRepository.save(product);
13   }
14
15   public Flux<Product> getAllProducts() {
16       return productRepository.findAll();
17   }
18
19   public Mono<Product> getProductById(String id) {
20       return productRepository.findById(id);
21   }
22
23   public Mono<Product> updateProduct(String id, Product product) {
24       return productRepository.findById(id)
25               .flatMap(existingProduct -> {
26                   existingProduct.setName(product.getName());
27                   existingProduct.setPrice(product.getPrice());
28                   return productRepository.save(existingProduct);
29               });
30   }
31
32   public Mono<Void> deleteProduct(String id) {
33       return productRepository.deleteById(id);
34   }
35 }
```

In the controller layer, we build reactive APIs using annotations provided by Spring WebFlux, such as '@RestController' and '@RequestMapping'. The controller methods are annotated with '@GetMapping', '@PostMapping', '@PutMapping', and '@DeleteMapping' to handle HTTP GET, POST, PUT, and DELETE requests, respectively.

```
1  import org.springframework.web.bind.annotation.*;
2
3  @RestController
4  @RequestMapping("/products")
5  public class ProductController {
6      private final ProductService productService;
7
8      public ProductController(ProductService productService) {
9          this.productService = productService;
10     }
11
12     @PostMapping
13     public Mono<Product> createProduct(@RequestBody Product product) {
14         return productService.createProduct(product);
15     }
16
17     @GetMapping
18     public Flux<Product> getAllProducts() {
19         return productService.getAllProducts();
20     }
21
22     @GetMapping("/{id}")
23     public Mono<Product> getProductById(@PathVariable String id) {
```

```
24        return productService.getProductById(id);
25     }
26
27     @PutMapping("/{id}")
28     public Mono<Product> updateProduct(@PathVariable String id, @RequestBody
          Product product) {
29        return productService.updateProduct(id, product);
30     }
31
32     @DeleteMapping("/{id}")
33     public Mono<Void> deleteProduct(@PathVariable String id) {
34        return productService.deleteProduct(id);
35     }
36  }
```

This illustrates a complete reactive flow from the database layer to the controller, utilizing non-blocking operations throughout. Implementing CRUD operations in Spring WebFlux involves utilizing reactive repositories, encapsulating business logic within a service that interacts with these repositories, and finally, creating controller endpoints to handle HTTP requests reactively.

By following this approach, applications can achieve scalability, improve performance, and handle concurrent data streams effectively, making them well-suited for modern web applications with high data throughput requirements.

8.6   Error Handling in Spring WebFlux Applications

Error handling in Spring WebFlux applications is an essential aspect that ensures the robustness and resilience of reactive APIs. Spring WebFlux provides various mechanisms to handle errors gracefully, allowing developers to manage exceptions and maintain a seamless flow of data streams in reactive applications. This chapter discusses strategies for error handling, including the use of the onErrorMap, onErrorResume, and global error handling techniques that are pivotal in developing reactive Spring applications.

Let's start with the reactive stream error handling operators provided by Project Reactor. These operators allow errors to be handled in the data flow without breaking the reactive chain. The onErrorMap operator is used to transform an error into a different exception. For instance, it can be used to map a low-level database exception to a more generic error that can be easily serialized and understood by the client.

201

```
1  flux.onErrorMap(e -> new CustomException("Custom message", e));
```

The above snippet demonstrates how to use the onErrorMap to convert any exception that occurs in the reactive stream into a CustomException.

Another powerful operator for error handling in reactive streams is onErrorResume. It allows the application to provide a fallback strategy in case of errors. This could be returning a default value, or, in the case of APIs, a default response object.

```
1  flux.onErrorResume(e -> Mono.just(new DefaultItem()));
```

This code snippet illustrates the use of onErrorResume to return a default item when an error occurs, ensuring the data stream remains uninterrupted.

For global error handling across the entire Spring WebFlux application, developers can take advantage of Spring's @ControllerAdvice annotation. This approach allows for centralized error handling, avoiding duplication of error handling logic across multiple reactive endpoints.

```
1  @ControllerAdvice
2  public class GlobalErrorHandler {
3
4      @ExceptionHandler(CustomException.class)
5      public ResponseEntity<String> handleCustomException(CustomException e) {
6          return ResponseEntity.status(HttpStatus.BAD_REQUEST).body(e.getMessage());
7      }
8  }
```

Here, a global error handler is defined using @ControllerAdvice. It captures exceptions of type CustomException thrown by any controller within the application and returns a BAD REQUEST response with the custom error message.

Furthermore, Spring WebFlux supports functional endpoint routing, which introduces a different approach to error handling. When utilizing functional endpoints, error handling can be integrated directly into the routing configuration.

```
1  RouterFunction<ServerResponse> route = RouterFunctions
2      .route(RequestPredicates.GET("/endpoint"), request ->
3          ServerResponse.ok().body(flux, Item.class)
4          .onErrorResume(e -> ServerResponse.status(HttpStatus.INTERNAL_SERVER_ERROR).
                   build())
5      );
```

The above example demonstrates configuring an endpoint with functional routing and incorporating `onErrorResume` directly. This enables immediate handling of errors within the route definition, providing a concise way to manage exceptions.

Error handling in Spring WebFlux applications is multifaceted, offering a variety of tools and strategies to effectively manage exceptions and maintain the integrity of data streams. By utilizing operators such as `onErrorMap` and `onErrorResume`, along with global error handling mechanisms and functional routing capabilities, developers can ensure that their reactive Spring applications are not only robust and resilient but also provide meaningful feedback to clients in the event of errors.

8.7   Functional Endpoint Routing in WebFlux

Functional Endpoint Routing in Spring WebFlux is a powerful and flexible mechanism for defining API routes and their handling functions in a more functional style, as compared to the annotation-driven approach. This model promotes a cleaner separation of concerns and enhances the composability of routing configurations. It allows developers to configure routes in a more expressive manner, leveraging Java's functional programming capabilities.

In traditional Spring MVC or even in the annotated controllers of Spring WebFlux, endpoints are typically defined using annotations like `@GetMapping` or `@PostMapping` on methods within controller classes. While this approach is straightforward and familiar to many developers, it intertwines the routing information with the business logic, making it less modular and, in some cases, harder to maintain.

The functional routing API in WebFlux, on the other hand, defines routes as a separate concern, explicitly tying URLs to handler functions without the need for annotations on controller methods. This approach enables a clear and concise way to define routing rules and handler functions that can be easily composed and dynamically modified if needed.

To start defining functional endpoints, one must become familiar with the two primary components of this model: the `RouterFunction` and the `HandlerFunction`.

- A RouterFunction is responsible for associating a request to a HandlerFunction based on specific criteria (e.g., path, HTTP method).

- A HandlerFunction is essentially a function that takes a ServerRequest and returns a Mono<ServerResponse>. This function contains the actual code to handle the request.

An essential construct for creating routes in a functional style is the RouterFunctions class, which provides static methods for route definition. Similarly, HandlerFunctions is a helper class for creating handler functions.

Let's look at a simple example to illustrate the definition of functional endpoints. Assume we are tasked with creating a basic API that returns a greeting message.

```
1  RouterFunction<ServerResponse> route =
2      RouterFunctions.route(RequestPredicates.GET("/greet"),
3          request -> ServerResponse.ok().body(BodyInserters.fromValue("Hello, WebFlux!
              ")));
```

In this example, we define a route for HTTP GET requests to the path "/greet". The associated handler function creates a successful (200 OK) response, including a greeting message in the body.

It's also possible to organize routes more efficiently by grouping them. For instance, you can define multiple related routes together, which can contribute to cleaner code, especially for larger applications.

```
1  RouterFunction<ServerResponse> routerFunction =
2      RouterFunctions
3          .route(RequestPredicates.GET("/greet"), request ->
4              ServerResponse.ok().body(BodyInserters.fromValue("Hello, WebFlux!")))
5          .andRoute(RequestPredicates.GET("/goodbye"), request ->
6              ServerResponse.ok().body(BodyInserters.fromValue("Goodbye, WebFlux!")));
```

In this extended example, we define an additional route for the path "/goodbye" alongside the initial greeting route, demonstrating how routes can be chained together to build a comprehensive routing table in a functional style.

It's worth noting that the functional endpoint routing model is entirely optional within Spring WebFlux. Developers can choose between this model and the more traditional annotated controllers based on the specific needs of their applications or personal preference. However, adopting this model might lead to a more organized and modular codebase, particularly for applications with complex routing requirements.

By leveraging the capabilities of the functional routing in WebFlux, developers can significantly enhance the modularity, readability, and maintainability of their reactive Spring applications.

8.8 Securing Spring WebFlux APIs

Securing APIs is crucial to protect resources from unauthorized access and ensure that data is safe. Spring WebFlux integrates seamlessly with Spring Security, a powerful and customizable authentication and access-control framework, to secure reactive applications. This section will discuss configuring Spring Security in a Spring WebFlux application, implementing authentication, enforcing authorization rules, and applying best practices for securing reactive APIs.

Firstly, to add Spring Security to a Spring WebFlux project, the `spring-boot-starter-security` dependency must be included in the project's build configuration file. This automatically configures a basic security setup, which can be customized according to specific requirements.

```
1  <dependency>
2      <groupId>org.springframework.boot</groupId>
3      <artifactId>spring-boot-starter-security</artifactId>
4  </dependency>
```

With Spring Security in place, the next step is to create a configuration class to customize the security settings. This involves extending the `WebSecurityConfigurerAdapter` class and overriding the `configure` method. However, for reactive applications, `SecurityWebFilterChain` must be used to configure security rules. The `SecurityWebFilterChain` is a functional way to specify security rules, ideal for reactive applications.

```
1   @Configuration
2   @EnableWebFluxSecurity
3   public class SecurityConfig {
4
5       @Bean
6       public SecurityWebFilterChain springSecurityFilterChain(ServerHttpSecurity http
            ) {
7           http
8               .authorizeExchange()
9               .pathMatchers("/api/public/**").permitAll()
10              .pathMatchers("/api/secure/**").authenticated()
11              .and()
12              .httpBasic().and()
13              .formLogin();
14          return http.build();
```

```
15      }
16  }
```

In this configuration, public endpoints are accessible without authentication, while secure endpoints require authentication. Spring Security supports basic authentication and form login by default, as illustrated above, but can be extended to support JWT, OAuth2, and other authentication mechanisms.

Now, let's delve into implementing authentication. Spring Security supports a variety of authentication mechanisms. For reactive APIs, authentication data is often encapsulated in JSON Web Tokens (JWT). The use of `ReactiveAuthenticationManager` allows the authentication process to be non-blocking and to fit into the reactive programming model. The authentication manager validates the incoming JWT, ensures it's not expired, and extracts the user details and authorities.

Authorization, on the other hand, refers to the process of deciding whether an authenticated user has access to a particular resource. In Spring WebFlux, this can be achieved using method-level security annotations such as `@PreAuthorize` or by configuring the access rules within the `SecurityWebFilterChain`. For fine-grained control over endpoints, method-level security is very effective.

```
1  @PostMapping("/api/secure/data")
2  @PreAuthorize("hasRole('ADMIN')")
3  public Mono<ResponseEntity<Object>> secureData(@RequestBody Data data) {
4      // Implementation omitted
5  }
```

In this example, only users with the ADMIN role can access the secure endpoint. The use of reactive types like `Mono` and `Flux` ensures that the method fits well into the reactive processing model.

Lastly, to enhance API security, consider the following best practices:

- Enforce HTTPS to secure data in transit.

- Validate and sanitize input data to prevent injections and other attacks.

- Use CORS to restrict resources to trusted domains only.

- Implement rate limiting to protect against brute-force attacks.

- Keep dependencies up-to-date to mitigate known vulnerabilities.

206

Securing Spring WebFlux APIs involves configuring Spring Security to fit the reactive programming model, implementing authentication and authorization, and adhering to security best practices. By taking these steps, developers can build secure, resilient, and scalable reactive APIs that safeguard sensitive information and resources.

8.9 Integrating Reactive Client with WebFlux

In this section, we will discuss the integration of a reactive client with Spring WebFlux. For applications to fully leverage the non-blocking nature of reactive programming, both the server and the client components must support reactive streams. Spring WebFlux includes the WebClient class, a non-blocking, reactive client for performing HTTP requests. The main advantage of using WebClient over traditional blocking clients is its ability to operate in event-driven environments, providing more efficient resource utilization and improved overall performance.

The use of WebClient in a Spring WebFlux application involves several key steps: configuring the WebClient instance, creating HTTP requests, handling responses, and incorporating error handling.

Configuring WebClient: Before making any requests, it is necessary to create and configure an instance of `WebClient`. Configuration options include setting the base URL, default headers, error handling strategies, and more. Here is an example of creating a `WebClient` bean with a base URL:

```
@Bean
public WebClient webClient(WebClient.Builder builder) {
    return builder.baseUrl("http://example.org/api")
                .defaultHeader(HttpHeaders.CONTENT_TYPE, MediaType.
                    APPLICATION_JSON_VALUE)
                .build();
}
```

Creating HTTP Requests: With the `WebClient` instance configured, requests can be made to various endpoints. The WebClient provides methods for each HTTP method (e.g., get, post, put, delete). An important aspect of these methods is their return type, `Mono` or `Flux`, representing a single or multiple responses, respectively. Here is an example of a GET request that retrieves a list of items:

```
Flux<Item> items = webClient.get()
                .uri("/items")
                .retrieve()
```

207

```
4              .bodyToFlux(Item.class);
```

Handling Responses: The `retrieve` method of `WebClient` provides a way to handle the response body. The `bodyToMono` and `bodyToFlux` methods are used to deserialize the response body into objects. For example, to retrieve an item by id, one might use:

```
1  Mono<Item> item = webClient.get()
2                      .uri("/items/{id}", itemId)
3                      .retrieve()
4                      .bodyToMono(Item.class);
```

Handling errors involves specifying actions or fallbacks in cases where the response indicates a failure. WebClient supports various mechanisms for error handling, such as the `onStatus` method, which allows for handling specific HTTP status codes:

```
1  webClient.get()
2      .uri("/items/{id}", itemId)
3      .retrieve()
4      .onStatus(HttpStatus::is4xxClientError, response -> Mono.error(new
           ClientException("Client Error")))
5      .onStatus(HttpStatus::is5xxServerError, response -> Mono.error(new
           ServerException("Server Error")))
6      .bodyToMono(Item.class);
```

Integrating Reactive Client with WebFlux: The integration of a reactive client within a WebFlux application allows for creating fully reactive systems that can communicate over HTTP. This capability is particularly useful in microservices architecture, where services need to make non-blocking calls to other services. For instance, a WebFlux service handling user requests might need to fetch data from another service:

```
1  Mono<User> fetchUserData(String userId) {
2      return webClient.get()
3                  .uri("/users/{userId}", userId)
4                  .retrieve()
5                  .bodyToMono(User.class);
6  }
```

To summarize, integrating a reactive client with Spring WebFlux enhances the reactive capabilities of an application, enabling efficient, non-blocking HTTP calls. By utilizing WebClient for HTTP communication, applications can achieve higher scalability and responsiveness, essential qualities for modern web applications. Throughout this process, it is critical to effectively configure the WebClient, handle request and response data reactively, and implement robust error handling mechanisms.

8.10 WebFlux and Database Reactive Transactions

In dealing with database transactions within a reactive context, it is foundational to grasp the intricacies involved in applying classical transaction management strategies to non-blocking, event-driven paradigms. Traditional synchronous transaction management techniques do not directly translate to the reactive world. This section elucidates the challenges and solutions in implementing database transactions within Spring WebFlux applications, specifically focusing on reactive transactions.

In reactive programming, data streams are processed in a non-blocking manner, necessitating a reevaluation of transaction boundaries and their management. Reactive transaction management in Spring is facilitated through the Reactor context, ensuring that transactions are handled in a reactive flow. The TransactionOperator is pivotal in this context, acting as a wrapper around the reactive sequences to apply transactional boundaries.

To begin, configuring a reactive transaction manager is essential. Spring WebFlux supports Reactive Transaction Managers tailored for reactive data access repositories such as R2DBC, Reactive MongoDB, and others. An example is the R2dbcTransactionManager for databases supporting R2DBC, which is a specification designed for reactive database access.

```
1  @Bean
2  public ReactiveTransactionManager transactionManager(ConnectionFactory
       connectionFactory) {
3    return new R2dbcTransactionManager(connectionFactory);
4  }
```

In this code snippet, a Bean is defined to provide a ReactiveTransactionManager configured with an R2DBC ConnectionFactory. Such a factory is responsible for creating connections to the database in a non-blocking manner.

Using the TransactionOperator is critical for declaratively managing transaction boundaries around a reactive stream. The TransactionOperator can be created by passing the ReactiveTransactionManager instance to its static create method. Once an operator is available, it can wrap a reactive pipeline within a transactional context.

```
1  TransactionOperator operator =
2      TransactionOperator.create(transactionManager);
3
4  Mono<Void> transactionalMono = operator.transactional(myReactiveRepository.save(
       entity));
```

This code demonstrates wrapping a reactive repository save operation within a transaction. The transactional method ensures that the operation is executed within the scope of a reactive transaction, committing or rolling back based on the completion signal of the reactive pipeline.

Error handling within reactive transactions is also an area that requires attention. When an error occurs within a transactional reactive pipeline, it is essential to rollback the transaction to maintain data consistency. The reactive programming model handles error propagation and handling through its event-driven architecture, allowing for clean and concise error handling mechanisms.

```
1  operator.transactional(
2      myReactiveRepository.save(entity)
3      .doOnError(e -> log.error("Error saving entity", e))
4  ).onErrorResume(e -> Mono.just(new EntityFallback()))
```

In this modified example, doOnError is used to log any errors that occur during the save operation, while onErrorResume provides a mechanism to return a fallback value in case of errors, ensuring the reactive stream can gracefully handle failures within the transaction.

Managing reactive database transactions within Spring WebFlux requires leveraging specific transaction management strategies that respect the non-blocking nature of the framework. The ReactiveTransactionManager and TransactionOperator play crucial roles in facilitating this process, allowing developers to define transactional boundaries within reactive streams effectively. Through careful management of transactions within a reactive context, applications can maintain data integrity and consistency, even in the face of errors, making Spring WebFlux a robust choice for reactive microservices and applications interacting with databases.

8.11 Building Real-time WebSocket APIs with WebFlux

WebSocket protocol facilitates full-duplex communication channels over a single, long-standing connection, enabling the server to send

210

real-time updates to clients without the need for repeated polling. The integration of WebSocket with Spring WebFlux offers a powerful mechanism for building reactive, real-time web applications. This section will discuss the essential steps to construct and deploy WebSocket APIs using Spring WebFlux, highlighting key configurations, handling of messaging semantics, and ensuring efficient resource management.

The initial phase in setting up WebSocket support in a Spring WebFlux project involves dependencies inclusion. Spring Boot's starter-webflux dependency inherently supports WebSocket, but for explicit WebSocket configurations, including the spring-boot-starter-websocket is recommended. This ensures the availability of WebSocket-specific annotations and functional programming models for use within the application.

```
1  <dependency>
2      <groupId>org.springframework.boot</groupId>
3      <artifactId>spring-boot-starter-websocket</artifactId>
4  </dependency>
```

After incorporating the necessary dependency, configuring a WebSocket handler is the next crucial step. A WebSocket handler is responsible for managing WebSocket connections, including opening, message exchange, and closing of connections. Spring Framework provides the `WebSocketHandler` interface, requiring the overriding of the `handle` method. This method serves as the entry point for processing incoming WebSocket messages.

```
1  @Component
2  public class ReactiveWebSocketHandler implements WebSocketHandler {
3
4      @Override
5      public Mono<Void> handle(WebSocketSession session) {
6          return session.send(session.receive()
7              .map(msg -> session.textMessage("Echo: " + msg.getPayloadAsText())));
8      }
9  }
```

The above example demonstrates a simple echo handler, returning received messages prefixed with "Echo:". This illustrates the reactive programming model within the WebSocket context, employing `Mono` and `Flux` for handling single and stream of events, respectively.

With the WebSocket handler defined, mapping this handler to a specific URL endpoint is achieved through WebSocket configuration. The Spring Framework's `WebSocketHandlerRegistry` facilitates the registration of handlers and their corresponding URL mappings.

```
1  @Configuration
```

```
2   @EnableWebSocket
3   public class WebSocketConfig implements WebSocketConfigurer {
4
5       @Autowired
6       private WebSocketHandler webSocketHandler;
7
8       @Override
9       public void registerWebSocketHandlers(WebSocketHandlerRegistry registry) {
10          registry.addHandler(webSocketHandler, "/ws/echo").setAllowedOrigins("*");
11      }
12  }
```

The @EnableWebSocket annotation activates WebSocket processing capability within Spring's web application context, empowering WebSocketConfigurer to define handler mappings. The example above maps the echo handler to the /ws/echo URL path, allowing cross-origin requests with setAllowedOrigins("*").

In WebSocket-based communication, managing client connections and broadcasting messages to multiple subscribers are common requirements. Spring WebFlux and Project Reactor provide extensive support for such scenarios. Utilizing Flux to represent a stream of messages, one can create publisher-subscriber models where messages are broadcasted to all connected clients.

```
1   private final FluxProcessor<String, String> broadcaster = DirectProcessor.create().
        serialize();
2   private final FluxSink<String> sink = broadcaster.sink();
3
4   public void broadcast(String message) {
5       sink.next(message);
6   }
```

In this construct, DirectProcessor serves as a hot source of messages, emitting data to currently subscribed clients. The sink is used to push messages into the processor, effectively broadcasting to all subscribers. Incorporating this mechanism within a WebSocket handler allows the implementation of various real-time messaging features, such as live chat rooms or data dashboards.

Leveraging Spring WebFlux to build WebSocket APIs enables the creation of highly responsive and real-time web applications. By following the outlined steps—dependency inclusion, WebSocket handler implementation, and handler registration—developers can efficiently integrate real-time communication capabilities into their Spring WebFlux projects. Careful consideration of messaging semantics and connection management is essential to ensure optimal performance and resource utilization. Through reactive programming principles and Spring's comprehensive support for WebSocket communication, developers are

212

well-equipped to tackle the challenges of developing modern, real-time web applications.

8.12 Performance Monitoring and Optimization for WebFlux APIs

Performance monitoring and optimization play critical roles in the lifecycle of any Reactive API developed with Spring WebFlux. Given the non-blocking and asynchronous nature of these applications, traditional methods for monitoring and optimization might not always yield the expected insights or outcomes. It is imperative to approach these tasks with techniques and tools specifically designed or adapted for reactive programming paradigms to ensure the APIs remain responsive, resilient, and efficiently scalable under varying loads.

Firstly, understanding the key metrics for monitoring is essential. These include, but are not limited to, the number of active threads, memory usage, response times, error rates, and back-pressure events. Tools like Micrometer, integrated within Spring Boot Actuator, provide a rich set of functionalities to capture these metrics. Micrometer acts as an application metrics facade that supports numerous monitoring systems, allowing developers to instrument their code with dimensional metrics with minimal overhead.

Monitoring the number of active threads and memory usage is vital in a reactive environment. Due to the non-blocking nature of WebFlux, applications can serve numerous concurrent requests with significantly fewer threads compared to traditional servlet-based applications. However, it is still possible to encounter resource leaks or inefficient use of system resources, which can degrade performance.

For monitoring active threads and memory usage, consider the following example:

```
@Bean
MeterBinder processMemoryMetrics() {
    return new ProcessMemoryMetrics();
}

@Bean
MeterBinder processThreadMetrics() {
    return new ProcessThreadMetrics();
}
```

The above code snippets demonstrate how to register custom metrics for monitoring process memory and thread usage using Micrometer within a Spring WebFlux application.

Response times and error rates are direct indicators of the API's health and user experience. Tracking these metrics allows developers to identify slow-performing endpoints or areas within the application where errors frequently occur. This insight facilitates targeted optimizations to improve performance and reliability. Tools like Spring Boot Actuator in combination with Micrometer effortlessly expose these metrics, which can then be visualized using platforms such as Prometheus and Grafana.

Back-pressure, a crucial component in reactive streams, must be monitored to prevent system overloads by ensuring that producers do not overwhelm consumers. Reactive systems should gracefully handle back-pressure by scaling horizontally or throttling requests, rather than simply failing. Monitoring tools that can tap into the reactive stream's back-pressure mechanisms are vital for observing system behavior under load and making necessary adjustments.

For effective performance optimization, identifying and addressing bottlenecks is key. Profiling tools that support reactive applications can help in pinpointing issues such as thread contention, blocking calls, and inefficient resource utilization. Techniques such as implementing caching at strategic points, optimizing database queries, and fine-tuning the number of threads allocated for non-blocking tasks are essential strategies.

Regarding database interactions, leveraging non-blocking drivers and ensuring the database interactions themselves do not become the bottleneck is crucial. For example, when using R2DBC with a reactive repository, you can efficiently manage database connections and operations in a non-blocking manner, enhancing performance.

Monitoring and optimizing the performance of Spring WebFlux APIs require a deep understanding of reactive programming principles, as well as the effective use of specialized tools and techniques. By focusing on critical metrics, employing the right tools for monitoring, and adopting a proactive approach to optimization, developers can significantly enhance the responsiveness, efficiency, and scalability of their reactive APIs. Ensuring that these APIs can handle the demands of today's data-driven applications.

Chapter 9

Reactive Database Access with R2DBC

R2DBC pioneers the reactive access to SQL databases, bridging the gap between the traditional blocking nature of database interactions and the non-blocking, event-driven paradigms of reactive programming. It provides a robust framework for managing database operations asynchronously, facilitating scalable and efficient data access patterns. This chapter delves into the essentials of configuring and utilizing R2DBC within reactive applications, covering connection management, executing CRUD operations reactively, and transaction management. Through practical examples and discussions, it equips developers with the knowledge to harness reactive database access, significantly enhancing the responsiveness and performance of applications that rely on SQL data stores.

9.1 Introduction to R2DBC

Reactive Programming constitutes a paradigm shift in how developers think about and handle asynchronous data streams and event-driven programming. Within this paradigm, R2DBC (Reactive Relational Database Connectivity) emerges as a significant development, specifically designed to extend reactive programming capabilities to SQL database interactions. Unlike traditional JDBC (Java Database Connectivity), which operates on a blocking model, R2DBC is non-blocking and fully reactive. This characteristic fundamentally transforms the way applications interact with databases, particularly in the context of scalable, high-performance applications.

Let's start with understanding the core issue R2DBC addresses. Applications today demand high responsiveness and non-blocking I/O operations to handle large volumes of concurrent users and transactions efficiently. The blocking nature of JDBC, where threads wait idly for database operations to complete, is ill-suited for these requirements. It leads to inefficient resource utilization, as a significant portion of system resources is dedicated to idle threads during database I/O operations. In contrast, R2DBC operates on a non-blocking model, ensuring threads can be freed up for other tasks while waiting for database operations to conclude, thus significantly improving resource utilization and application throughput.

To dive deeper into the mechanics of R2DBC, it employs a push model where data is emitted by the database driver as and when it becomes available, contrary to the pull model used by JDBC, where data is requested explicitly. This model aligns perfectly with reactive streams specifications, enabling backpressure—a mechanism where the consumer can signal the producer about how much data it can handle—to be naturally integrated into database interactions. This ensures that applications remain responsive under load without overwhelming system resources.

Integrating R2DBC into applications, particularly those built with the Spring Framework, is streamlined by the inherent support for reactive programming in Spring Boot. The Spring Data R2DBC module provides a high-level abstraction for R2DBC operations, simplifying the complexity involved in reactive database access. It allows for a seamless integration of R2DBC within the Spring ecosystem, leveraging the capabilities of Spring Data to perform database operations reactively.

In this section, we will discuss the configuration and usage patterns of R2DBC with Spring Boot. The configuration involves setting up R2DBC connection factories, which are responsible for creating and managing database connections in a non-blocking manner. These connection factories can be configured programmatically or via application properties, enabling flexibility in how connections are managed.

```
1  // Example of configuring a ConnectionFactory in Spring Boot
2  @Configuration
3  public class R2dbcConfiguration {
4
5      @Bean
6      public ConnectionFactory connectionFactory() {
```

```
7       return ConnectionFactories.get(
8           ConnectionFactoryOptions.builder()
9               .option(DRIVER, "pool")
10              .option(PROTOCOL, "postgresql") // Example for PostgreSQL
11              .option(HOST, "localhost")
12              .option(PORT, "5432")
13              .option(USER, "user")
14              .option(PASSWORD, "password")
15              .option(DATABASE, "reactive_db")
16              .build());
17      }
18 }
```

This configuration highlights the flexibility and ease with which R2DBC can be integrated into Spring applications, enabling developers to focus on business logic rather than boilerplate code for database connectivity.

Utilizing R2DBC for executing CRUD operations reactively further exemplifies the shift from imperative to reactive programming. Operations that would traditionally block the executing thread now return immediately, with results being processed asynchronously as they become available.

```
1  // Example of a simple reactive query with R2DBC
2  Mono<Person> findPersonById(ConnectionFactory connectionFactory, Integer id) {
3      return Mono.from(connectionFactory.create())
4          .flatMap(conn -> Mono.from(conn
5              .createStatement("SELECT * FROM person WHERE id = :id")
6              .bind("id", id)
7              .execute()))
8          .flatMap(result -> Mono.from(result
9              .map((row, meta) -> new Person(row.get("id", Integer.class),
10                                  row.get("name", String.class)))));
11 }
```

The example above demonstrates a reactive query to fetch a person by their ID, leveraging R2DBC's API to execute a non-blocking database operation and process the results reactively.

R2DBC represents a revolutionary approach to database interaction within the realm of reactive programming, breaking the traditional blocking barriers of JDBC and enabling efficient, scalable, and responsive applications. By leveraging R2DBC, developers can harness the power of reactive streams for database operations, paving the way for a new era of application performance and scalability.

217

9.2 Setting up R2DBC with Spring Boot

Let's start with the fundamental steps required to integrate R2DBC into a Spring Boot application. R2DBC, as a specification, allows reactive programming with SQL databases, enabling developers to manage database interactions in a non-blocking manner. Spring Boot, with its auto-configuration capabilities, simplifies the process of setting up R2DBC, making it accessible even to those new to reactive programming principles.

First, to include R2DBC in a Spring Boot project, dependencies must be added to the project's build configuration. Assuming Maven is the build tool being used, the following dependencies need to be incorporated in the pom.xml file:

```
1   <dependency>
2       <groupId>org.springframework.boot</groupId>
3       <artifactId>spring-boot-starter-data-r2dbc</artifactId>
4   </dependency>
5   <dependency>
6       <groupId>io.r2dbc</groupId>
7       <artifactId>r2dbc-pool</artifactId>
8   </dependency>
9   <dependency>
10      <groupId>io.r2dbc</groupId>
11      <artifactId>r2dbc-driver-name</artifactId>
12      <version>driver-version</version>
13  </dependency>
```

Here, the spring-boot-starter-data-r2dbc starter includes the necessary Spring Data R2DBC bindings. The r2dbc-pool dependency is for connection pooling, and the last dependency should be replaced with the specific R2DBC driver for the SQL database being used, such as r2dbc-mysql or r2dbc-postgresql, along with its version.

Next, configuring the database connection is essential. This involves specifying the URL, username, password, and other relevant settings specific to the database and the R2DBC driver. These configurations are typically placed in the application.properties or application.yml file of the Spring Boot project. An example configuration for a PostgreSQL database might look like this:

```
1   spring
2     r2dbc
3       url r2dbcpostgresql//localhost5432/databaseName
4       username user
5       password password
6       pool
7         initial-size 5
```

```
8 │    max-size 20
```

The `url` field follows the R2DBC URL scheme, which includes the database type, host, port, and database name. The `pool` configuration is optional but recommended for configuring the initial and maximum size of the connection pool.

With dependencies added and configurations set, the application can now leverage the reactive capabilities of R2DBC. For instance, to perform a simple query using R2DBC's `DatabaseClient`, one could add the following code snippet to a service class:

```
1  @Autowired
2  DatabaseClient databaseClient;
3
4  public Flux<String> findNamesByTitle(String title) {
5      return databaseClient.sql("SELECT name FROM people WHERE title = :title")
6              .bind("title", title)
7              .map((row, metadata) -> row.get("name", String.class))
8              .all();
9  }
```

This example uses the `DatabaseClient` to execute a SQL query reactively, binding a parameter to avoid SQL injection, and mapping the results to a reactive stream of names. The return type `Flux<String>` indicates a reactive stream of strings, which will be emitted as query results become available.

Setting up R2DBC with Spring Boot involves adding specific dependencies, configuring database connection properties, and then using the provided reactive APIs to interact with the database. By following these steps, developers can efficiently set up a reactive database access layer in their Spring Boot applications. This setup not only bolsters the scalability and performance of the application by utilizing non-blocking database interactions but also aligns with the reactive programming paradigm that is increasingly prevalent in modern software development.

9.3 Configuring Database Connections

Proper configuration of database connections is pivotal in harnessing the power of R2DBC for reactive database access. This section will discuss the essentials of establishing and managing database connections using R2DBC within the context of Spring Boot applications. A well-configured connection setup ensures efficient utilization of resources, enhancing the application's responsiveness and scalability.

In R2DBC, the connection factory is the core interface responsible for creating connections to the database. Spring Boot simplifies the configuration of the connection factory through application properties and auto-configuration mechanisms. First, it is necessary to include the R2DBC starter and database driver dependencies in the pom.xml or build.gradle file of the Spring Boot project. For instance, to use PostgreSQL, one might include:

```
1  <dependency>
2      <groupId>org.springframework.boot</groupId>
3      <artifactId>spring-boot-starter-data-r2dbc</artifactId>
4  </dependency>
5  <dependency>
6      <groupId>io.r2dbc</groupId>
7      <artifactId>r2dbc-postgresql</artifactId>
8      <scope>runtime</scope>
9  </dependency>
```

Following the addition of dependencies, the next step involves configuring the database connection properties in the application.properties or application.yml file. These properties include the database URL, username, and password, among others. An example configuration for a PostgreSQL database could be:

```
1  spring.r2dbc.url=r2dbc:postgresql://localhost:5432/mydatabase
2  spring.r2dbc.username=myuser
3  spring.r2dbc.password=mypassword
```

This configuration instructs Spring Boot to auto-configure a connection factory that connects to the specified database using the provided credentials. The URL format usually follows the pattern r2dbc:database://host:port/database, where the database-specific segment might vary depending on the database being used.

Connection pooling is a critical aspect to consider for managing database connections efficiently, especially in high-load scenarios. Connection pools manage a set of connections that can be reused, reducing the overhead of establishing connections for each database operation. R2DBC offers integration with connection pool libraries, such as R2DBC Pool. To utilize connection pooling, additional dependencies must be added, and the pool settings must be configured adequately. For instance:

```
1  <dependency>
2      <groupId>io.r2dbc</groupId>
```

220

```
3      <artifactId>r2dbc-pool</artifactId>
4    </dependency>
```

And the corresponding pool settings in `application.properties` might include:

```
1    spring.r2dbc.pool.initial-size=5
2    spring.r2dbc.pool.max-size=20
3    spring.r2dbc.pool.max-idle-time=30m
```

These settings configure the initial size of the connection pool, the maximum number of connections the pool can contain, and the maximum idle time for a connection before it is closed, respectively.

Ensuring secure and efficient database connection management involves monitoring and fine-tuning the connection settings based on the application's specific requirements and the operational environment. Developers should consider factors like connection timeout settings, the expected load, and the database's performance characteristics when configuring the connection pool. Additionally, it is beneficial to leverage Spring Boot's actuator endpoints to monitor connection pool metrics and identify potential connection management issues in real time.

Finally, error handling and exception translation mechanism provided by Spring Framework can be utilized to handle database access errors gracefully. Spring Data R2DBC integrates with Spring's error handling infrastructure, translating database-specific exceptions into a consistent, Spring-specific DataAccessException hierarchy. This abstraction facilitates error handling and allows developers to write cleaner, more portable error handling code.

Configuring database connections using R2DBC in Spring Boot applications involves specifying connection properties, managing dependencies, and optionally configuring connection pooling for efficient resource utilization. By adhering to best practices for connection management and monitoring, developers can ensure that reactive applications leveraging R2DBC maintain high performance and scalability, even under significant load.

9.4 Implementing CRUD Operations with R2DBC

Implementing CRUD (Create, Read, Update, Delete) operations is a fundamental aspect of interacting with databases in any application. With R2DBC, these operations are executed reactively, which requires a different approach than the traditional blocking model. This section will discuss how to perform these operations using R2DBC within a Spring Boot application.

Firstly, to enable R2DBC in a Spring Boot application, one must include the necessary dependencies for R2DBC along with the database driver in the pom.xml or build.gradle file. This setup allows Spring Boot to configure the reactive database context automatically.

```
1  <dependency>
2      <groupId>org.springframework.boot</groupId>
3      <artifactId>spring-boot-starter-data-r2dbc</artifactId>
4  </dependency>
5  <dependency>
6      <groupId>io.r2dbc</groupId>
7      <artifactId>r2dbc-postgresql</artifactId>
8      <version>LATEST_VERSION</version>
9  </dependency>
```

After configuring the dependencies, the next step involves creating a repository interface for your entity. This interface extends the ReactiveCrudRepository<T, ID> interface provided by Spring Data R2DBC, where T is the entity type and ID is the type of the entity's identifier.

```
1  public interface UserRepository extends ReactiveCrudRepository<User, Long> {
2  }
```

With the repository in place, implementing CRUD operations becomes straightforward. Spring Data R2DBC provides a robust set of reactive methods for common operations. Below are examples of executing these operations.

Create: To insert a new entity into the database, you can use the save method provided by the ReactiveCrudRepository.

```
1  User user = new User("John", "Doe");
2  userRepository.save(user).subscribe();
```

Read: For reading data from the database, several methods are available, such as findById(ID id) for fetching a single entity and findAll() for fetching all entities.

```
1  Mono<User> user = userRepository.findById(1L);
2  Flux<User> users = userRepository.findAll();
```

Update: Updating an entity involves fetching it from the database, modifying its properties, and then saving it back to the database.

```
1  userRepository.findById(1L)
2      .map(user -> {
3          user.setLastName("Smith");
4          return user;
5      })
6      .flatMap(userRepository::save)
7      .subscribe();
```

Delete: The delete method can be used to remove an entity from the database either by passing the entity itself or its identifier.

```
1  userRepository.deleteById(1L).subscribe();
```

It's important to note that all the CRUD operations return a Mono or Flux instance, representing a single or multiple values over time, respectively. These types are fundamental to Reactor, the reactive library used by Spring WebFlux and R2DBC.

To conclude, implementing CRUD operations with R2DBC in a Spring Boot application is a straightforward process thanks to the abstractions provided by Spring Data R2DBC. By leveraging these reactive patterns, applications can achieve better scalability and responsiveness, especially in I/O-bound operations like database access. Understanding these examples and integrating them into your application can significantly improve how it interacts with SQL databases reactively.

9.5 Advanced Query Techniques

In this section, we will discuss the application of advanced query techniques using R2DBC. These techniques enhance the capability to manage complex data retrieval and manipulation scenarios within a reactive programming context. Given R2DBC's non-blocking nature, these advanced methods ensure efficient data access patterns, leveraging the full potential of reactive programming to handle SQL databases.

The primary focus here will be on dynamic queries, batch operations, streaming results, and the usage of stored procedures. Each of these techniques addresses specific scenarios and challenges that emerge when dealing with large and complex datasets in a reactive application.

Dynamic Queries

Dynamic queries enable the construction of SQL queries at runtime based on various conditions, such as user inputs or application states. This flexibility is critical in scenarios where the query structure is not known at compile time. In R2DBC, dynamic queries can be efficiently managed using the R2DBC Entity Template or the DatabaseClient API.

```
1  DatabaseClient databaseClient = DatabaseClient.create(connectionFactory);
2  String dynamicQuery = "SELECT * FROM products WHERE category = :category";
3  databaseClient.sql(dynamicQuery)
4      .bind("category", "electronics")
5      .map((row, metadata) -> row.get("name", String.class))
6      .all()
7      .subscribe(product -> System.out.println(product));
```

In the above example, a dynamic query is constructed and executed to fetch products belonging to a specific category. The query parameters are bound at runtime, showcasing the flexibility of dynamic queries.

Batch Operations

Batch operations are essential for executing multiple SQL statements in a single round-trip to the database. This technique is particularly useful for bulk insert or update operations. R2DBC supports batch operations, which can significantly improve performance when dealing with large volumes of data.

```
1  ConnectionFactory connectionFactory = ConnectionFactories.get("r2dbc:pool:mysql://
       localhost/test");
2  connectionFactory.create()
3      .flatMapMany(connection ->
4          connection.createBatch()
5              .add("INSERT INTO products(name, category) VALUES('Product 1', 'Category
                   1')")
6              .add("INSERT INTO products(name, category) VALUES('Product 2', 'Category
                   2')")
7              .execute())
8      .subscribe();
```

The example demonstrates how to create and execute a batch operation with R2DBC. Multiple SQL statements are added to the batch and executed in a non-blocking manner.

Streaming Results

224

Streaming results allows the processing of query results as they become available, rather than waiting for the entire result set. This technique is highly beneficial for processing large datasets, as it reduces memory usage and improves response times.

```
1  databaseClient.sql("SELECT * FROM large_dataset")
2      .map((row, metadata) -> row.get("data", String.class))
3      .all()
4      .subscribe(data -> process(data));
```

In the above example, data from a large dataset is streamed and processed row by row. This approach showcases how R2DBC enables efficient handling of large data volumes in a reactive manner.

Stored Procedures

Using stored procedures combines complex business logic into a single callable unit within the database, which can be invoked from an R2DBC application. This encapsulation of logic at the database level can lead to performance optimizations and cleaner application code.

```
1  databaseClient.sql("CALL FetchProductDetails(:productId)")
2      .bind("productId", 1001)
3      .fetch()
4      .rowsUpdated()
5      .subscribe(count -> System.out.println("Rows updated: " + count));
```

The example illustrates the invocation of a stored procedure with R2DBC, passing a parameter and processing the result. This demonstrates how stored procedures can be seamlessly integrated into a reactive application.

Advanced query techniques in R2DBC unlock a wide range of possibilities for efficiently handling complex data access patterns in reactive applications. By leveraging dynamic queries, batch operations, streaming results, and stored procedures, developers can significantly enhance the scalability, performance, and responsiveness of their applications. It is essential to carefully consider the specific requirements of each use case to effectively apply these techniques and achieve the desired outcomes.

Given R2DBC's evolving landscape, remaining current with its documentation and community best practices is advisable to fully exploit these advanced query capabilities.

9.6   Transaction Management in R2DBC

Transactional support in reactive systems represents a significant shift from the traditional imperative model, with nuances that are essential to grasp for ensuring data consistency and reliability in reactive applications. The R2DBC specification accommodates transactions within the reactive paradigm, providing mechanisms that align well with the non-blocking, event-driven nature of reactive programming.

Transactions in a database context refer to a sequence of operations performed as a single logical unit of work. If any operation within this sequence fails, the transaction is aborted, and the database state is rolled back to its initial state, ensuring data integrity. The traditional blocking nature of transaction management, however, does not fit well within the reactive model, requiring a fresh approach to transactional semantics that R2DBC offers.

In R2DBC, transaction management is inherently non-blocking and leverages the reactive streams model. It allows the initiation, execution, and completion (commit or rollback) of transactions to be handled asynchronously, ensuring that database operations do not block the application's event loop, thereby preserving scalability and responsiveness.

```
1  Mono<Void> transactionalOperation(R2dbcEntityTemplate template) {
2      return template.inTransaction(session -> {
3          return session.insert(new Entity("value1"))
4                  .then(session.update(new Entity("value2")))
5                  .then();
6      });
7  }
```

The above example illustrates a simple transaction that inserts and updates an entity within a single logical operation. Notably, the inTransaction method is utilized to execute multiple database operations reactively within a transaction. The operations are chained using then, indicating the dependency between operations and ensuring that they are executed sequentially within the transaction context.

Error handling within transactions in R2DBC leverages the standard error handling capabilities of Reactor. In the event of an error, the transaction is automatically rolled back, and the error is propagated through the reactive streams to be handled by the application.

```
1  template.inTransaction(session ->
2      session.insert(new Entity("value1"))
3              .then(Mono.error(new RuntimeException("Simulated error")))
```

```
4            .then(session.update(new Entity("value2")))
5    )
6    .onErrorResume(e -> {
7        // Error handling logic
8        return Mono.just(new SomeFallbackResult());
9    });
```

This snippet demonstrates error handling within a transactional context. A simulated error interrupts the transaction, triggering an automatic rollback. The onErrorResume operator allows for the integration of custom error handling logic, providing a path for graceful error recovery or fallback operations.

Implementing transactional boundaries explicitly is also possible in scenarios where finer control over transactions is required. This is achieved by obtaining a transactional Connection and manually beginning and committing transactions.

```
1    connection.beginTransaction()
2        .thenMany(connection
3            .execute("INSERT INTO table (column) VALUES (value)")
4            .then(connection.commitTransaction())
5        )
6        .onErrorResume(transactionError -> connection.rollbackTransaction()
7            .then(Mono.error(transactionError))
8        );
```

In this example, a transaction is started with beginTransaction, followed by the execution of a database operation. The transaction is committed with commitTransaction if the operation succeeds, or rolled back with rollbackTransaction in case of an error. This explicit control over transactions allows developers to fine-tune transactional semantics to satisfy specific requirements.

In summary, R2DBC's transaction management extends the reactive programming model to database operations, offering both declarative and programmatic transaction management strategies. Through reactive streams, R2DBC ensures non-blocking transaction execution, enhancing both the performance and scalability of reactive applications. Developers must understand these transactional semantics and patterns to effectively leverage reactive database access and maintain data consistency and integrity in reactive systems.

9.7   R2DBC with Spring Data

R2DBC with Spring Data seamlessly integrates reactive programming models with relational database access, leveraging the power of Spring Data's repository abstraction to simplify data access layer implementations. This integration brings forth the robustness of Spring Data repositories, combined with the non-blocking architecture of R2DBC, thus providing a comprehensive solution for reactive database access in applications.

To start implementing R2DBC with Spring Data, it is essential to include the necessary dependencies in the project's build configuration file. For a Maven project, the following dependencies need to be added to the pom.xml file:

```
1   <dependency>
2       <groupId>org.springframework.boot</groupId>
3       <artifactId>spring-boot-starter-data-r2dbc</artifactId>
4   </dependency>
5   <dependency>
6       <groupId>io.r2dbc</groupId>
7       <artifactId>r2dbc-spi</artifactId>
8       <version>0.8.4.RELEASE</version>
9   </dependency>
10  <dependency>
11      <groupId>io.r2dbc</groupId>
12      <artifactId>r2dbc-pool</artifactId>
13      <version>0.8.4.RELEASE</version>
14  </dependency>
```

With the dependencies set up, the next step involves configuring the database connection. This is achieved by specifying the connection properties in the application.properties or application.yml file of the Spring Boot application. A typical configuration for a PostgreSQL database might look as follows:

```
1   spring.r2dbc.url=r2dbc:postgresql://localhost:5432/mydatabase
2   spring.r2dbc.username=myusername
3   spring.r2dbc.password=mypassword
4   spring.r2dbc.pool.initial-size=5
5   spring.r2dbc.pool.max-size=20
```

The configuration specifies the URL, username, and password required to establish a connection to the database. Additionally, it configures a connection pool with an initial size of 5 connections, expandable up to 20 connections under load.

After configuring the database connection, the next step involves creating repository interfaces for domain entities. Spring Data

228

R2DBC repositories extend from the `ReactiveCrudRepository` or `R2dbcRepository` interface, providing methods for standard CRUD operations without requiring the implementation code. For instance, a repository interface for a `Person` entity may be defined as follows:

```
public interface PersonRepository extends ReactiveCrudRepository<Person, Long> {
    Flux<Person> findByLastName(String lastName);
}
```

This interface extends `ReactiveCrudRepository`, specifying `Person` as the domain type and `Long` as the ID type. It also defines a custom query method `findByLastName`, which returns a `Flux<Person>` reactive stream for each person with the matching last name.

Apart from standard CRUD operations, Spring Data R2DBC supports complex query definitions using the `@Query` annotation. This feature allows for specifying custom SQL queries directly within the repository interface. For example:

```
@Query("SELECT * FROM person WHERE age >= :age")
Flux<Person> findPersonsOlderThanAge(@Param("age") int age);
```

This query method retrieves persons older than a specified age, demonstrating the flexibility of Spring Data R2DBC in executing custom queries reactively.

Transaction management in R2DBC with Spring Data is handled declaratively using the `@Transactional` annotation. This annotation ensures that operations within the annotated method are executed within a single transaction context, allowing for rollback in case of errors. For reactive transactions, the `TransactionalOperator` can be used programmatically to control transaction boundaries.

Error handling and exception translation in Spring Data R2DBC are facilitated by the `DatabaseClient` abstraction, which translates database-specific exceptions into Spring's unified data access exception hierarchy. This allows for consistent handling of data access exceptions across different database systems.

Integrating R2DBC with Spring Data provides a powerful toolset for developing reactive applications that interact with relational databases. By abstracting the boilerplate code associated with database access and providing a familiar programming model, it significantly reduces the complexity of implementing reactive data access layers, making it an invaluable addition to the reactive programmer's toolkit.

9.8   Error Handling and Exception Translation

In this section, we will discuss the mechanisms for handling errors and translating exceptions within the context of R2DBC and reactive programming. Error handling is an integral part of developing resilient applications, especially when dealing with asynchronous database access. Unlike traditional imperative programming models, reactive programming introduces new paradigms for error management that developers must grasp to ensure application stability and responsiveness.

R2DBC, being a specification designed for reactive database access, interacts with databases in a non-blocking manner. This implies that all operations return a `Publisher` which will eventually signal completion, data emission, or an error. The key challenge in reactive error handling is to comprehensively understand and respond to errors in a way that maintains the non-blocking and asynchronous nature of the reactive stream.

Error Signal in Reactive Streams

The Reactive Streams API defines that errors are part of the data stream and are propagated downstream as error signals. When an error occurs within a stream, it is wrapped into an exception and immediately signaled downstream to the subscriber. The subscriber can then decide how to handle the error based on its type or content. This approach is in stark contrast to traditional try-catch block mechanisms and necessitates a different mindset for error handling.

Exception Translation in R2DBC

A noteworthy aspect of using R2DBC is the need to translate database-specific exceptions into a more generic and understandable form. This is crucial for maintaining the portability of the code across different database implementations.   R2DBC provides a mechanism for exception translation through the `R2dbcExceptionTranslator` interface.   This interface allows developers to implement custom translation of database-specific exceptions to a more generalized `DataAccessException` hierarchy, which is consistent with Spring's data access abstraction.

```
1   public interface R2dbcExceptionTranslator {
```

```
2    DataAccessException translate(String task, @Nullable String sql, R2dbcException
         ex);
3  }
```

Implementing a custom exception translator involves interpreting the error codes and messages provided by the database driver and converting them into instances of `DataAccessException` or its subclasses. This enables the application to handle exceptions in a unified manner, abstracting away the database-specific details.

Error Handling Operators in Reactor

Project Reactor, the reactive library used by Spring and R2DBC, provides several operators for handling errors within a reactive stream. These operators allow developers to elegantly manage errors, apply fallback strategies, or recover from errors without breaking the flow of the stream. Some of the key operators include:

- `onErrorResume`: Allows substitution of a new Publisher when an error occurs.

- `onErrorReturn`: Enables returning a default value when an error is encountered.

- `doOnError`: Provides a mechanism to perform side-effects, such as logging, upon an error.

- `retry`: Facilitates retrying an operation that failed due to an exception.

```
1  // Example of using onErrorResume to provide a fallback strategy
2  databaseClient.sql("SELECT * FROM non_existent_table")
3    .fetch()
4    .all()
5    .onErrorResume(e -> Flux.empty()) // Fallback to an empty Flux on error
6    .subscribe(data -> System.out.println(data));
```

Implementing Global Error Handling

For broader error management, especially in web applications using Spring WebFlux, developers can implement global error handlers using the `WebExceptionHandler` interface. This approach centralizes error handling logic, allowing for uniform response to errors across different parts of the application.

```
1   @Component
2   public class GlobalErrorHandler implements WebExceptionHandler {
3       @Override
4       public Mono<Void> handle(ServerWebExchange exchange, Throwable ex) {
5           // Implement custom error handling logic
6           // Convert exceptions to HTTP responses, log errors, etc.
7           return Mono.error(new CustomException("An error occurred", ex));
8       }
9   }
```

Effective error handling and exception translation in R2DBC and reactive programming require a different approach compared to traditional imperative programming. By leveraging the error handling operators provided by Reactor, implementing custom exception translation, and using global error handlers, developers can build resilient and responsive applications that gracefully handle errors in a reactive context.

9.9 Performance Considerations for Reactive Database Access

Performance optimization is crucial for developing high-throughput, low-latency applications, especially when accessing databases reactively. This section will discuss performance considerations for reactive database access, focusing on connection pooling, batching operations, statement caching, and monitoring.

Connection management is a fundamental aspect of database interactions. Traditional blocking databases use a model where each thread is bound to a single connection. This model does not scale well in a non-blocking, event-driven environment. R2DBC overcomes this limitation by implementing a non-blocking connection pool. Utilizing connection pools efficiently is key to achieving high performance in reactive applications. Connection pools enable reusing database connections, reducing the overhead of establishing connections for each database operation. However, configuring the connection pool size is critical. Too small a pool might lead to insufficient resources during peak loads, whereas too large a pool can consume unnecessary resources and may lead to database server overload.

r2dbc-pool provides a convenient way to manage connection pools in reactive applications. It is vital to monitor and tune the connection pool settings according to application requirements and database server capacity. Optimal settings can vary based on the workload and specific use cases.

```
// Example of configuring a connection pool with r2dbc-pool
ConnectionPoolConfiguration configuration = ConnectionPoolConfiguration.builder()
    .maxIdleTime(Duration.ofMillis(1000))
    .maxSize(20)
    .build();
ConnectionPool pool = new ConnectionPool(configuration);
```

Batching operations can significantly improve performance by reducing the number of round trips between the application and the database server. R2DBC supports batching operations through the `Batch` statement. Combining multiple operations into a single batch reduces network latency and allows databases to optimize execution plans.

```
// Example of batching operations with R2DBC
Batch batch = connection.createBatch();
batch.add("INSERT INTO person (id, name) VALUES (1, 'John Doe')");
batch.add("INSERT INTO person (id, name) VALUES (2, 'Jane Doe')");
Mono<Void> result = batch.execute().then();
```

Statement caching is another optimization technique that can improve performance. Preparing statements is an expensive operation, involving parsing and compiling the SQL query on the database server. Caching prepared statements for reuse can eliminate this overhead for frequently executed queries. R2DBC does not directly support statement caching, so it is up to the application developers to implement caching mechanisms if needed.

Monitoring is essential for identifying performance bottlenecks and optimizing reactive database access. Metrics such as query execution time, connection pool utilization, and back pressure signals can provide insights into the database layer's performance. Spring Boot Actuator and Micrometer offer tools for monitoring reactive applications and their interactions with the database.

```
# Example of metrics that can be monitored
- database.query.execution.time
- r2dbc.pool.acquired
- r2dbc.pool.idle
- r2dbc.pool.pending
```

Optimizing performance for reactive database access involves several considerations, including efficient connection management, operation batching, statement caching, and comprehensive monitoring. By addressing these factors, developers can significantly enhance the responsiveness and scalability of reactive applications.

9.10 Migrating from JDBC to R2DBC

Migrating from JDBC (Java Database Connectivity) to R2DBC (Reactive Relational Database Connectivity) represents a significant shift in how applications communicate with SQL databases. While JDBC has been the traditional, established method for database operations in Java applications, its synchronous and blocking nature does not align with the reactive programming paradigm. R2DBC, on the other hand, offers non-blocking database access, which is more suitable for reactive applications demanding scalability and efficient resource utilization.

To initiate the migration process, it is essential to understand the fundamental differences between JDBC and R2DBC. JDBC operates on a blocking model, where the application thread waits for the database operation to complete. This approach can lead to inefficient use of resources in highly concurrent applications. R2DBC eliminates this bottleneck by adopting a non-blocking approach, where database operations are executed asynchronously, allowing application threads to be repurposed for other tasks while waiting for database operations to complete.

The first step in migrating an application from JDBC to R2DBC is to replace the JDBC dependencies with R2DBC dependencies in your project's build configuration file. For a Maven project, this involves removing the JDBC driver dependency and adding the corresponding R2DBC driver dependency. Here is an example of replacing a PostgreSQL JDBC driver with an R2DBC driver in a Maven pom.xml file:

```
1   <dependencies>
2       <!-- Remove JDBC driver dependency -->
3       <dependency>
4           <groupId>org.postgresql</groupId>
5           <artifactId>postgresql</artifactId>
6           <scope>runtime</scope>
7       </dependency>
8
9       <!-- Add R2DBC Postgres driver dependency -->
10      <dependency>
11          <groupId>io.r2dbc</groupId>
12          <artifactId>r2dbc-postgresql</artifactId>
13          <version>LATEST_VERSION</version>
14      </dependency>
15  </dependencies>
```

After updating the project dependencies, the next step is to configure the database connection for R2DBC. Unlike JDBC, which uses a blocking driver manager or data source to establish connections, R2DBC utilizes connection factories configured programatically or declaratively through application properties. A Spring Boot application can be configured as follows in the `application.properties` file:

```
1  spring.r2dbc.url=r2dbc:postgresql://localhost:5432/database
2  spring.r2dbc.username=user
3  spring.r2dbc.password=pass
```

The code changes required to migrate from JDBC to R2DBC are far from trivial, as they necessitate adopting a reactive programming model throughout the application. This involves revisiting all database interaction code and converting synchronous operations into asynchronous ones. For instance, a simple query execution in JDBC might look like this:

```
1  public List<User> findAllUsers(Connection conn) throws SQLException {
2      Statement stmt = conn.createStatement();
3      ResultSet rs = stmt.executeQuery("SELECT * FROM users");
4
5      List<User> users = new ArrayList<>();
6      while (rs.next()) {
7          users.add(new User(rs.getLong("id"), rs.getString("name")));
8      }
9      return users;
10 }
```

In contrast, the equivalent R2DBC operation would be:

```
1  public Flux<User> findAllUsers(ConnectionFactory connectionFactory) {
2      return Mono.from(connectionFactory.create())
3          .flatMapMany(connection ->
4              Flux.from(connection.createStatement("SELECT * FROM users")
5                  .execute())
6                  .flatMap(result ->
7                      result.map((row, rowMetadata) ->
8                          new User(row.get("id", Long.class), row.get("name", String.
                                   class)))))
9          .doFinally(signalType -> connection.close());
10 }
```

Notice the transition from utilizing `List` to `Flux`. This change reflects the shift to a reactive model, where data is handled in a non-blocking and asynchronous fashion.

Transaction management also changes significantly. In JDBC, transactions are managed imperatively using the connection's transaction APIs. R2DBC, however, integrates transactions into the reactive stream, allowing for declarative transaction management that aligns with the reactive paradigms.

Finally, testing strategies need adjustment. Traditional blocking interactions with the database can be easily tested using straightforward JUnit tests that execute synchronously. However, with R2DBC, testing

235

requires the use of tools and frameworks that support reactive streams, such as Project Reactor's StepVerifier, to verify the outcomes of reactive sequences.

```
1  @Test
2  public void testFindAllUsers() {
3      ConnectionFactory connectionFactory = ConnectionFactories.get("r2dbc:pool:
           postgresql://localhost/test");
4      assertThat(Flux.from(findAllUsers(connectionFactory)).collectList().block()).
           hasSize(2);
5  }
```

Migrating from JDBC to R2DBC is a substantial endeavor that impacts not only the technical aspects of database access but also the fundamental approach to designing and testing applications. The migration enables applications to fully leverage the reactive programming model, leading to more scalable, responsive, and resource-efficient applications. However, it requires thorough planning, careful execution, and likely, a significant learning curve for teams accustomed to synchronous, blocking database access patterns.

9.11   Testing R2DBC Applications

Testing R2DBC applications requires a comprehensive strategy that covers unit, integration, and end-to-end tests. Effective testing ensures that the reactive interactions with the database operate as expected under various conditions. This section will discuss approaches and best practices for testing applications using R2DBC, alongside the implementation of tests using popular frameworks.

Test Setup

Before delving into specific testing methodologies, it is crucial to establish a conducive testing environment. For R2DBC applications, this often involves spinning up a test database that mimics the production database schema. Docker containers or in-memory databases like H2 can be utilized for this purpose. Using Spring Boot's test utilities, one can configure a TestContainer or an H2 database instance to startup before the tests run.

```
1  @Testcontainers
2  @SpringBootTest
3  public class R2dbcApplicationTests {
4
```

```
 5    @Container
 6    static PostgreSQLContainer container = new PostgreSQLContainer("postgres:latest")
 7      .withDatabaseName("testdb")
 8      .withUsername("test")
 9      .withPassword("test");
10
11    @DynamicPropertySource
12    static void properties(DynamicPropertyRegistry registry) {
13      registry.add("spring.r2dbc.url", () -> container.getJdbcUrl().replace("jdbc", "
             r2dbc"));
14      registry.add("spring.r2dbc.username", () -> container.getUsername());
15      registry.add("spring.r2dbc.password", () -> container.getPassword());
16    }
17
18    // Additional test cases
19  }
```

Unit Testing Repositories

Unit testing repositories involving R2DBC can be achieved using the
DatabaseClient with a mock connection factory. Spring Data R2DBC's
support for MockConnectionFactory can be leveraged to simulate the
database layer, allowing for the testing of repository methods without
needing an actual database connection.

```
 1  public class MyRepositoryTest {
 2
 3    private MyRepository repository;
 4    private MockConnectionFactory connectionFactory;
 5
 6    @BeforeEach
 7    public void setup() {
 8      connectionFactory = new MockConnectionFactory();
 9      DatabaseClient databaseClient = DatabaseClient.create(connectionFactory);
10      repository = new MyRepository(databaseClient);
11    }
12
13    @Test
14    public void testFindById() {
15      // Configure the mock connection factory
16      // Execute repository method and verify outcome
17    }
18  }
```

Integration Testing

While unit tests verify the correctness of business logic in isolation,
integration tests ensure that the application components work together
as expected. For R2DBC applications, integration testing involves
invoking repository methods and verifying that data is correctly saved,
updated, fetched, or deleted in the database. Spring's @DataR2dbcTest

annotation can be used to simplify the configuration required for
R2DBC integration tests.

```
1   @DataR2dbcTest
2   public class UserRepositoryIntegrationTest {
3
4     @Autowired
5     private UserRepository repository;
6
7     @Test
8     public void testCreateUser() {
9       User user = new User(null, "John Doe", "john.doe@example.com");
10      Mono<User> savedUser = repository.save(user);
11
12      StepVerifier.create(savedUser)
13        .expectNextMatches(user -> user.getId() != null && "John Doe".equals(user.
            getName()))
14        .verifyComplete();
15    }
16  }
```

End-to-End Testing

End-to-end testing verifies that the entire application, including its
interaction with the database, works as expected. This type of testing is
critical for ensuring that the system's integrations are functioning correctly and can involve using WebTestClient to simulate web requests.

```
1   @SpringBootTest(webEnvironment = SpringBootTest.WebEnvironment.RANDOM_PORT)
2   @ActiveProfiles("test")
3   public class UserApiEndToEndTest {
4
5     @Autowired
6     private WebTestClient webTestClient;
7
8     @Test
9     public void testCreateUserApi() {
10      webTestClient.post().uri("/users")
11        .contentType(MediaType.APPLICATION_JSON)
12        .bodyValue("{ \"name\": \"Jane Doe\", \"email\": \"jane.doe@example.com\" }")
13        .exchange()
14        .expectStatus().isOk()
15        .expectBody()
16        .jsonPath("$.id").isNotEmpty()
17        .jsonPath("$.name").isEqualTo("Jane Doe");
18    }
19  }
```

Testing R2DBC applications is a multifaceted process that requires the
implementation of unit, integration, and end-to-end tests. Each testing
level serves a distinct purpose, from verifying the functionality of individual components to ensuring the application performs as expected
in real-world scenarios. Through the thoughtful application of testing

practices detailed in this section, developers can build robust, reactive applications with confidence in their reliability and performance.

9.12   Real-World Use Cases and Patterns

In the domain of software development, the integration of R2DBC into real-world applications epitomizes a paradigm shift towards embracing non-blocking, event-driven architectures. This section will discuss various use cases and patterns where R2DBC significantly enhances application performance, resilience, and scalability.

Highly Scalable Web Applications: With the exponential growth of internet users, web applications must serve an increasing number of requests simultaneously. Traditional blocking databases become a bottleneck under heavy load, leading to increased response times and decreased user satisfaction. R2DBC, with its non-blocking nature, allows for handling an extensive number of concurrent database operations, thereby improving application scalability. This is particularly beneficial for social media platforms, e-commerce sites, and online gaming portals where high throughput and low latency are critical.

```
1  // Example of a non-blocking query using R2DBC
2  Mono<Customer> customer = connectionFactory.create()
3      .flatMap(connection ->
4          connection.createStatement("SELECT id, name FROM customer WHERE id = $1")
5              .bind("$1", customerId)
6              .execute()
7      )
8      .flatMap(result -> result.map((row, rowMetadata) -> new Customer(row.get("id",
              Integer.class), row.get("name", String.class))))
9      .next();
```

Microservices Architecture: In a microservices architecture, different services communicate over the network, often requiring access to their own or shared databases. Utilizing R2DBC in a reactive microservices ecosystem facilitates non-blocking I/O operations, contributing to the overall responsiveness and efficiency of the system. This is particularly useful when services perform compound operations that involve multiple database calls, as R2DBC minimizes the latency impact of these operations.

```
{
  "id": 1,
  "name": "John Doe"
}
```

Real-time Data Processing Applications: Applications that require real-time data processing, such as financial tickers, IoT data streams, and instant messaging apps, benefit greatly from R2DBC's reactive capabilities. By efficiently managing backpressure and facilitating asynchronous data flows, R2DBC enables these applications to provide timely updates and maintain high levels of performance.

- Streaming financial data to client applications

- Processing and storing IoT sensor data

- Real-time chat message delivery

Data Integration and ETL Processes: Extract, Transform, Load (ETL) processes and data integration tasks often involve complex data manipulations and transfers between different systems. The asynchronous execution model of R2DBC can dramatically reduce the processing time of these operations, supporting more frequent data updates and enabling near real-time analytics.

Algorithm 2: Pseudocode for reactive ETL process

Data: sourceDataFlux
Result: Transformed and loaded data
1 initialization
2 **while** *data in sourceDataFlux* **do**
3 $\quad$ extractData()
4 $\quad$ transformData()
5 $\quad$ loadData()

Batch Operations and Bulk Inserts: Performing batch operations or bulk inserts traditionally involves blocking I/O operations that can degrade application performance. R2DBC addresses this challenge by providing reactive APIs that allow these operations to be executed non-blockingly, thus maintaining the responsiveness of the application even during extensive data manipulation tasks.

```
Flux.just("INSERT INTO log (date, level, message) VALUES ($1, $2, $3)")
    .flatMap(sql -> connection.createStatement(sql)
        .bind("$1", logEntry.getDate())
        .bind("$2", logEntry.getLevel())
        .bind("$3", logEntry.getMessage())
        .execute())
    .subscribe();
```

240

R2DBC's reactive programming model offers numerous advantages for modern applications, from enhancing scalability and performance in web applications to enabling more efficient data processing in microservices architectures and real-time applications. By embracing R2DBC, developers can build more responsive, efficient, and scalable applications, ready to meet the demands of today's digital landscape.

Chapter 10

Testing and Debugging Reactive Applications

Testing and debugging are critically important in the development of reactive applications, where asynchronous data flows and concurrency introduce unique challenges. This chapter focuses on the methodologies and tools that can be employed to effectively test and debug reactive applications, ensuring their correctness, performance, and reliability. It covers unit testing of reactive streams, integration testing strategies, the use of virtual time for scheduling tests, and debugging techniques that cater to the asynchronous nature of reactive programming. Through a detailed exploration of these topics, developers will learn how to approach testing and debugging in a way that aligns with the principles of reactive systems, enabling the delivery of high-quality, resilient software.

10.1 Overview of Testing Reactive Applications

Testing reactive applications presents a distinct set of challenges compared to traditional synchronous systems. The asynchronous, non-blocking nature of reactive programming paradigms requires a different approach to ensure the reliability and performance of applications.

This section discusses the intricacies of testing reactive systems, focusing on the unique characteristics that influence testing strategies and the selection of appropriate tools and methodologies.

Reactive programming, particularly with frameworks like RxJava and Spring Boot, introduces a model where data streams and the propagation of changes are first-class citizens. The fundamental shift towards an event-driven architecture means that the state of the application is continually evolving in response to incoming events. This dynamism, while powerful, introduces complexity in testing scenarios that are typically static and well-defined in synchronous systems.

The primary challenge in testing reactive applications is dealing with the inherent asynchronicity. Traditional testing approaches often assume a linear execution flow, where inputs lead to immediate outputs. In contrast, reactive systems operate on data streams that may emit items at unpredictable intervals. This can lead to race conditions and timing issues in tests that are not designed to handle asynchronous behavior.

To address these challenges, developers must leverage testing frameworks and libraries that explicitly support reactive paradigms. These tools provide mechanisms to control and manipulate the scheduler, which manages the execution of asynchronous tasks. By using a virtual time scheduler, for instance, tests can simulate the passage of time in a controlled manner, making it possible to deterministically test asynchronous operations without real delays. This approach not only reduces the complexity of testing reactive flows but also significantly speeds up the execution of test suites.

Listing 10.1: Example of unit testing a reactive flow with virtual time

```
@Test
public void testReactiveFlowWithVirtualTime() {
    TestScheduler scheduler = new TestScheduler();
    TestObserver<Long> testObserver = Observable.interval(1, TimeUnit.MINUTES,
        scheduler)
                                    .take(2)
                                    .test();
    // Move the scheduler forward by 1 minute
    scheduler.advanceTimeBy(1, TimeUnit.MINUTES);
    testObserver.assertValueCount(1);
    // Move the scheduler forward by another minute
    scheduler.advanceTimeBy(1, TimeUnit.MINUTES);
    testObserver.assertValueCount(2);
}
```

The above example demonstrates how to use virtual time to test a reactive flow that emits items over time. By controlling the scheduler, the test can assert the state of the stream at specific simulated time points, thus verifying the behavior of the reactive flow under test.

Another critical aspect of testing reactive applications is the handling of error conditions and exception handling paths. Due to the asynchronous execution model, exceptions may be propagated through data streams and require explicit handling. Tests must ensure that error conditions are correctly managed, and that the application behaves as expected when anomalies occur. This involves verifying that error signals are properly propagated through reactive chains and that fallback mechanisms, such as retry logic or default values, are effectively invoked.

Integration testing of reactive applications also poses unique challenges. The interconnectedness of reactive components, often involving external services and databases, requires a holistic approach to ensure the entire system functions correctly in concert. Tools like Testcontainers offer a solution by enabling lightweight, disposable instances of external dependencies, such as databases or message brokers, to be used during tests. This facilitates the creation of realistic testing environments where reactive flows can be exercised end-to-end.

```
Tests completed: 45
Passed: 45
Failed: 0
```

The code output example shown illustrates the ideal result of a successful test suite execution, where all tests pass without any failures. Achieving this level of reliability in testing reactive applications necessitates a deep understanding of the reactive paradigm and a conscientious application of appropriate testing strategies.

Testing reactive applications demands a paradigm shift in how tests are designed and executed. The unpredictability introduced by asynchronous data flows requires specialized tools and methodologies that cater to the dynamics of reactive systems. By embracing virtual time for deterministic scheduling, meticulously handling error conditions, and leveraging integration testing with realistic environments, developers can ensure the correctness, reliability, and performance of reactive applications. As reactive programming continues to gain traction, the importance of effective testing strategies cannot be overstated, laying the foundation for the development of robust, resilient software.

10.2   Unit Testing Reactive Flows with JUnit

Unit testing is a fundamental practice in software development, serving as the first line of defense against bugs. In the context of reactive programming, unit testing ensures that the asynchronous, non-blocking, and event-driven behaviors of applications behave as expected. This section will discuss how to apply unit testing to reactive flows using JUnit, which, when combined with Project Reactor's `StepVerifier`, provides a powerful toolkit for validating reactive streams.

JUnit 5, the latest generation of the widely-used testing framework for Java, introduces numerous features and improvements that make it particularly well-suited for testing reactive applications. Among these, the ability to write expressive and flexible tests, support for lambda expressions, and the introduction of nested tests offer a significant boost in productivity when dealing with complex reactive flows.

Testing Reactive Streams with `StepVerifier`

`StepVerifier` is a utility provided by Project Reactor that simplifies the process of verifying the behavior of reactive streams. It allows developers to describe expected events in the stream's lifecycle, such as signal emissions, completions, and error occurrences. To use `StepVerifier`, one first creates a scenario of expected events and then attaches it to the reactive stream to be tested.

```
1  StepVerifier.create(myFlux)
2     .expectNext("Expected Value")
3     .expectError(MyException.class)
4     .verify();
```

In the example above, `StepVerifier` is used to test a `Flux` (a type of reactive stream that represents 0 to N items). The test specifies that the `Flux` should emit "Expected Value" and then terminate with a specific error, `MyException`. The `verify()` method initiates the test by subscribing to the `Flux`.

Combining JUnit 5 and `StepVerifier` for Reactive Tests

JUnit 5's flexibility and `StepVerifier`'s expressiveness together provide a robust framework for testing reactive applications. Below is an illustrative example of how to combine these tools:

```
1  @Test
2  void myReactiveTest() {
3      Flux<String> myFlux = Flux.just("Value1", "Value2");
4      StepVerifier.create(myFlux)
5          .expectNext("Value1")
```

```
6        .expectNext("Value2")
7        .verifyComplete();
8    }
```

In the snippet, a `Flux` emitting two values is tested to ensure it emits "Value1" and "Value2" in sequence and then completes successfully. The `@Test` annotation from JUnit demarcates the method as a test case. The simplicity and readability of this approach enable rapid development and maintenance of tests for reactive flows.

Handling Time-sensitive Operations

One of the common challenges in testing reactive applications is dealing with time-dependent behavior. Project Reactor and JUnit 5 offer solutions for this as well. By using virtual time scheduling, tests can simulate time passage and verify time-sensitive operations without delay. Here's how to apply virtual time with `StepVerifier`:

```
1    @Test
2    void timeBasedOperationTest() {
3        StepVerifier.withVirtualTime(() -> Mono.delay(Duration.ofHours(1)))
4            .expectSubscription()
5            .thenAwait(Duration.ofHours(1))
6            .expectNextCount(1)
7            .verifyComplete();
8    }
```

In the above test, a `Mono` that delays its emission for one hour is verified to work as expected using virtual time. The `thenAwait` method simulates the passage of one hour.

Unit testing reactive flows demands an understanding of both the nature of asynchronous programming and the tools at one's disposal. By leveraging JUnit 5 and Project Reactor's `StepVerifier`, developers can write expressive, robust, and concise tests. This not only aids in ensuring the correctness of reactive streams but also significantly enhances the maintainability and quality of the software being developed.

10.3 Integration Testing Strategies

Integration testing plays a pivotal role in ensuring that different parts of a reactive application work together as expected. Unlike unit testing, which focuses on individual components in isolation, integration testing addresses the interactions between components and external

247

systems. This is particularly important in the context of reactive programming, where the non-blocking nature and the asynchronous data flows can lead to intricate inter-component dynamics.

To effectively test these interactions in a reactive context, it is essential to employ strategies that can handle asynchronous operations and ensure that the tests are both comprehensive and reliable. This section discusses several integration testing strategies, such as using embedded servers, leveraging test slices, employing Testcontainers, and incorporating virtual time.

Using Embedded Servers

One common approach for integration testing in reactive applications is the use of embedded servers. Frameworks such as Spring WebFlux support the creation of lightweight, embedded instances of the application server, which can be started and stopped within the test environment. This provides a realistic setting for testing the interactions between the application components and the server, including the handling of HTTP requests and responses in a non-blocking manner.

For example, testing a reactive REST controller with an embedded server could be achieved as follows:

```
1   @SpringBootTest(webEnvironment = WebEnvironment.RANDOM_PORT)
2   class ReactiveControllerIntegrationTest {
3
4     @Autowired
5     private WebTestClient webTestClient;
6
7     @Test
8     void testReactiveEndpoint() {
9       webTestClient.get().uri("/reactive-endpoint")
10          .exchange()
11          .expectStatus().isOk()
12          .expectBody(String.class).isEqualTo("Response from reactive endpoint");
13    }
14  }
```

This test starts an embedded server on a random port and uses WebTestClient to perform non-blocking web requests, validating the response of the reactive controller.

Leveraging Test Slices

Spring Boot provides a feature known as test slices which allows for more focused integration testing by loading only certain parts of the application context. Test slices are particularly useful in reactive applications for testing layers such as web, data, or services in isolation, reducing the overall overhead and execution time of the tests.

For instance, to test the reactive repository layer with a database slice:

```
1   @DataJpaTest
2   class ReactiveRepositoryTest {
3
4     @Autowired
5     private ReactiveRepository repository;
6
7     @Test
8     void testRepositoryOperation() {
9       // Perform test operations on the repository
10    }
11  }
```

@DataJpaTest annotation configures an in-memory database for testing, loading only the components necessary for testing the repository layer, thus making the test faster and more focused.

Employing Testcontainers

For integration testing involving external services or databases, Testcontainers offer a powerful solution. Testcontainers are lightweight, throwaway instances of common databases, Selenium web browsers, or other services that run in Docker containers. They can be programmatically started and stopped within your test code, ensuring a consistent and isolated environment for each test execution.

A simple example of using Testcontainers for testing a reactive application with a PostgreSQL database might look like this:

```
1   class ReactiveServiceTestcontainersTest {
2
3     static PostgreSQLContainer<?> postgresqlContainer = new PostgreSQLContainer<>("
          postgres:latest");
4
5     @BeforeAll
6     static void setup() {
7       postgresqlContainer.start();
8       System.setProperty("spring.datasource.url", postgresqlContainer.getJdbcUrl());
9       // Additional configuration to connect to the containerized database
10    }
11
12    @AfterAll
13    static void cleanup() {
14      postgresqlContainer.stop();
15    }
16
17    // Test methods follow
18  }
```

In this example, a PostgreSQL container is started before all tests and stopped after all tests have completed, providing a real database environment without any manual setup or external dependencies.

Incorporating Virtual Time

Another valuable strategy for integration testing reactive applications is the use of virtual time. Virtual time simulates the passage of time, allowing tests involving delays or timeouts to run instantly rather than waiting for real time to pass. This can significantly accelerate the execution of tests that involve time-based operations.

Frameworks like the Reactor provide support for virtual time, which can be leveraged in tests as follows:

```
1  @Test
2  public void testWithVirtualTime() {
3    StepVerifier.withVirtualTime(() -> Mono.delay(Duration.ofHours(3)))
4        .thenAwait(Duration.ofHours(3))
5        .expectNextCount(1)
6        .verifyComplete();
7  }
```

This test simulates a 3-hour delay using virtual time, completing almost instantaneously while ensuring the reactive pipeline behaves as expected over the time-delayed operation.

Integration testing in the context of reactive programming requires a thoughtful approach that accounts for the asynchronous and non-blocking nature of reactive applications. By employing strategies such as using embedded servers, leveraging test slices, employing Testcontainers, and incorporating virtual time, developers can create effective and efficient integration tests. These strategies ensure that the different parts of a reactive application work together seamlessly, meeting the demands of high-performance, resilient systems.

10.4   Testing with Testcontainers for Reactive Services

In this section, we will discuss the utilization of Testcontainers for conducting integration tests within reactive applications. Testcontainers is a Java library that supports JUnit tests by providing lightweight, throwaway instances of common databases, Selenium web browsers, or anything else that can run in a Docker container. It is particularly useful for integration testing of reactive services where the service might interact with an external system or service.

Consideration of reactive applications necessitates a nuanced approach to integration testing. Reactive applications, by nature, leverage asynchronous and non-blocking operations. Due to this, conventional blocking tests might not be efficiently applicable or might require significant adjustments to accommodate the reactive paradigm.

Testcontainers simplifies this process by allowing the creation of real runtime environments that mirror the application's operational context. This versatility provides a more accurate assessment of the application's behavior under real-world conditions.

Setup and Configuration

To start using Testcontainers, include the Testcontainers dependency in your project's build configuration. Assuming the use of Maven for managing dependencies, this can be achieved by adding the following to your pom.xml file:

```
1  <dependency>
2      <groupId>org.testcontainers</groupId>
3      <artifactId>testcontainers</artifactId>
4      <version>1.15.3</version>
5      <scope>test</scope>
6  </dependency>
```

This dependency declaration enables your project to access Testcontainers functionality for writing integration tests.

Executing a Simple Test Case

A fundamental example might involve a reactive application that interacts with a PostgreSQL database. The goal is to test the application's repository layer without connecting to a live database.

First, the PostgreSQL container is defined and started in the test class, as shown below:

```
1  @Test
2  public void testRepositoryInteraction() {
3      PostgreSQLContainer<?> postgresqlContainer =
4          new PostgreSQLContainer<>("postgres:latest")
5              .withDatabaseName("integration-tests-db")
6              .withUsername("sa")
```

```
 7        .withPassword("password");
 8
 9    postgresqlContainer.start();
10
11    // Configure the application to use the container's database
12    // and perform your tests here
13
14    assertTrue(/* your assertion here */);
15
16    postgresqlContainer.stop();
17 }
```

This code snippet demonstrates initiating a PostgreSQL container with a specific version, along with custom configuration for database name, username, and password. The container is started, providing a real PostgreSQL instance for the test. After executing the test assertions, it is essential to stop the container, ensuring that resources are not unduly consumed.

Leveraging Testcontainers for End-to-End Testing

Integrating Testcontainers into end-to-end testing scenarios enhances the testing fidelity of reactive systems. Consider a microservices architecture where services interact asynchronously. Deploying instances of dependent services and their associated databases or other dependencies in containers can simulate the full interaction cycle in a controlled environment.

This approach allows the testing of the complete reactive flow, from the initial request through backend service interactions, to the final response delivery. It provides valuable insights into the system's behavior under conditions that closely replicate production settings.

Challenges and Considerations

While Testcontainers significantly streamline the process of setting up real-world testing environments, there are considerations to bear in mind. Resource consumption is a primary concern, as each container is a full instance of the service or database it represents. Careful resource management and test optimization can help mitigate potential issues, ensuring that integration tests do not become a bottleneck in the development process.

Moreover, the dynamism and flexibility of reactive systems introduce complexity in ensuring that test environments accurately reflect production environments. The versioning of Docker images and the configuration of Testcontainers need careful management to maintain consistency across development and testing environments.

Testcontainers offer a powerful capability for testing reactive services, providing an agile and reliable means of conducting integration and end-to-end tests. By facilitating the creation of dynamic, ephemeral testing environments, Testcontainers enable developers to confidently validate the behavior of reactive applications. With careful management and strategic integration into the testing lifecycle, the challenges inherent in testing reactive systems can be effectively addressed, leading to the development of robust, high-quality reactive services.

10.5 Debugging Techniques for Reactive Streams

Debugging reactive streams introduces a unique set of challenges due to their asynchronous nature. Traditional debugging techniques such as step-by-step execution might not be as effective because of the non-blocking operations and the scheduler's control over thread execution. This section will discuss strategies and tools specifically designed to aid in debugging reactive applications.

Firstly, it is essential to introduce the concept of logging and how it can be leveraged to understand the behavior of reactive streams. Logging provides insights into the stream's operations and the data flowing through it. For frameworks like Project Reactor, which is heavily utilized in reactor-based programming, the log() operator can be used. This operator is placed in the reactive chain and logs various events such as subscription, onNext signals, errors, and completion signals.

```
1  Flux<String> flux = Flux.just("A", "B", "C")
2                     .log();
```

Upon execution, the console will output log messages that include the aforementioned signals, providing clear visibility into the stream's behavior at runtime.

```
onSubscribe(FluxArray.ArraySubscription)
request(unbounded)
onNext(A)
```

253

```
onNext(B)
onNext(C)
onComplete()
```

Another powerful technique involves using breakpoints in a way that respects the asynchronous nature of reactive programming. Tools like IntelliJ IDEA allow developers to place conditional asynchronous breakpoints that activate only when a specific condition is met. These conditions can be based on the characteristics of the elements within the stream, enabling targeted inspection of data under precise circumstances.

In addition to logging and strategic breakpoints, Reactor's Hooks.onOperatorDebug() can be a lifesaver during debugging sessions. When activated, this global hook enhances the stack trace information for each operator in the reactive chain. It allows developers to trace errors back to their source in the code more efficiently, addressing one of the most significant challenges in debugging reactive applications: identifying the origin of exceptions.

```
1  Hooks.onOperatorDebug();
```

However, this increased detail comes at the cost of performance and should be used sparingly, primarily in a development or debugging context.

Testing with virtual time is another crucial concept in the debugging process, particularly useful for handling time-based operations without the need to wait for real-time delays or timeouts. Virtual time allows simulating the passage of time instantaneously, enabling the rapid execution of tests that involve delays or time windows.

```
1  StepVerifier.withVirtualTime(() -> Mono.delay(Duration.ofHours(3)))
2          .expectSubscription()
3          .thenAwait(Duration.ofHours(3))
4          .expectNextCount(1)
5          .verifyComplete();
```

This example demonstrates using virtual time to test a Mono that emits a value after a delay of three hours.

Finally, the visualization of reactive streams can significantly aid in understanding complex flows. Tools such as Project Reactor's debug agent provide a graphical representation of the reactive chain, showcasing the flow of data and the interactions between different components. This visual aid is invaluable for grasping the behavior of intricate streams and identifying areas that may contribute to unexpected behavior or performance bottlenecks.

By employing these strategies, developers can navigate the complexities of debugging reactive streams. The combination of advanced logging, conditional breakpoints, detailed error tracking, virtual time testing, and flow visualization equips developers with a robust toolkit for tackling the challenges posed by reactive programming. Embracing these techniques will enhance the ability to deliver reliable, high-quality reactive applications.

10.6 Using Spring Boot Actuator for Monitoring

Monitoring is a fundamental aspect of maintaining the reliability and performance of reactive applications. Spring Boot Actuator stands out as an integral part of the Spring Boot ecosystem, providing a series of built-in endpoints allowing developers to monitor and interact with their application. This section will discuss how to leverage Spring Boot Actuator to effectively monitor reactive applications, focusing on endpoints relevant to reactive streams and how to customize Actuator to suit specific monitoring needs.

Spring Boot Actuator exposes a range of endpoints for various operational insights, such as health indicators, metrics, log levels, and environment properties. To utilize Spring Boot Actuator, it is first necessary to include the Actuator dependency in your Spring Boot project's build configuration. The implementation begins by adding:

```
1  <dependency>
2      <groupId>org.springframework.boot</groupId>
3      <artifactId>spring-boot-starter-actuator</artifactId>
4  </dependency>
```

Upon including the Actuator dependency, several endpoints are automatically enabled by default, such as '/health', '/info', and '/metrics'. However, to fully exploit the capabilities of Actuator, especially in the context of reactive applications, further configurations might be required.

The '/metrics' endpoint is particularly noteworthy. It provides a wealth of information regarding the application's performance, including details about the JVM, garbage collection, and HTTP metrics. For

255

reactive applications, metrics related to thread pools, executor services, and queue sizes are crucial. They offer insights into the concurrency and parallelism aspects of the application, which are pivotal for diagnosing and resolving performance bottlenecks.

To access detailed metrics for reactive streams, custom metrics can be defined and registered with the global registry of Micrometer, Spring Boot's default metrics engine. Here's how you might capture the latency of a reactive endpoint:

```
1  @Autowired
2  private MeterRegistry registry;
3
4  public Mono<String> getReactiveData() {
5      return Mono.just("data")
6              .doOnSubscribe(sub -> registry.timer("reactive.endpoint.latency").record
                  (() -> {
7                  // reactive operation
8              }));
9  }
```

This custom metric, named 'reactive.endpoint.latency', measures the latency of a simulated operation within a reactive pipeline.

Spring Boot Actuator's '/health' endpoint provides application health information, which might include disk space, database connectivity, and custom health indicators. For reactive applications, defining a custom health indicator to monitor the status of non-blocking components is possible and recommended:

```
1   @Component
2   public class ReactiveComponentHealthIndicator implements HealthIndicator {
3
4       @Override
5       public Mono<Health> health() {
6           // Implementation to check the health of reactive components
7           boolean componentHealthy = // your health check logic here
8           if (componentHealthy) {
9               return Mono.just(Health.up().build());
10          } else {
11              return Mono.just(Health.down().withDetail("error", "Component is not
                    healthy").build());
12          }
13      }
14  }
```

In addition to these, Spring Boot Actuator can be extended to include custom endpoints. For instance, to provide insights specific to the application's reactive architecture, a custom endpoint can be created:

```
1  @Component
2  @Endpoint(id = "reactiveDetails")
3  public class ReactiveDetailsEndpoint {
4
```

```
5    @ReadOperation
6    public Mono<Map<String, Object>> reactiveDetails() {
7        Map<String, Object> details = new HashMap<>();
8        // Populate details map with relevant information
9        return Mono.just(details);
10   }
11 }
```

This custom endpoint, accessible via '/actuator/reactiveDetails', could aggregate and expose information pertinent to the application's reactive elements, offering a tailored view into its operational state.

Careful configuration of Spring Boot Actuator is essential to harness its full potential in monitoring reactive applications. It requires tuning the Actuator's properties, such as defining which endpoints are enabled, their access levels, and customizing their behavior through properties in 'application.properties' or 'application.yml'. Here is an example configuration:

```
1  management
2    endpoints
3      web
4        exposure
5          include health, info, metrics, reactiveDetails
```

This configuration snippet enables the health, info, metrics, and custom 'reactiveDetails' endpoints, making them accessible over HTTP.

Spring Boot Actuator is a powerful tool for monitoring reactive applications. It offers a wide range of endpoints for operational insights and allows for extensive customization to tailor monitoring to the specific needs of reactive systems. By leveraging Actuator in conjunction with proper application design and development practices, developers can significantly improve the observability, reliability, and performance of their reactive applications.

10.7 Performance Testing Reactive Applications

Performance testing in the context of reactive applications is an essential process that measures the responsiveness, scalability, and stability of an application under a particular workload. Given the asynchronous and non-blocking nature of reactive programming, traditional performance testing methodologies need to be adapted to accurately reflect the behavior and performance characteristics of reactive applications.

Performance testing of reactive applications involves simulating various scenarios to assess how the system behaves under stress or heavy load. Unlike imperative programming models, reactive systems are designed to handle a large number of concurrent data streams and operations. Therefore, the focus of performance testing shifts towards assessing backpressure handling, latency under load, throughput, and memory usage.

Testing Methodologies:

To begin with, it is crucial to establish a baseline performance metric for the application under normal conditions. This baseline provides a reference point against which the impact of stress conditions can be measured. One effective way to establish a baseline is by employing the use of `Gatling` or `JMeter`, well-known tools for performance testing that can simulate a large number of users accessing the application concurrently.

```
1  val scn = scenario("BasicSimulation")
2    .exec(http("Request_1")
3    .get("/"))
4    .pause(5)
5
6  setUp(scn.inject(atOnceUsers(100))).protocols(httpProtocol)
```

The above `Gatling` script simulates 100 users accessing the root endpoint of the application simultaneously, allowing for a simple performance test that establishes a throughput baseline.

Performance Metrics:

Several key metrics are critical in assessing the performance of reactive applications:

- Throughput - measuring the number of requests that the application can handle within a given time.

- Latency - the time taken for a request to be processed.

- Memory Usage - assessing the application's memory footprint under load conditions.

- Error Rate - the percentage of requests that result in errors under stress.

These metrics offer a comprehensive view of the application's performance and are invaluable in identifying bottlenecks and areas for optimization.

Analyzing Performance under Load:

After establishing baseline metrics, the next step involves incrementally increasing the load to observe how the application behaves. This process, commonly referred to as stress testing, is pivotal for identifying the application's breaking point and how it manages backpressure. Reactive applications should ideally degrade gracefully under stress, providing mechanisms to shed load or prioritize critical operations.

```
setUp(
  scn.inject(
    nothingFor(4.seconds),
    atOnceUsers(100),
    rampUsers(1000) over (30.seconds)
  ).protocols(httpProtocol)
)
```

The above script demonstrates a ramp-up scenario where the number of users accessing the application increases from 0 to 1000 over 30 seconds, a typical pattern for assessing scalability and stability.

Utilizing Virtual Time:

Testing with real-time scenarios can be time-consuming and often impractical for time-sensitive applications. Virtual time testing, a concept introduced in reactive programming, allows for simulating the passage of time in a controlled environment. This methodology is particularly useful for unit and integration tests where the objective is to simulate and observe behaviors under various temporal conditions without the long wait times.

```
@Test
public void virtualTimeTest() {
    StepVerifier.withVirtualTime(() -> Mono.delay(Duration.ofHours(3)))
        .expectSubscription()
        .expectNoEvent(Duration.ofHours(2))
        .thenAwait(Duration.ofHours(1))
        .expectNextCount(1)
        .verifyComplete();
}
```

Performance testing for reactive applications requires a nuanced approach that accounts for the specific characteristics of reactive programming. By effectively utilizing tools like `Gatling` and harnessing the capabilities of virtual time testing, developers can gain deep insights into their application's performance under various conditions. This process not only ensures that the reactive application can handle real-world scenarios but also aids in tuning the system for optimal performance and scalability.

10.8 Error Handling and Exception Testing

Error handling and exception testing in reactive programming requires a sophisticated understanding of how exceptions propagate in asynchronous, non-blocking systems. Given the nature of reactive streams, where data flows from publishers to subscribers, it is vital to ensure that exceptions do not break the chain of operations, affecting the stability and resilience of the application.

In reactive systems, error handling is often implemented using dedicated error channels. These channels allow exceptions to be treated as data, enabling the application to gracefully react to errors without terminating the reactive flow. This approach is fundamentally different from traditional try-catch blocks used in imperative programming paradigms.

To effectively test error handling in reactive applications, developers must simulate various exception scenarios and verify that the application reacts correctly. This involves asserting not only the occurrence of exceptions but also the continuation of the reactive stream where appropriate.

Listing 10.2: Simulating an Exception in a Reactive Stream

```
Flux<String> simulateException = Flux.just("data1", "data2")
    .concatWith(Mono.error(new RuntimeException("Simulated exception")))
    .onErrorResume(e -> Mono.just("fallback data"));

StepVerifier.create(simulateException)
    .expectNext("data1")
    .expectNext("data2")
    .expectNext("fallback data")
    .verifyComplete();
```

The above code snippet demonstrates a common pattern in testing the handling of exceptions within a reactive stream. The Mono.error method simulates an exception, while the onErrorResume operator provides a fallback mechanism, ensuring the stream's continuity. The StepVerifier is used to assert the expected behavior of the stream in response to the exception.

An important aspect of testing reactive applications is the verification of logging and monitoring mechanisms in place for error reporting. This often involves the integration of external tools and services designed to capture and analyze error data in a reactive context.

```
2023-04-01 10:00:00 ERROR - Simulated exception encountered in reactive stream
```

The above log entry is an example of a simulated exception being recorded during a test. It is critical to verify that the application correctly logs exceptions, providing sufficient context for debugging and analysis.

In addition to simulating exceptions, effective exception testing in reactive systems also involves asserting the behavior of the application under partial failure conditions. In distributed systems, for instance, a downstream service might become temporarily unavailable. Testing how the reactive application handles such scenarios, possibly by employing fallback mechanisms or retries, is fundamental to ensuring resilience.

Listing 10.3: Testing Partial Failure Handling with Retries

```
1  Flux<String> resilientFlux = Flux.just("request")
2      .flatMap(req -> callExternalService(req)
3          .retry(2)
4          .onErrorReturn("default response"));
5
6  StepVerifier.create(resilientFlux)
7      .expectNext("default response")
8      .verifyComplete();
```

This code snippet illustrates the testing of a reactive stream's resilience to partial failures, employing retries and fallback strategies. The callExternalService simulates an external call that may fail, while the retry mechanism ensures multiple attempts before defaulting to a fallback response.

Error handling and exception testing in reactive programming are pivotal to developing robust, resilient applications capable of maintaining functionality under adverse conditions. Through the strategic simulation of exceptions, verification of error handling mechanisms, and the testing of partial failure scenarios, developers can ensure that reactive applications gracefully manage errors, thereby enhancing stability and reliability.

10.9 Mocking and Stubbing Reactive Components

Mocking and stubbing are essential practices in the realm of testing, particularly when dealing with the intrinsic complexities of reactive applications. These techniques allow developers to simulate the behaviors of components within a reactive system, facilitating isolation and verification of specific functionalities without the need for the entire application context. This proves invaluable in situations where testing components require interactions with external services, databases, or any other dependencies that are either time-consuming, costly, or complex to orchestrate in a test environment.

When it comes to reactive applications, the asynchronous and non-blocking nature of reactive streams introduces additional considerations. Traditional mocking frameworks might not be inherently suited to handle the fluid dynamics of reactive streams. Therefore, leveraging frameworks that understand and integrate well with the reactive paradigm is crucial. Project Reactor, for instance, offers tools such as `StepVerifier` that are designed specifically for testing reactive streams, providing a fluent API to assert specific states and events within a reactive sequence.

Integrating Mocking Frameworks

The first step in mocking reactive components involves integrating a mocking framework that is compatible with reactive types, such as Mockito. Mockito allows the creation of mock objects for interfaces or classes, facilitating the stubbing of reactive methods' return values. Here is an example showcasing how to mock a reactive repository within a service layer test:

```
1  @Test
2  public void testFindAllUsers() {
3      Flux<User> userFlux = Flux.just(new User("John Doe"), new User("Jane Doe"));
4      UserRepository mockRepository = Mockito.mock(UserRepository.class);
5
6      Mockito.when(mockRepository.findAll()).thenReturn(userFlux);
7
8      UserService userService = new UserService(mockRepository);
9      StepVerifier.create(userService.findAllUsers())
10         .expectNextMatches(user -> user.getName().equals("John Doe"))
11         .expectNextMatches(user -> user.getName().equals("Jane Doe"))
12         .verifyComplete();
13 }
```

In the example above, `Mockito.when()` is used to stub the `findAll()` method of the `UserRepository` to return a predefined Flux of User objects. The `StepVerifier` is then used to assert that the `UserService` reacts as expected when the stubbed repository method is invoked.

Stubbing Asynchronous Behavior

A critical aspect of mocking in a reactive context is the ability to stub asynchronous and latency-prone operations in a manner that reflects their non-blocking nature. For instance, one might want to simulate a delayed response from a mocked service method to verify timeout handling or resilience logic in dependent components. This can be achieved using Project Reactor's `Mono.delay` or `Flux.delay` along with Mockito:

```
1   @Test
2   public void testDelayedServiceResponse() {
3       UserService mockService = Mockito.mock(UserService.class);
4       Mono<User> delayedUserMono = Mono.delay(Duration.ofSeconds(5))
5           .thenReturn(new User("Delayed User"));
6
7       Mockito.when(mockService.findUserById(Mockito.anyString()))
8           .thenReturn(delayedUserMono);
9
10      // Further testing logic
11  }
```

By combining Mockito's stubbing capabilities with Reactor's constructs for expressing time, developers can comprehensively simulate complex behavior in reactive streams.

Best Practices

While mocking and stubbing are invaluable, certain best practices should be adhered to, ensuring effective testing:

- Focus on behavior rather than implementation details when stubbing methods. The test should verify that the correct behavior occurs when certain conditions are met, without being overly specific about how that behavior is achieved.

- Limit the scope of mocks to external dependencies or components whose behavior is not being directly tested. Excessive mocking can lead to brittle tests that are overly sensitive to implementation changes.

263

- Use `StepVerifier` to assert post-conditions and outcomes of reactive streams thoroughly. `StepVerifier` provides a powerful and expressive framework for testing reactive types, allowing precise timing control and state inspection.

In summary, mocking and stubbing reactive components require a nuanced approach that accommodates the asynchronous and event-driven characteristics of reactive applications. By leveraging suitable frameworks and adhering to best practices, developers can effectively isolate, test, and verify the behavior of components within a reactive system.

10.10 End-to-End Testing of Reactive Applications

Testing is a critical phase in the software development lifecycle, particularly for reactive applications, which are asynchronous and event-driven in nature. End-to-end (E2E) testing assumes paramount significance as it verifies the integration and interaction of individual components within an application in a scenario that closely mimics real-world use. This section focuses on the principles, strategies, and best practices for conducting E2E testing of reactive applications, emphasizing how to navigate the challenges posed by their asynchronous nature.

To start, it is essential to have a clear understanding of the purpose of E2E testing in the context of reactive applications. Unlike unit and integration tests that focus on smaller units of code and their interaction respectively, E2E tests evaluate the system as a whole. This approach verifies that different parts of the application work together seamlessly to deliver the desired functionality, and that the system behaves as expected when operated in an environment similar to production.

E2E testing of reactive applications often involves simulating real user interactions with the system, which may include user interface interactions, backend processing, database transactions, and calling external APIs. The asynchronous and non-blocking nature of reactive applications adds complexity to this process, as tests must handle operations that do not complete instantaneously.

A successful strategy for E2E testing reactive applications includes the following components:

- **Choosing the Right Tools:** Selecting testing frameworks and tools that are designed to work with reactive applications is crucial. These tools should be capable of handling asynchronous operations and assertions. Examples include Selenium for web UI testing, which can be coupled with tools like WebdriverIO or Protractor that offer support for handling asynchronous browser tasks.

- **Creating Test Environments:** Setting up test environments that replicate the production environment as closely as possible ensures that the E2E tests provide accurate results. This includes configuring databases, external services, and other infrastructure components.

- **Simulating Real-World Scenarios:** Test cases should be designed to mimic real user interactions, covering a broad spectrum of user behaviors, including edge cases. This ensures that the system is tested in scenarios that are likely to occur in production.

- **Asynchronous Control Flow:** Test scripts must be able to manage asynchronous operations, waiting for them to complete before proceeding. This is achieved through the use of promises, callbacks, or async/await syntax, depending on the capabilities of the programming language and testing framework.

- **Data Management:** Effective data management strategies, such as setting up test data before test execution and cleaning up after tests to maintain isolation, are vital to ensure the reliability of E2E tests.

- **Monitoring and Logging:** Implementing comprehensive monitoring and logging throughout the testing process can help in identifying and diagnosing issues that occur during test execution.

To demonstrate how to write E2E test scenarios for a reactive application, consider the following example written in a generic testing framework:

```
1  // Example of an end-to-end test for a reactive application
2  describe('User Registration Flow', () => {
3    it('should register a new user successfully', async () => {
4      const uniqueEmail = `testUser${Date.now()}@example.com`;
5      const registrationData = {
6        email: uniqueEmail,
7        password: 'password123',
8        confirmPassword: 'password123'
```

```
 9    };
10
11    await navigateToRegistrationPage();
12    await fillRegistrationForm(registrationData);
13    await submitRegistrationForm();
14
15    const registrationSuccessMessage = await waitForElement('successMessage');
16    expect(registrationSuccessMessage).toContain('Registration successful');
17    });
18  });
```

In the example above, asynchronous operations are handled using the async/await syntax, ensuring that the test waits for each operation to complete before proceeding. This approach is essential for testing reactive applications, where many operations are non-blocking and return promises or observables.

Implementing comprehensive E2E testing for reactive applications involves overcoming challenges related to asynchronous operations, data management, and environment setup. However, by selecting appropriate tools, designing tests that mimic real-world usage, and applying best practices for managing asynchronous control flow and test data, developers can ensure the reliability and effectiveness of their reactive applications. Through meticulous planning and execution of E2E tests, the goal of delivering high-quality, resilient software that meets user expectations can be achieved.

10.11 Automating Reactive Testing with CI/CD

Automating the testing process is a cornerstone of modern software development, especially when it comes to the complex nature of reactive applications. Continuous Integration and Continuous Deployment (CI/CD) pipelines provide a framework for automating the testing and deployment of software, ensuring that changes are reliably and efficiently integrated into production systems. This process is crucial for reactive applications, where the asynchronous and non-blocking nature of the code can introduce subtle bugs that are difficult to detect without comprehensive testing strategies.

In a CI/CD pipeline for reactive applications, the first step involves setting up a version control system (VCS) such as Git. Every push to the repository triggers the CI/CD pipeline, which starts with the execution of automated tests. It's imperative to structure the pipeline to run different types of tests in a logical sequence, usually starting with fast-executing tests and progressing to more comprehensive and time-consuming tests. This strategy helps to quickly catch and fix any breaking changes, minimizing the impact on the development workflow.

```
1   // Example of unit test for a Mono in a reactive application
2   @Test
3   public void givenMono_whenSuccess_thenExpectValue() {
4       String expectedValue = "RxJava";
5       Mono<String> testMono = Mono.just(expectedValue);
6       StepVerifier.create(testMono)
7           .expectNext(expectedValue)
8           .verifyComplete();
9   }
```

This code snippet demonstrates how to write a unit test for a reactive stream using 'Mono' from Project Reactor. 'StepVerifier' is used to assert the emitted items, ensuring that the reactive flow behaves as expected under test conditions. Such unit tests are the first to run in the CI/CD pipeline, providing immediate feedback on the impact of code changes.

After unit tests, integration tests play a critical role in verifying the interaction between components in a reactive system. These tests are more comprehensive and require additional setup, often necessitating the use of tools like Testcontainers to spin up dependencies such as databases or other services in Docker containers.

```
1   // Example of integration test with Testcontainers
2   @Test
3   public void givenReactiveService_whenRequest_thenExpectResponse() {
4       // Setup Testcontainer environment
5       MySQLContainer<?> mysqlContainer = new MySQLContainer<>(DockerImageName.parse("
            mysql:latest"));
6       mysqlContainer.start();
7
8       // Application context setup and test execution
9       // Assumed to be implemented
10  }
```

The CI/CD pipeline also incorporates steps for deploying the application to staging environments, where end-to-end tests can validate the application's behavior from the user's perspective. This step often requires orchestration tools such as Kubernetes and Helm to manage the deployment process across different environments effectively.

Performance testing is another critical component of the pipeline for reactive applications. Tools like Gatling or JMeter can simulate high-load scenarios to ensure the application maintains responsiveness and robustness under stress. These tests are particularly important for reactive applications, where the non-blocking nature and backpressure handling mechanisms need to withstand heavy loads.

```
---- Response Time Distribution ------------------------------------------
> t < 800 ms                                    953 (95%)
> 800 ms < t < 1200 ms                           47 (5%)
> t > 1200 ms                                     0 (0%)
> failed                                          0 (0%)
```

This output example from a performance test shows the distribution of response times, indicating that the majority of requests are processed within the acceptable threshold, an essential insight for reactive application development.

Finally, the CI/CD pipeline automates the deployment of the application to production environments, leveraging blue-green deployments or canary releases to minimize downtime and reduce risk. Monitoring and logging tools are also integrated into the production environment to ensure ongoing observability and reliability.

Automating reactive testing within a CI/CD pipeline not only streamlines the development process but also ensures that the unique challenges of reactive applications are addressed consistently, contributing to the delivery of high-quality, resilient, and scalable software solutions.

10.12 Common Pitfalls and How to Avoid Them

In the development of reactive applications, certain common pitfalls can significantly hamper the efficiency, reliability, and scalability of the system. This section will discuss these pitfalls and provide guidance on how to avoid them.

- **Blocking Calls in a Non-Blocking Context:** One of the most common mistakes in reactive programming is introducing blocking calls within a non-blocking flow. This not only defeats the purpose of a reactive system but can also cause significant performance issues due to thread starvation.

  To avoid this, always ensure that all operations within the reactive pipeline are non-blocking. If integration with a blocking API is unavoidable, use constructs like Mono.fromCallable() and subscribe on a separate scheduler that is specifically designated for blocking tasks, e.g., `Schedulers.boundedElastic()`.

- **Overusing Thread Pools:** While it might be tempting to create a separate thread pool for every operation that might seem blocking, overuse of thread pools can lead to increased complexity and decreased application throughput.

  It is advisable to understand the default schedulers provided by the reactive framework being used and leverage them effectively. Only create additional schedulers when there is a clear necessity, and ensure they are reused across the application where possible.

- **Not Handling Backpressure Properly:** Backpressure is a mechanism to prevent overwhelming a consumer with data from a faster producer. Neglecting backpressure strategies can lead to memory issues or lost messages.

  To manage backpressure, use operators that allow managing the demand from consumers, such as `onBackpressureDrop()`, `onBackpressureBuffer()`, or `onBackpressureLatest()`. Furthermore, utilize backpressure-aware components throughout the application to ensure a resilient data flow.

- **Improper Error Handling:** Error handling in a reactive stream can become complex due to the asynchronous nature of the operations. Failing to properly handle errors can lead to silent failures or unexpected system behavior.

  Employ error-handling operators such as `onErrorResume()`, `onErrorReturn()`, and `doOnError()` to gracefully handle exceptions and maintain the integrity of the reactive pipeline. Always assume that errors can happen at any point and plan for them accordingly.

- **Mismanagement of Resources:** Reactive applications often deal with external resources such as database connections or network sockets. Without proper management, these resources can lead to leaks and hinder application performance.

  Utilize resource management features offered by the reactive framework, such as `Mono.using()` or `Flux.usingWhen()`, to ensure that resources are properly created and disposed of in alignment with the lifecycle of the reactive stream.

- **Testing Negligence:** Due to the asynchronous and non-blocking nature of reactive applications, traditional testing approaches might not be effective. Neglecting thorough testing can lead to undetected issues in production.

Adopt a testing strategy that includes unit tests for individual components, integration tests that simulate the interaction between components, and end-to-end tests that verify the system as a whole. Leverage testing utilities provided by the reactive framework to mock, stub, and verify reactive flows under test conditions.

To mitigate these pitfalls, developers must cultivate a deep understanding of the reactive paradigm, its benefits, and its potential drawbacks. Knowing when and how to apply the principles of reactive programming is essential for building high-quality, resilient, and scalable applications. By recognizing common mistakes and employing the strategies outlined, developers can navigate the complexities of reactive system development with confidence.